Class Construction in C and C++

Object-Oriented Programming Fundamentals

Roger Sessions

International Business Machines Corporation
Austin, Texas

PRENTICE HALL, Englewood Cliffs, New Jersey 07632

Library of Congress Cataloging-in-Publication Data

SESSIONS, ROGER.
   Class construction in C and C + + : object-oriented programming
fundamentals / Roger Sessions.
      p.   cm.
   Includes bibliographical references and index.
   ISBN 0-13-630104-5
   1. Object-oriented programming. 2. C (Computer program language)
3. C + + (Computer program language) I. Title.
   QA76.64.S42   1992
   005.1—dc20   91–48099
                                     CIP

Cover design: *Lundgren Graphics, Ltd.*
Source: *Image Bank*
Illustrator: *Sandra Lilippucci*
Copy editor: *Maria Caruso*
Acquisitions editor: *Greg Doench*
Editorial assistant: *Rene Wilkins*
Prepress buyer: *Mary E. McCartney*
Manufacturing buyer: *Susan Brunke*

Trademarks...
L^AT_EX is a trademark of Addison-Wesley.
PCT_EX is a trademark of Personal T_EX, Inc.
T_EX is a trademark of the American Mathematical Society.
IBM is the registered trademark of International Business Machines Corporation.

© 1992 by Prentice-Hall, Inc.
A Simon & Schuster Company
Englewood Cliffs, New Jersey 07632

The publisher offers discounts on this book when ordered in
bulk quantities. For more information, write: Special
Sales/Professional Marketing, Prentice Hall, Professional &
Technical Reference Division, Englewood Cliffs, NJ 07632.

Printed in the United States of America

10 9 8 7 6 5 4 3 2 1

ISBN   0-13-630104-5

PRENTICE-HALL INTERNATIONAL (UK) LIMITED, *London*
PRENTICE-HALL OF AUSTRALIA PTY. LIMITED, *Sydney*
PRENTICE-HALL CANADA INC., *Toronto*
PRENTICE-HALL HISPANOAMERICANA, S.A., *Mexico*
PRENTICE-HALL OF INDIA PRIVATE LIMITED, *New Delhi*
PRENTICE-HALL OF JAPAN, INC., *Tokyo*
SIMON & SCHUSTER ASIA PTE. LTD., *Singapore*
EDITORA PRENTICE-HALL DO BRASIL, LTDA., *Rio de Janeiro*

Contents

In order to find one's place in the infinity of being,
one must be able both to separate and to unite.

- I Ching
Chun Hexagram — Difficulty at the Beginning
Translated by Richard Wilhelm and Cary F. Baynes

Preface

This book is about object-oriented programming and how the concepts of object-oriented programming can be applied in C and in C++. The book's goal is to demystify object-oriented programming; to show that object-oriented programming is really just a common sense extension of structured programming; to show that many of the principles of object-oriented programming are applicable to any language; and to show that there are just a few new language features in C++ that must be learned to start using the language effectively.

There are two parts to learning object-oriented programming. The first is learning the object-oriented paradigm. The second is learning an object-oriented language, in this case, C++.

Learning both a new paradigm and a new language can be a daunting goal. The object-oriented paradigm is for most of us a new way of thinking about programming. The new language we are interested in, C++, is generally regarded as quite complex, with many new syntactic enhancements over and above C, a language most consider already complicated enough.

This book simplifies the material through two approaches. The first is by separating the paradigm from the language. The second is by focusing on only the important language features.

Separating the paradigm from the language means teaching as much of the object-oriented paradigm as possible using standard C code. This allows the reader to become familiar with the concepts of object-oriented programming without having to deal with the overhead of a new language.

Once the paradigm is firmly established, we start discussing C++. We look at where C has weaknesses in implementing object-oriented concepts, and how C++ supplements C to address these weaknesses. We purposely ignore the syntactic fluff of C++ which has little to do with object-oriented programming.

Many influential authors suggest using C++ as a better C, even if one never makes the shift to object-oriented programming. Their reasoning is that C++ is a superset of C, and therefore any C programmer can start using C++ immediately by just using the C subset of C++. Then, one can gradually make more and more use of the new C++ language features as one learns them. Since so few of the new language features are directly related to object-oriented programming, this argument goes, why wait to make the paradigm shift?

This argument has one major flaw. The most important advance offered by C++ is not its myriad collection of C enhancements, but its direct support for the object-oriented paradigm. The programmer who successfully makes the paradigm shift, but does not know every last C++ feature, will be far ahead of the programmer who memorizes every C++ ampersand and keyword, but never learns the new approach to thinking about programming.

This book focuses on the paradigm. We discuss those C++ language features which are essential to the paradigm and ignore those that are not. Those features which we do cover are covered in considerable depth, much greater depth than can be covered in books which cover every detail of the language.

The purpose of this book is to get you to use object-oriented programming. To teach you the important features of C++. To teach you those features well. You will then have plenty of time to learn the details, and there are plenty of books available from which you can learn it.

This book is targeted at two main groups of readers. The first is the C programmer who wants to learn object-oriented programming and C++. The second is the large group of C++ programmers who have never made the paradigm shift, who use C++ but only to write better procedural code than they could have written in C.

This book teaches object-oriented programming by looking at a lot of object-oriented code. This book includes over 7000 lines of code, almost all of which is shown as fully running programs complete with output. Almost every feature we discuss is demonstrated by actual running code.

Overview of Book

This book can be thought of as having three parts. The first part (Chaps. 1–5) teaches the C programmer the basic concepts of object-oriented programming, all in the C programming language. The second part (Chaps. 6–9) teaches the fundamentals of using C++. The final part (Chaps. 10–12) examines selected C++ issues in much greater depth. This last part will be of interest even to seasoned C++ programmers.

The next chapter, Chapter 1, provides a quick refresher course in the more advanced features of C. Although readers are expected to already be familiar with

C, many will not have used some of the more advanced features of the language such as pointers to functions and dynamic memory allocation. These features are used extensively in object-oriented programming, and all such features are reviewed in this chapter.

Chapter 2 reviews the concepts of structured programming. We consider a reasonably complex problem, counting excessively used words in a text file. This chapter gives a fully coded structured solution to this problem.

Chapter 3 introduces object-oriented programming. It defines most of the new object-oriented terminology in terms designed to be comfortable to the C programmer. It discusses the meaning of object-oriented programming. It recodes the problem of the previous chapter using an object-oriented solution, still in C, giving us a concrete example to contrast structured and object-oriented approaches to programming. The main purpose of this chapter is to give an intuitive understanding of what we mean by the term object-oriented programming.

Chapter 4 introduces more rigor to the concept of object-oriented programming in C. We discuss how programs must be organized to allow multiple instantiations of classes and maximum flexibility in the use of classes. As an example of a well organized object-oriented program, we look at software designed to manage a doctor's waiting room. This program uses many object-oriented data structures designed with minimal compile time limitations.

Chapter 5 discusses some of the problems one faces using C to develop object-oriented programming. Since C++ was developed primarily to address these limitations, this chapter essentially discusses the design goals of C++. Understanding the issues C++ was designed to address makes it easier to understand the new syntax of the language, and why the features work the way they do.

Chapter 6 gives an introduction to object-oriented programming in C++. This chapter covers the basics: defining classes, instantiating objects, and invoking methods. We look at C++ code designed to manage point of sale transactions as an example of how C++ can be used to solve real life problems.

Chapter 7 discusses inheritance, or class derivation. Inheritance is difficult to program in C, so this concept is introduced now for the first time. Class derivation is an important feature of C++, providing a fundamental technique for writing generic and reusable code.

Chapter 8 discusses method resolution in C++ in more depth. It compares virtual and non virtual resolution, and shows how virtual resolution compares to the C techniques of using function pointers to achieve code generality. The linked list class introduced earlier is recoded to make full use of inheritance and virtual resolution.

Chapter 9 discusses a collection of issues all having to do with managing memory in C++. We discuss the relationship between memory allocation and memory construction, between deallocation and destruction. We show how the

C++ programmer can take full control over allocation, construction, deallocation, and destruction. We discuss related issues such as reference and constant variable types and assignment operators.

Chapter 10 shows how the most popular C++ precompiler actually works. We look at the C code the precompiler emits, and compare this code to our own versions of C classes. This chapter gives some valuable insight into why C++ works the way it does, and why it has some of the problems it has.

Chapter 11 discusses some of the problems with C++. This is not to denigrate the language, only to point out some of the tradeoffs the language makes.

Chapter 12 gives a full, complex example coded in C++. The example is a text processing program. It is difficult to appreciate how C++ is used in a real programming environment without looking at a real problem. This chapter solves a problem, a real problem, with a nontrivial solution. This chapter includes over 18 class definitions and 1700 lines of code. By looking at this code in detail, we can appreciate the complexities of trying to apply object-oriented programming, and the design issues one typically faces.

Finally, an epilogue. This gives an overview of what this book has not covered, and points the reader in some directions for following up on areas of interest.

Acknowledgments

I owe a great deal to a great many people for their support in writing this book.

I especially thank my wife, Alice Sessions, who has not only supported the effort emotionally, but spent many hours at the word processor entering and editing text. She also found many of the opening chapter quotations.

Other members of my family have taken a keen interest in this work. My daughter Emily critiqued quotations and helped choose the title. My son Michael kept reminding me to "work on the book."

The book has benefited greatly from some very thorough reviews by some very knowledgeable people. I am grateful to Stephen Dewhurst of Glockenspiel, Doug Lea of SUNY at Oswego, and Clovis Tondo of IBM at Boca Raton for their many helpful suggestions.

I appreciate the support of IBM in this writing. IBM has allowed me to use their hardware and software, and has provided an environment which greatly nourishes the creative process. Tony Dvorak, Mike Kiehl, Larry Loucks, and others have encouraged and supported publishing activity. My co-workers have been very helpful. Hari Madduri and Craig Becker especially have provided me with valuable in depth critiques of earlier revisions of this manuscript. Mike Conner was the first to point out to me the problems of C++ library version incompatibility, one of the topics in the C++ Problems chapter.

Although IBM has kindly supported this effort, it has exerted no editorial control. The views expressed here reflect those of the author, and not necessarily those of IBM.

Prentice Hall is, as always, a pleasure to work with. I am greatly indebted to my editor Greg Doench for his encouragement, and to his assistant Joan Magrabi for coordinating most of the activity of this book.

Clovis Tondo of IBM Boca Raton designed this book and prepared it for typesetting. The final camera ready copy was printed with the Chelgraph IBX typesetter by TYPE 2000, 16 Madrona Avenue, Mill Valley, California 94941.

It seems only appropriate to thank the many writers' hangouts of Austin, Texas where so much of this book was written and edited. These are all spots, where, for the price of a expresso or an inexpensive meal, one can take over a table, spread out a ream or two of paper, and lose oneself for hours in the process of writing. These establishments include Martin Brothers Cafe, Chez Fred, Kerbey Lane Cafe, La Zona Rosa, Texas French Bread Bakery, Elephant Club, University of Texas Student Union, Upper Crust Bakery, Campus Cafe, and of course, the quintessential Austin writer's hangout, Captain Quackenbush's Intergalactic Dessert and Expresso Emporium. Thanks to all of you for your tolerance, and to the many other establishments I have yet to discover.

Finally, I thank the many publishers who have kindly consented to allow me to reprint from these copyrighted materials:

Don Quixote by Cervantes, translated by Samuel Putnam, Copyright © 1951 Viking Press. Reprinted with permission.

Hinduism by R. C. Zaehner, Copyright © 1966 Oxford University Press. By permission of Oxford University Press.

Microprocessors and Microsystems (1990) Vol. 14 No. 3, pp. 149–152, Copyright © 1990, Butterworth-Heinemann Ltd. Reprinted with permission.

On the Composition of Well-Structured Programs by Niklaus Wirth in *ACM Computing Surveys*, December 1974. Copyright © 1974 by Association for Computing Machinery, Inc. Reprinted with permission.

Tao Te Ching by Lao Tsu, translated by Gia-Fu Feng and Jane English, Published by Vintage Books, Copyright © 1972 by Gia-Fu Feng and Jane English. Reprinted with permission.

The Analects of Confucius translated by Arthur Waley, Copyright © 1938 by George Allen & Unwin, Ltd. Reprinted with permission.

The I Ching translated by Richard Wilhelm and Cary F. Baynes, Copyright © 1977 by Princeton University Press. Reprinted with permission.

The Annotated Mother Goose edited by William S. Baring-Gould and Cecil Baring-Gould, Copyright © 1971 NAL/Dutton. Reprinted with permission.

Tzu-kung asked how to become Good. The Master said, A craftsman, if he means to do good work, must first sharpen his tools.

- The Analects of Confucius
Translated by Arthur Waley

Chapter 1

C Refresher

1.1 Introduction

Although this book assumes readers have a working knowledge of the C programming language, some of the more advanced features of the language may be unfamiliar to some readers. This chapter reviews some important features of the language which we depend on in developing the techniques of this book.

If you have been using C extensively in a production environment, you may have no need of this chapter at all. If you have just finished your first course in the language, you may want to study this chapter carefully. If you fall someplace in the middle, as most readers will, browse through the chapter and study those sections which seem new to you. As you continue in this book, return to this chapter on an "as needed" basis.

If you find yourself unable to understand C programming techniques not covered in this chapter, unable to understand the material in this chapter, or unable to complete the exercises at the end of this chapter, you may need to review a C introductory text.

1.2 typedef

C provides a standard collection of types. When a variable is declared, it can be declared to be any of the built in C types. For example,

1

```
int size;
```

declares a variable `size` to be the standard C type `int`. We can also declare new types using the **typedef** construct. These new types can then be used in variable declarations such as

```
name myName;
name yourName;
```

The general rule for using a **typedef** to define a desired type is

1. Define a variable of the desired type.

2. Place **typedef** in the front of the line.

For example,

```
char name[100];
```

declares a variable which is a 100 character array.

```
typedef char name[100];
```

declares a type which is a 100 character array. The lines

```
name myName;
name yourName;
```

then declare two variables of type **name** which, based on our **typedef**, are 100 character arrays. These declarations are exactly equivalent to

```
char myName[100];
char yourName[100];
```

but have two advantages. First, the declarations are simpler. Second, type changes are easier.

By collecting **typedef**s, in a small number of header files, we can update our types in one location and propagate them quickly throughout the system. Suppose, for example, we have 20 variables of type **name** scattered throughout our system, and we then discover that we need 110 characters instead of 100 for a name. We can update every variable of type **name** by making this one change

```
typedef char name[110];   /* Changed from 100 */
```

Without the **typedef**, we must hunt through possibly hundreds of declarations like

```
char myName[100];
char who[110];
char what[100];
char where[98];
```

and decide on an individual basis which of these variables were meant to hold names and therefore need updating, a time consuming and error prone process.

1.3 Structures and Structure Pointers

Programs are often responsible for coordinating large amounts of data. One way of managing the complexity of data is to package together related data items into what is called a structure. For example, we could define an employee structure that contains an employee name, address, social security number, and manager name. A program which manipulates ten thousand employee names, ten thousand employee addresses, ten thousand social security numbers, and ten thousand manager names is a complicated program. A program which manipulates ten thousand employee structures is a simple program. The volume of data is similar for both programs, but the latter manages the complexity of the data by using structures.

The term *structure* is commonly used to refer to both the definition and the allocation of data structures. The definition of a structure defines the size and contents of a given structure, without actually allocating memory. The allocation takes an existing definition and allocates memory for such a structure. The definition of a structure is done exactly once per structure type. The allocation may be done any number of times, including zero.

A structure is defined using the syntax

```
struct structureName {
  type1 item1;
  type2 item2;
  etc.
};
```

The definition of our employee structure looks like

```
struct employeeStructure {
  char name[100];
  char address[100];
  char ssnum[20];
  char manager[100];
};
```

A structure is allocated using the syntax

```
struct definedStructureName thisStructureName;
```

We can define an instance of the `employeeStructure` named `mary` by

```
struct employeeStructure mary;
```

Once a structure has been allocated, we refer to its elements using this syntax

```
structure.item
```

For example, we could print **mary**'s name by

```
printf("Name: %s\n", mary.name);
```

We can also define variables which contain the addresses of structures. The syntax for this is

```
struct structName *varName;
```

so we could have

```
struct employeeStructure mary;        /* Allocate mary */
struct employeeStructure sam;         /* Allocate sam */
struct employeeStructure *currentEmp; /* Allocate Pointer */
currentEmp = &mary;                   /* Set Pointer to mary */
```

Logically, you would expect to be able to refer to a member of a structure being pointed to by this syntax:

```
(*varName).item
```

or in this case,

```
(*currentEmp).name
```

but C provides this more convenient equivalent syntax

```
varName->item
```

or in this case,

```
currentEmp->name
```

When we pass a structure into a function, we almost always pass in the address of the structure, and receive it as a pointer. The following types of code fragments are very common.

```
struct employeeStructure mary;
struct employeeStructure sam;
/* ... */
printEmp(&mary);
printEmp(&sam);
}
void printEmp(employee *thisEmp)
{
/* ... */
```

We also frequently see structures **typedef**ed. The following statement

```
    typedef struct employeeStructure employee;
```

defines **employee** to be a valid C type, in that it can be used to define other variables. With this **typedef**, we can replace these lines

```
    struct employeeStructure mary;      /* Allocate mary */
    struct employeeStructure sam;       /* Allocate sam */
    struct employeeStructure *currentEmp; /* Allocate Pointer */
    currentEmp = &mary;                 /* Set Pointer to mary */
```

by these

```
    employee mary;          /* Allocate mary */
    employee sam;           /* Allocate sam */
    employee *currentEmp;   /* Allocate Pointer */
    currentEmp = &mary;     /* Set Pointer to mary */
```

The following program shows all of these techniques in use.

```
    #include <stdio.h>
    #include <stdlib.h>

/* Define an employee structure.
   ---------------------------- */
    struct employeeStructure {
      char name[100];
      char address[100];
      char ssnum[20];
      char manager[100];
    };
    typedef struct employeeStructure employee;

/* Function declarations.
   ---------------------- */
    void printEmp(employee *thisEmp);

int main()
{
/* Allocate memory for mary and sam.
   -------------------------------- */
    employee mary;
    employee sam;
```

```
   /* Initialize mary.
      ---------------- */
      strcpy(mary.name, "Mary");
      strcpy(mary.address, "Austin, Tx.");
      strcpy(mary.ssnum, "123-45-6789");
      strcpy(mary.manager, "CEO");

   /* Initialize sam.
      --------------- */
      strcpy(sam.name, "Sam");
      strcpy(sam.address, "Austin, Tx.");
      strcpy(sam.ssnum, "456-78-9012");
      strcpy(sam.manager, mary.name);

   /* Print mary and sam.
      ------------------- */
      printEmp(&mary);
      printEmp(&sam);
      return 0;
   }
   /* Print an employee record.
      ------------------------- */
   void printEmp(employee *thisEmp)
   {
      printf("-------------------------------------------------\n");
      printf("                  Name: %s\n", thisEmp->name);
      printf("               Address: %s\n", thisEmp->address);
      printf("Social Security Number: %s\n", thisEmp->ssnum);
      printf("               Manager: %s\n", thisEmp->manager);
   }
```

When we run this program, we get this output

```
-------------------------------------------
                  Name: Mary
               Address: Austin, Tx.
Social Security Number: 123-45-6789
               Manager: CEO
-------------------------------------------
                  Name: Sam
               Address: Austin, Tx.
Social Security Number: 456-78-9012
               Manager: Mary
```

Structures provide a handy way of packaging together related information. The structure definition defines how the packaging is to be done. The structure allocation declares instances of such packages. It is very important not to confuse the definition and the declaration of a structure.

1.4 Dynamic Memory Allocation

In the previous section's program, we had these lines allocating memory for structures

```
employee mary;
employee sam;
```

This is an example of compile time memory allocation, or to be more precise, memory whose allocation is determined at compile time. We call this kind of memory allocation *static* memory allocation. It is also possible to allocate memory for structures at run time, which we call *dynamic* memory allocation. Dynamic allocation is common in situations where the maximum number of structures is unknown (such as a linked list of unknown length) or when it is too costly to allocate the entire memory at once (such as a large array of structures).

Dynamic memory allocation is a four step process. First, you define the structure. Second, you declare a pointer to the structure. Third, you ask the system to make a runtime memory allocation (usually through the function `malloc()`), and set the pointer to the memory the system allocates. Fourth, you inform the system when you no longer need the memory (usually through the function `free()`).

Other than the process of allocation and deallocation, dynamically allocated structures behave exactly like statically allocated structures.

The function `malloc()` is used to dynamically allocate memory. It takes a single parameter, the number of bytes needed. Typically one determines the number of bytes needed using the precompiler directive `sizeof()`, which takes as its argument a valid data type.

The function `free()` is paired with `malloc()`. Memory that is allocated with `malloc()` is freed with `free()`. The function `free()` takes a single parameter, the address of the memory block being freed. The following code segment demonstrates how these functions are coordinated:

```
struct employeeStructure {
  char name[100];
  char address[100];
  char ssnum[20];
  char manager[100];
};
```

```
typedef struct employeeStructure employee;
employee *thisEmp;
thisEmp = malloc(sizeof(employee));
/* ... */
free(thisEmp);
```

The mary/sam program rewritten to use dynamic allocation looks like this

```
#include <stdio.h>
#include <stdlib.h>

/* Define an employee structure.
   --------------------------- */
   struct employeeStructure {
     char name[100];
     char address[100];
     char ssnum[20];
     char manager[100];
   };
   typedef struct employeeStructure employee;

/* Function declarations.
   -------------------- */
   void printEmp(employee *thisEmp);

int main()
{
/* Allocate memory for mary and sam.
   ------------------------------- */
   employee *mary;   /* Now pointer */
   employee *sam;    /* Ditto */

   mary = malloc (sizeof (employee));
   sam  = malloc (sizeof (employee));

/* Initialize mary.
   -------------- */
   strcpy(mary->name, "Mary");
   strcpy(mary->address, "Austin, Tx.");
   strcpy(mary->ssnum, "123-45-6789");
   strcpy(mary->manager, "CEO");
```

```
/* Initialize sam.
   --------------- */
strcpy(sam->name, "Sam");
strcpy(sam->address, "Austin, Tx.");
strcpy(sam->ssnum, "456-78-9012");
strcpy(sam->manager, mary->name);

/* Print mary and sam.
   ------------------ */
printEmp(mary);
printEmp(sam);
return 0;
}
```

The `printEmp()` function is unchanged.

1.5 Generic Pointers

We often find the need for a pointer of unknown type. The generic C pointer is
`void *`. A `void *` variable can contain the address of anything. We have already
seen `void *` being used as a generic pointer in the last section, in this line

```
mary = malloc(sizeof(employee));
```

`malloc()` is defined as returning `void *`, and `mary` is defined to be an
`employee *`. Normally C does not allow a pointer of one type to be assigned the
value of a pointer of a different type without an explicit typecast. The exception is
when one of the pointers is a `void *`.

We may also use a `void *` when a variable may hold the address of any of a
number of datatypes. One such example is the function `printIt()`, in this file

```
#include <stdio.h>
#include <stdlib.h>

#define EMPLOYEE 0
#define SALE 1

struct employeeStructure {
  char name[100];
};
typedef struct employeeStructure employee;
```

```
struct saleStructure {
  int   number;
  char itemDescription[100];
};
typedef struct saleStructure sale;

void printIt(void *itemToPrint, int type)
{
    employee *thisEmp;
    sale *thisSale;

    if (type == EMPLOYEE) {
       thisEmp = itemToPrint;
       printf("Employee Name: %s\n", thisEmp->name);
    }
    if (type == SALE) {
       thisSale = itemToPrint;
       printf("  Number Sold: %d Item Description: %s\n",
          thisSale->number, thisSale->itemDescription);
    }
}
```

Since `printIt()` doesn't know which of two address types it will be called with, it uses the generic address, which will accept either.

The main program uses `printIt()` with both types of addresses:

```
void printIt(void *itemToPrint, int type);
int main()
{
    employee *salesPerson;
    sale *thisSale;

    salesPerson = malloc(sizeof(employee));
    thisSale = malloc(sizeof(sale));

    strcpy(salesPerson->name, "Helen");
    strcpy(thisSale->itemDescription, "Tea Pot");
    thisSale->number = 2;
    printIt(salesPerson, EMPLOYEE);
    printIt(thisSale, SALE);
    return 0;
}
```

The program gives this output

```
Employee Name: Helen
   Number Sold: 2 Item Description: Tea Pot
```

Once `printIt()` has decided what type of address it has been passed, it sets an appropriate local variable to the parameter. This is strictly a documentation aid. We could have referred to

```
((employee *)itemToPrint)->name
```

rather than

```
thisEmp->name
```

but the latter seems more readable.

1.6 Prototyping Functions

All functions should be prototyped before they are used. Prototyping a function means defining to the compiler the name of the function, the return type, and the types of any parameters. This allows the compiler to detect many, but not all, errors in the use of the function before they cause run time problems. The syntax for prototyping is

```
returnType functionName(paramType1 dummyName1, ...);
```

We saw an example of this function prototype in the last section

```
void printIt(void *itemToPrint, int type);
```

which said that the function `printIt()` has no return value and takes two parameters. The first can be any address. The second must be an integer. The name of the parameter is optional. The `printIt()` prototype could have been written

```
void printIt(void *, int);
```

but we usually include the dummy parameter names for documentation purposes.

We can see how helpful prototyping is in this example. First, we define two structures:

```
struct employeeStructure {
  char name[100];
};
typedef struct employeeStructure employee;
```

```
struct saleStructure {
  int   number;
  char itemDescription[100];
};
typedef struct saleStructure sale;
```

then give this prototype for `printEmp()`:

```
void printEmp(employee *thisEmp);
```

We can see from the implementation of `printEmp()` that it truly expects only one type of address

```
void printEmp(employee *thisEmp)
{
    printf("Employee Name: %s\n", thisEmp->name);
}
```

This code segment illustrates four invocations of `printEmp()`. The first one is correct. The next three contain errors, two of which will be flagged by the compiler. These two can be flagged only because the function was prototyped.

```
employee *salesPerson;
sale *thisSale;
int n;

printEmp(salesPerson);          /* OK */
printEmp(thisSale);             /* Compile Error */
n = printEmp(salesPerson);      /* Compile Error */
printEmp((employee *)thisSale); /* Run Time Error */
```

The last invocation is an error, but is not detected. The compiler wrongly assumes that because the code has typecast a `sale` address to an `employee` address, that the code knows what it is doing.

1.7   Boolean Functions

A boolean variable is a variable which can be interpreted as true or false. In C, 0 is considered false. Anything else is considered true. A boolean thus can contain two significant values: zero, and nonzero. Any of the integer family of types and any pointer can be treated as a boolean.

A function can also be considered to return a boolean, as can an expression. Any boolean variable, function, or expressions can be used wherever C expects a truth value. Most typically, this is inside an `if` statement.

It is fairly obvious that the following function can be treated as a boolean:

```
int validMonth1(int month)
{
   if (month>=1 && month <=12) return 1;
   else return 0;
}
```

but less obvious is that the following also is a valid boolean:

```
char *validMonth2(int month)
{
   char *months[12] = {
      "January", "February", "March", "April",
      "May", "Junk", "July", "August",
      "September", "October", "November", "December"
   };
   if (month>=1 && month <= 12) return months[month-1];
   else return 0;
}
```

Look closely at `validMonth2()`. It either returns 0 (a valid address) or some nonzero address. Any nonzero address is, when treated as a boolean, considered to be true. Note that 0 has a unique position among integers. It is the *only* integer value which can safely be assigned to any pointer variable, and this is designed just so that pointers can be interpreted as booleans.

The following program shows these functions being used as booleans:

```
#include <stdio.h>
int validMonth1(int month);
char *validMonth2(int month);
int main()
{
   int testMonth;
   char *result;

   testMonth = 2;
   if (validMonth1(testMonth))
      printf("%d is valid month\n", testMonth);
   if (validMonth2(testMonth))
      printf("%d is valid month\n", testMonth);
   if (result = validMonth2(testMonth))
      printf("%d is %s\n", testMonth, result);
   return 0;
}
```

The program gives this output

```
2 is valid month
2 is valid month
2 is February
```

1.8   Passing by Value

In C, when a function is called, the parameters are passed by value. This mean that the function gets its own local copy of each of the parameters. Any updates the function makes to parameters are made to its local copies. There are no exceptions to this rule. The following code demonstrates this rule:

```
#include <stdio.h>
void incrBy2(int n);
int main()
{
  int n;
  n = 2;
  printf("in main...... n: %d\n", n);
  incrBy2(n);
  printf("in main...... n: %d\n", n);
  return 0;
}
void incrBy2(int n)
{
  n = n + 2;
  printf("In incrBy2... n: %d\n", n);
}
```

The output shows that the update of **n** by `incrBy2()` is not seen by the calling code.

```
in main...... n: 2
In incrBy2... n: 4
in main...... n: 2
```

1.9   Updating Function Parameters

Not withstanding the previous section, there are times when a function needs to return more information than just its return value. If we cannot update any of the parameters, how is this to be accomplished? The answer is through addresses.

We always have the option of indirect updates through a variable's address. The following program, for example, updates **n** through such indirection:

```
#include <stdio.h>
int main()
{
  int n;
  int *addressOfn;

  addressOfn = &n;
  n = 2;
  printf("n: %d\n", n);
  *addressOfn = 4;
  printf("n: %d\n", n);
  return 0;
}
```

giving this output

```
n: 2
n: 4
```

We can use this same technique with function parameters. If we set up a parameter to be not a variable, but the address of a variable, then our function can indirectly update the variable to which the address points. This does not alter our assertion of the last section that parameters cannot be updated. The parameter is not updated. The variable it points to is updated.

This code uses this technique to create a function **timeScan()** , which takes a string such as "04:22", and calculates the minutes and seconds represented by the string.

```
#include <stdio.h>
#include <stdlib.h>

int timeScan(char *timeString, int *minutes, int *seconds);

int main()
{
  int minutes, seconds;
  char *thisTime = "1:34";
  if (timeScan(thisTime, &minutes, &seconds))
      printf("Time: %s is Valid... minutes: %d seconds: %d\n",
      thisTime, minutes, seconds);
```

```
    else
        printf("Time: %s is Not Valid\n", thisTime);
    return 0;
}

int timeScan(char *timeString, int *minutes, int *seconds)
{
    int tminutes, tseconds;
    char colon;
    sscanf(timeString, "%d%1c%d", &tminutes, &colon, &tseconds);
    if (tminutes < 0 || tminutes > 60) return 0;
    if (tseconds < 0 || tseconds > 60) return 0;
    *minutes = tminutes;
    *seconds = tseconds;
    return 1;
}
```

The output from this is

```
Time: 1:34 is Valid... minutes: 1 seconds: 34
```

1.10   Logical Equality Operator

Boolean operators are a little unusual in that they return 0 or 1. As we have discussed, C interprets 0 as false, and nonzero, including 1, as true. This is demonstrated in the following program. Notice the difference between the first print statement, which shows a boolean operation, and the fourth, which shows a deceptively similar looking assignment operator.

```
#include <stdio.h>
int main()
{
    int n;
    n = 5;
    printf("n == 5 returns %d\n", n == 5);
    printf("n != 5 returns %d\n", n != 5);
    printf("n != 2 returns %d\n", n != 2);
    printf("n = 5  returns %d\n", n = 5);
    return 0;
}
```

The program gives this output

```
n == 5 returns 1
n != 5 returns 0
n != 2 returns 1
n = 5   returns 5
```

1.11   Static Data

When data is declared locally inside a function, the data is by default automatic. Automatic data is allocated when the function is entered, and deallocated when the function is exited. There is no reason to expect that further entries into the function will allocate data from the same memory locations as earlier function entries. It is also quite likely that, even if the memory is allocated from the same location, that other code would have used those locations in the interim. Therefore, one cannot assume that upon entry the local variable states are as they were left at last exit.

When a consistent state is needed across invocations, one uses the `static` keyword. This informs the compiler that allocation is to be stable. The memory assigned to static local variables is assigned permanently and will not be used by other segments. Any initialization of static variables is done just once. The following function uses a static local variable to keep track of whether the function has already been called.

```c
void testFunction(void)
{
  static int alreadyCalled = 0;
  if (!alreadyCalled)
     printf ("First time call of testFunction\n");
  alreadyCalled = 1;
}
```

This main program demonstrates its use

```c
#include <stdio.h>
void testFunction(void);
int main()
{
  testFunction();
  testFunction();
  testFunction();
  return 0;
}
```

and gives this output

```
First time call of testFunction
```

If we change the declaration of `alreadyCalled`, as in

```
void testFunction(void)
{
  int alreadyCalled = 0;      /* Not static anymore. */
  if (!alreadyCalled)
     printf ("First time call of testFunction\n");
  alreadyCalled = 1;
}
```

we get a very different result:

```
First time call of testFunction
First time call of testFunction
First time call of testFunction
```

As we can see here, `alreadyCalled` is now initialized with every entry of `testFunction()`.

Static variables are sometimes used to allocate blocks accessed from more than one function. One such example is this version of `getString()`

```
char *getString(void)
{
  static char charArray[100];
  strcpy(charArray, "String courtesy of getString");
  return charArray;
}
```

used by this main program

```
#include <stdio.h>
char *getString(void);
int main()
{
  char *myString;
  myString = getString();
  printf("%s\n", myString);
  return 0;
}
```

giving this output

```
String courtesy of getString
```

If we redefine `charArray` to be nonstatic, as

```
char *getString(void)
{
  char charArray[100];      /* Not static anymore. */
  strcpy(charArray, "String courtesy of getString");
  return charArray;
}
```

we get a main program which prints a string of garbage characters.

1.12   Scope Rules

Every variable has a specific scope, that is, a body of code within which the variable can be referenced. There are three main scopes we will consider. A variable has *local* scope if it is declared within a function. A variable with local scope can be referenced only from within the declaring function. A variable has *file* scope if it is declared in the file before any functions are declared, and specified as `static`. A variable with file scope can be referenced from within any function whose code resides in the declaring file. A variable has *global* scope if it is declared like a file scope variable, but without the static qualifier. Such a variable can be referenced in any function who declares the variable with the `extern` qualifier.

The following program, made up of two code files, uses both local and global variables. The first file is

```
#include <stdio.h>

char *globalString;
void testFunction(void);
int main()
{
    char *mainString = "String from main program";
    globalString = mainString;
    printf("In main, globalString: %s\n", globalString);
    testFunction();
    printf("In main, globalString: %s\n", globalString);
    return 0;
}
```

and the second is

```
#include <stdio.h>

extern char *globalString;
```

```
void testFunction(void)
{
  char *testFunString = "String from testFunction";
  globalString = testFunString;
}
```

The variable `globalString` is declared global in the first file, and **extern** in the second. Thus updates to `globalString` made by `testFunction()` are seen by the main program in the first file, as shown in this output

```
In main, globalString: String from main program
In main, globalString: String from testFunction
```

If we add the **static** qualifier to the declaration in the first file, as here

```
#include <stdio.h>

static char *globalString;
void testFunction(void);
int main()
{
    char *mainString = "String from main program";
    globalString = mainString;
    printf("In main, globalString: %s\n", globalString);
    testFunction();
    printf("In main, globalString: %s\n", globalString);
    return 0;
}
```

we get a different result. Now we get a link error, as the linker attempts to resolve the **extern** declaration in the second file against a similarly named variable with global scope. It can't find any, since the static qualifier says `globalString` has file scope only.

If the same variable name is defined with more than one scope, the most limiting scope always wins. So if a function declares a name locally that was also declared globally, any references made to the variable will be to the local version. We can see the difference this change makes to `testFunction()`

```
#include <stdio.h>
extern char *globalString;
```

```
void testFunction(void)
{
  char *globalString;          /* Local redeclaration. */
  char *testFunString = "String from testFunction";
  globalString = testFunString;
}
```

from this output

```
In main, globalString: String from main program
In main, globalString: String from main program
```

1.13 Function Pointers

There are two ways functions can be invoked in C: by name and by address. Invocation by name is by far the most common, and is used when the programmer knows unequivocally which function is to be called. There are other times when the programmer knows that some function needs to be invoked, and knows a great deal about the function that will be invoked, but does not know the name of the function. This is the time for call by address.

Often this technique is used to write highly generic functions which need to perform some small piece of nongeneric functionality. The nongeneric functionality is packaged into another function. The address of the nongeneric function is passed into the generic function as a parameter. When the times comes to perform the nongeneric functionality, the nongeneric function is invoked by address.

Let's consider writing a function to print out a null terminated array of pointers to objects of some unknown type. This function will look something like this

```
void printArray(void *thisArray[])
{
  int n;
  void *nextElement;
  for (n=0; thisArray[n]; n++) {
    nextElement = thisArray[n];
    /* print thisElement */
  }
}
```

The problem is that since we don't know what type of objects are stored in the array, we don't know what kind of code it takes to print one.

This function **printArray()** is a good example of a generic function needing some nongeneric functionality. Based on our earlier discussion, we add a second parameter whose type is the address of a print function which returns **void** and takes one parameter, a `void *`. Notice that although we don't know the name of the function, we do know quite a lot about it. We know its return type, its parameters, and, in a generic sense, what behavior is expected.

The declaration of a function pointer looks like

```
returnType (*pointerName)(typeParam1 dummyParam1, ...);
```

We invoke a function though its address with this syntax

```
(*pointerName)(param1,..);
```

Rewriting `printArray()` to use this additional parameter, we get

```
void printArray(
  void *thisArray[],
  void (*printFunction)(void *thisElement))
{
  int n;
  for(n=0; thisArray[n]; n++) {
     (*printFunction)(thisArray[n]);
  }
  printf("------------\n");
}
```

A client wanting to use `printArray()` must implement the necessary print functions. Two such print functions could be these

```
void printPerson(char *thisPerson)
{
  printf("Person: %s\n", thisPerson);
}

void printFlavor(char *thisFlavor)
{
  printf("Flavor: %s\n", thisFlavor);
}
```

The following program uses these print functions and `printArray()` to display two arrays:

```
#include <stdio.h>

void printPerson(char *thisPerson);
void printFlavor(char *thisFlavor);
void printArray(
  void *thisArray[],
  void (*printFunction)(void *thisElement));
```

```
int main()
{

  char *flavors[4] = {
    "Chocolate", "Strawberry", "Vanilla", 0
  };
  char *people[5] = {
    "Aristotle", "Lincoln", "Confucius", "Shakespeare", 0
  };
  printArray(flavors, printFlavor);
  printArray(people, printPerson);
  return 0;
}
```

giving this output:

```
Flavor: Chocolate
Flavor: Strawberry
Flavor: Vanilla
------------
Person: Aristotle
Person: Lincoln
Person: Confucius
Person: Shakespeare
------------
```

1.14 Exercises

Exercise 1.1 Write a program equivalent to the mary/sam program without using structures.

Exercise 1.2 Classify each line of the following program as either definition, allocation, or initialization.

```
struct animalType {
  char noise[100];
  char habitat[100];
};
typedef struct animalType animal;
animal Toto;
```

```
animal Lassie;
animal *myAnimal;
myAnimal = &Toto;
```

Exercise 1.3 Starting from the code shown in the last problem, write the next line, which should copy the string "Grrrrrrr" into the structure member **noise** of the structure pointed to by **myAnimal**.

Exercise 1.4 Write a program showing the following declaration in use:

```
employee currentEmps[100];
```

Exercise 1.5 Write a program showing the following declaration in use:

```
employee *currentEmps[100];
```

Exercise 1.6 Rewrite the **employee** definition so that instead of a manager's name being embedded into the employee record, a pointer to the manager's structure is embedded. Rewrite the program so that the overall logic and output of the program works as before.

Exercise 1.7 Given this employee structure

```
struct employeeStructure {
  char name[100];
  char ssnum[100];
  struct employeeStructure *manager;
};
typedef struct employeeStructure employee;
```

write a boolean function which, given an employee, returns a pointer to the manager's name, if there is a manager, or false if there is no manager.

Exercise 1.8 Given the structure definition in the last problem, and this one:

```
struct saleStructure {
  int number;
  char itemDescription[100];
};
typedef struct saleStructure sale;
```

write code to create arrays of **employees** and **sales**, and use the function **printArray()** discussed in Section 1.13 to print these arrays.

Exercise 1.9 Given the employee definition in problem 7, write a print function compatible with **printArray()** to print an array of **employees** along with their managers. Demonstrate the code in a test program.

This is the man all tattered and torn
That kissed the maiden all forlorn,
That milked the cow with the crumpled horn,
That tossed the dog,
That worried the cat,
That killed the rat,
That ate the malt,
That lay in the house that Jack built.

- The Annotated Mother Goose
Edited by William S. Baring-Gould and
Cecil Baring-Gould

Chapter 2

Structured Programming In C

The next two chapters explore the similarities and differences between classical structured programming and object-oriented programming. We will do this by solving a particular programming problem twice, one for each approach. This will allow us to clarify what we mean by object-oriented programming, and allow us to contrast the quality and reusability of structured and object-oriented code.

2.1   Introduction

Most of us appreciate the principles of program modularization. We may describe these principles as *top-down programming*, *step-wise refinement*, or *structured programming*. These terms are essentially synonymous, all describing a basic approach to program organization and development. They describe a commitment to logical, unidirectional program flow, and a belief that the quality of a program

27

is directly related to the care, skill and determination of the author.

Some practioners take a pragmatic approach to achieving program modularization, suggesting that specific programming rules be followed. Among the more familiar rules are these:

- Do not use GOTOs.

- Do not write functions which exceed a certain number of lines.

- Do not use global variables.

Many lines of unreadable, unmanageable, and unmaintainable code exist that adhere strictly to every one of these rules. We can also find examples of well organized, finely crafted code that technically violates all of these rules. Both novice and professional programmers can benefit by considering these rules as guidelines, rather than ends in themselves. The experienced programmer understands not only the rules, but the motivation behind the rules, and can recognize the exceptional situations when these rules should not apply.

No formal checklist exists that can reliably tell us if a program is well structured, although it is most likely well structured if a competent reader can follow the logic without becoming bogged down in the details.

The best organized programs seem the simplest. They appear to solve a series of obvious problems, and invoke in the reader a reaction of "What's the big deal — I can do that." It is the disheveled and disorganized programs that seem superficially impressive, because we tend to attribute our lack of understanding to intellectual superiority on the part of the author. Our respect for such programs is misplaced. Far greater skill is needed to maintain control of the programming process and to methodically craft each function as a self-contained problem with an understandable solution.

Good programmers are always aware of the limited capacity of the human mind. Our ability to appreciate relationships deteriorates as the number of items involved increases. Consider this "structured" description of a forest

- A forest is made up of trees and other plant life.

- Trees are made of leaves, branches, and trunks.

- Leaves are made up of a waterproof jacket, veins, and cells devoted to photosynthesis.

- The cells devoted to photosynthesis are made up primarily of structural molecules and molecules that capture energy.

- The structural molecules of these cells are mostly carbohydrates.

- The molecules that capture energy are primarily chlorophyll, a molecule similar in structure to hemoglobin.

Compare this structured description to the following, which considers the same view from an "un-structured" perspective:

> Many molecules go into a forest, including carbohydrates and chlorophyll. The carbohydrates and chlorophyll are found in the leaves. Leaves are parts of trees. Trees have branches and trunks in addition to leaves. The carbohydrates are mostly structural. The chlorophyll is a molecule specialized for capturing energy. The forest is made up of other plant life besides trees. The chlorophyll in the leaves is very similar in structure to hemoglobin. The chlorophyll is used by the leaves for photosynthesis. The leaves also have waterproof jackets and veins.

The structured forest description is intellectually manageable at all levels. The unstructured description leaves us floundering, without having any idea what we are talking about; we literally cannot see the forest for the trees.

2.2 Step-Wise Refinement

The term *step-wise refinement* is used by Niklaus Wirth to describe a structured approach to programming. We can actually describe a formal algorithm for this stepwise refinement process of program development. By carefully following this recursive algorithm, even the most complex problems are solvable in due time. The algorithm for stepwise refinement looks like this

```
solve_problem(problem)
{
  if (problem == trivial) write_solution;
  else {
    breakdown_problem_into_N_subproblems;
    define_relationship_between_subproblems;
    for (each_subproblem) solve_problem(subproblem);
  }
}
```

Let us look at an example of this refinement methodology. Consider writing a program named **scanline** to perform text scans. This program will ask the user for the name of a text file and a search string. The program will then print the file line by line. Each line will be preceded by three characters indicating the presence (or absence) of the search string. Lines containing the search string will be preceded by "-->", others by blanks.

A typical **scanline** run looks like this

```
run scanline
      Text File: meeting.900912
   Search String: Amanita
      Sunday's foray consisted of a pleasant walk
      through the Greenvale woods and surrounding
      meadows.  Participants were surprised at the
      quantity and quality of Agaricus campestris
      collected and by the relative sparseness of
-->   Amanitas.  The one exception was the hardwoods
      near the Hodgkins estate, which abounded
-->   in Amanita muscaria.  It was truly unfortunate
      that this stately mushroom could be appreciated
      only for its beauty, and not its culinary qualities.
```

   At the highest level, our problem is to produce **scanline**. Solving this problem
with the refinement methodology gives these results

1. **solve_problem()** is called with **scanline()**.

2. The problem is not trivial, so we break **scanline()** down into subproblems
   and define a new relationship, for example

```
solve_problem(scanline)
{
  get_user_input();
  open_text_file();
  scan_text_file();
  close_text_file();
}
```

3. **solve_problem()** is recursively called with each of the subproblems, starting
   with **get_user_input()**.

4. **solve_problem(get_user_input())** is trivial. It writes out two prompts
   and receives a string.

5. **solve_problem(open_text_file())** is also trivial.

6. **solve_problem(scan_text_file())** is not trivial. A new related series of
   subproblems is created.

```
solve_problem(scan_text_file)
{
  while ((input_line = read_line()) != DONE) {
    if (search_string_found()) write_arrow();
    else write_blank();
    write_input_line();
  }
}
```

7. Having defined this relationship for **scan_text_file()**, **solve_problem()** is recursively called with **read_line()**, **search_string_found()**, **write_arrow()**, **write_blank()**, and **write_input_line()**. Each of these subproblems is trivial, so we have finished **solve_problem()** of **scan_text_file()**.

8. We return to **solve_problem()**, having just completed the solution to **scan_text_file()**. We can **solve_problem()** once more with **close_text_file()**, which is trivial, and we are finished.

It should be clear that this algorithm yields the following function invocation hierarchy:

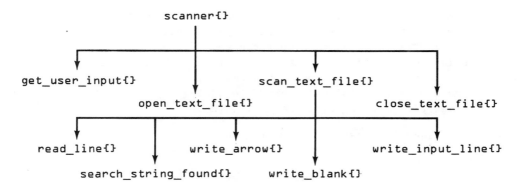

In the December 1974 issue of ACM Computing Surveys, Niklaus Wirth describes both the ideal and reality of this process very well.

> In passing, I should like to stress that we should not be led to infer that actual program conception proceeds in such a well organized, straightforward "top-down" manner. Later refinement steps may often show that earlier decisions are inappropriate and must be reconsidered.

But this neat, nested factorization of a program serves admirably well to keep the individual building blocks intellectually manageable, to explain the program to an audience and to oneself, to raise the level of confidence in the program, and to conduct informal, and even formal proofs of correctness.

2.3   Structured Programming Example

This section demonstrates the concept of structured programming through application to a more complex problem. Consider writing a program to scan text files looking for overused words. Say a word is overused if it appears more than once within any given span of 30 unique words.

Our program, called **scanner**, will, for each word in the text file,

1. Convert the word to lower case, so that words differing only in case will be considered the same.

2. If the word has recently been used, **scanner** will print both the word and the number of times the word appeared.

A typical input text file might look like the following:

```
User Friendly Software, Inc. announces the most completely
user friendly, powerful, object oriented software available.
A child can easily and simply create powerful object
oriented applications that can easily handle any need
completely, and still be completely user friendly through
the use of this object oriented technology.  To receive this
powerful software, simply mail this coupon.
```

The **scanner** analysis shows 21 overused words, 8 of which were used three times within a single 30 unique word span. The analysis should look like

```
                    Overused Word List
                    -------- ---- ----
        user (2)         friendly (2)        software (2)
    powerful (2)           object (2)        oriented (2)
         can (2)           easily (2)      completely (2)
         and (2)       completely (3)            user (3)
    friendly (3)              the (2)          object (3)
    oriented (3)             this (2)        powerful (3)
    software (3)           simply (2)            this (3)
```

```
Words Processed: 56 Overused Words Found: 21
Program Complete
```

2.4   Structured Solution (Overview)

A classic structured approach to this problem might yield a high level description of the problem like

```
program (scanner)
{
  set_up_program;
  open_appropriate_input_file;
  process_words_in_file;
  display_results;
  close_input_file;
}
```

Of the five subproblems in **scanner**, only **process_words_in_file** is non-trivial, and needs to be further refined.

```
process_words_in_file ()
{
  initialize_word_counts;
  while (file_is_not_empty) {
    read_next_word;
    increment_word_count;
    if (word_is_in_span) process_non_unique_word;
    else process_unique_word;
  }
}
```

The last three subproblems, checking a word span and processing unique and nonunique words, are all nontrivial subproblems. But we can't go any further with this process until we decide how we are going to implement a unique word span. We will implement a unique word span as a two-way linked list.

The concept of a two-way linked list is analogous in many ways to a train. A link in the list is like a car on the train. Finding an item in a two-way linked list is like finding an item on a train. Imagine for example that a passenger is trying to locate a friend on a train. The passenger has three choices at all times. The passenger can look in the current car. The passenger can move to the next car and look. The passenger can move back to the previous car and look. If the passenger decides to move to a new car, the same three choices must be faced again. The passenger can never skip a car, and can never reach a car other than by moving through the train. A program's view of a two-way linked list is similar to the passenger's view of the train.

Two pieces of "word" information will be stored in each link. The first is the character string of the word itself (converted, if necessary, to lower case). The second is a count of the number of times this word was overused. Each unique word in the file will be represented by at most one link in the list. The list will hold only unique words which are still of interest, that is, the last 30 unique words.

Position on the list will indicate chronological time of last reference. The first word on the list will be the most recent word encountered. The last word on the list will be the word encountered 30 unique words ago, and will no longer be relevant once the next unique word is read.

Having decided the implementation of a word span, we can complete the remaining three unsolved, nontrivial subproblems from scanner.

```
word_is_in_span()
{
  if (word_is_in_a_link) return TRUE;
  else return FALSE;
}
process_non_unique_word()
{
  promote_link_with_word_to_head_of_list;
  increment_occurrences_count;
  print_word;
}
process_unique_word()
{
  add_word_to_head_of_list;
  set_occurrences_count_to_1
}
```

2.5   Structured Solution (Details)

Using the scanner overview of the previous section, we can now fill in the details. A single file, scanner.c, will contain all scanner code. The code starts with some constants and include files.

```
/* Program Constants.
   ------------------- */
#define MAX_WORD_SIZE 50
#define MAX_LINKS 30

/* System Header Files.
   -------------------- */
#include <stdio.h>
#include <stdlib.h>
#include <string.h>
#include <ctype.h>
```

Next we define a word link. If you are unfamiliar with structures or pointers to structures, refer back to Section 1.3. If you are unfamiliar with **typedefs**, refer back to Section 1.2. In this structure, the pointers **previous** and **next** contain the addresses of the link before and after this link. Pictorially, we can represent a word link as

The C definition of this is

```
/* Linked List Definition.
   ----------------------- */
struct word_link_type {
   struct word_link_type *previous; /* Previous word.   */
   struct word_link_type *next;     /* Next word.       */
   char word[MAX_WORD_SIZE];        /* This word.       */
   int noccurs;                     /* Times overused.  */
};
typedef struct word_link_type *lp; /* Link Pointer */
```

Next we declare our functions. If you are unfamiliar with the ANSI standards for function prototyping, refer to Section 1.6.

```
/* Function Declarations.
   ---------------------- */
void get_input_filename(char *file_name);
void process_words(FILE *input, int *nwords, int *nowords);
int read_word(FILE *input, char *word_str);
```

```
lp check_word_list(lp head, char *word_str);
void update_list_and_promote
      (lp *head, lp *tail, lp found_link);
void add_word
      (lp *head, lp *tail, int *list_size, char *word_str);
void display_word(char *, int);
```

Next is our main program, which is a straightforward implementation of our highest level view of **scanner**. A few of the functions are easily implemented by any experienced C programmer and are not shown here. One of these is `get_input_filename()`, which asks the user for the name of a file. Another is `read_word()`, which returns the next word in the input file after conversion to lower case. A word is defined as a string of alpha-numeric characters terminated by one or more nonalpha-numeric characters. The third routine not shown is `display_word()` which displays a character string and an integer, three to a line. The function `display_word()` uses an internal, static variable to decide when a newline is necessary.

```
int main()
{
/* Local Declarations.
   ------------------- */
   int nwords = 0;      /* Number of words processed.      */
   int nowords = 0;     /* Number of overused words found. */
   char filename[100];  /* Name of input file.             */
   FILE *input;

/* Open Input File.
   --------------- */
   get_input_filename(filename);
   if (!(input = fopen(filename, "r"))) {
      printf("Error - Can't open input file: %s\n", filename);
      return -1;
   }
/* Process Words.
   ------------- */
   printf("\n");
   printf("%40s\n", "Overused Word List");
   printf("%40s\n", "-------- ---- ----");
   process_words(input, &nwords, &nowords);
```

```
/* Close up program.
   ----------------- */
fclose(input);
printf("\n\nWords Processed: %d  Overused Words Found: %d\n",
        nwords, nowords);
printf("Program Complete\n");
return 0;
}
```

The next function, `process_words()`, coordinates the word processing. Recall our earlier description of a linked list of words, where each link contains one word. A word includes the character string and word count, and placement on the list indicates time of reference. This function declares three pointers to links: **head**, pointing to the first link in the list; **tail**, pointing to the last link in the list; and **found_link** which refers to the current link of interest.

This function needs to update two of the parameters passed in from **main()**, **nwords** and **nowords**, which are, respectively, the counts of the total number of words and the number of words considered overused. Because these parameters will be updated, they are declared as pointers. If you are unfamiliar with this method of updating parameters, refer to Section 1.9. Similarly, `process_words()` calls several other functions which will need to update some of `process_words()`'s parameters. One of these is **update_list_and_promote()**, which will always update **head** and may update **tail**. Notice the difference between how **head** is passed to **check_word_list()**, which will not update **head**, and to **update_list_and_promote()**, which will.

```
    void process_words(
      FILE *input,    /* File from which to read.   */
      int *nwords,    /* Number of words processed. */
      int *nowords)   /* Number of overused words.  */
    {
    /* Local declarations.
       ------------------- */
      char word_str[MAX_WORD_SIZE];
                        /* Temp storage for word.     */
      lp found_link;    /* Link containing word.      */
      lp head = 0;      /* Head of word list.         */
      lp tail = 0;      /* Tail of word list.         */
      int list_size = 0; /* Number of elements in list. */
```

```
/* Loop as long as there are words in the file.
   --------------------------------------------- */
   *nwords = 0;
   *nowords = 0;

   while (read_word(input, word_str)) {

/*    If word is found, update list, otherwise add to head.
      ----------------------------------------------------- */
      (*nwords)++;
      found_link = check_word_list(head, word_str);
      if (found_link) {
         update_list_and_promote (&head, &tail, found_link);
         (*nowords)++;
      }
      else {
         add_word (&head, &tail, &list_size, word_str);
      }
   }
}
```

The next function looks for a specific word (`word_str`) in the word list. If it finds the word, it returns a pointer to the link containing the word. If not, it returns 0. Since the address of a valid link can never be 0, this function can be interpreted as returning **TRUE** if a word is on the list, **FALSE** otherwise. Although this function knows what a link looks like and how to follow a linked list of words, it does not know the address of the first link in the list. Thus **head** needs to be passed in from the calling function. This same variable, **head**, is used to step through the list, simply to avoid the declaration of another variable. This update however is strictly local. If you are unfamiliar with why this is so, refer back to Section 1.8.

```
lp check_word_list(
lp head,                  /* Head of list.   */
char *word_str)           /* String to find. */
{
   for (; head; head = head->next)
      if (!strcmp(head->word, word_str)) return head;
   return 0;
}
```

The next function is `update_list_and_promote()`. It is responsible for managing a link containing a found word (`found_link`). It updates the word count, coordinates the word display, and moves the word link to the head of the list. This function considers two situations to be special cases. The first special case occurs when `found_link` is already at the head of the list and no promotion is necessary. The second special case occurs when `found_link` is at the tail of the list. Then promotion involves resetting `tail`, which had been `found_link`, to the link preceding `found_link`.

A "promotion" is actually a series of pointer updates. This section of code should be examined carefully. It is very easy to make mistakes with this type of code. Any time saved by rushing through this implementation will be paid back dearly at debugging time. Pictorially, a promotion can be represented as the following series of events, where the `found_link` is represented by the double box.

A link is identified as "found."

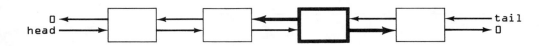

The link before is reset to bypass the found link.

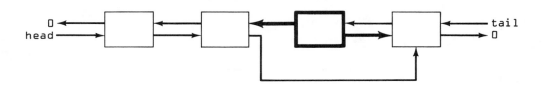

The found link prepares to move to the head of the list.

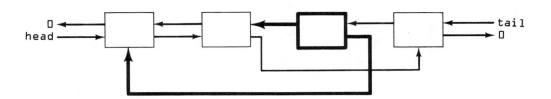

The **previous** pointer on the found link is set to zero, indicating it is now the head of the list.

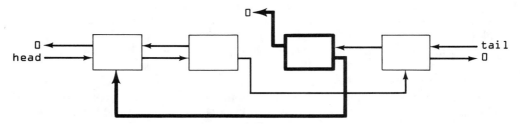

The **previous** pointer on the old head is reset to the new head.

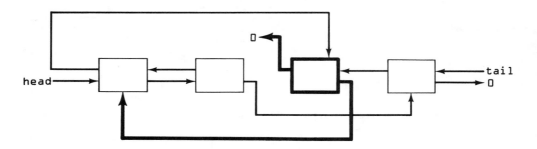

The **head** is reset to the new head.

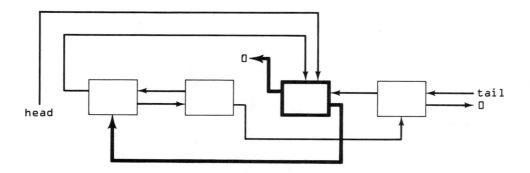

The link that used to follow the found link is reset to bypass the link.

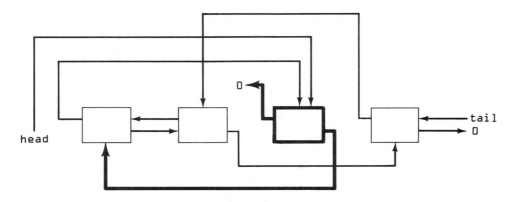

Rearranging this picture, with no further pointer updates, gives

There are two ways we can decide if a particular link is the head of the list. First, we can check the link's previous pointer. Second, we can check the address of the link against the address of the link known to be the head (contained in the variable **head**, which, recall, is of type pointer to link). Similarly, we can use the link's next pointer and the **tail** variable to decide if a particular link is the tail of the list. Both techniques are shown in this function.

```
void update_list_and_promote(
    lp *head,        /* Head of list.  */
    lp *tail,        /* Tail of list.  */
    lp found_link)   /* Link to update. */
{
/* Update link.
   ------------ */
    found_link->noccurs++;
    display_word(found_link->word, found_link->noccurs);
```

```
/* If this is the head, we are already promoted.
   ---------------------------------------------- */
   if (!found_link->previous) return;

/* If this is the tail, back up tail to previous link.
   ---------------------------------------------------- */
   if (found_link == (*tail)) (*tail) = (*tail)->previous;

/* Otherwise, update next link.
   --------------------------- */
   else found_link->next->previous = found_link->previous;

/* Promote found link to head.
   --------------------------- */
   found_link->previous->next = found_link->next;
   found_link->next = *head;
   found_link->previous = 0;
   (*head)->previous = found_link;

/* Update return variables.
   ----------------------- */
   *head = found_link;
   return ;
}
```

The next function, `add_word()`, adds a new word to the head of the word list. At least half of the code for this function is involved with efficiently allocating memory for new words in the list. If you are unfamiliar with dynamic memory allocation using `malloc()` and `free()` refer back to Section 1.4. Dynamic memory allocation is used extensively when working with complex data structures, and you need to understand it thoroughly before continuing.

Because of the nature of this algorithm, we only need to maintain information about the last 30 unique words encountered. This function could have been implemented by unconditionally allocating a new head link for the new word, and then freeing the last link. It is more efficient however, to reuse the memory for the new word. Typically, the tail will be available for reuse. Only the early calls, when the size of the list is under 30 words, will need to allocate a fresh link for the new word.

Once we have decided how to allocate memory for the new word, the remainder of the function is similar to `update_list_and_promote()`. Adding a word to an empty list is treated as a special case, since none of the link pointers need updating. When adding to a nonempty list, we make the new link the new head, and the old head the new second link. The pointer manipulations are less complex than for `update_list_and_promote()`, since only two instead of three links are involved, and no existing linkages are "broken." The pictogram is left for a reader exercise.

```
    void add_word(
        lp *head,               /* Head of list.             */
        lp *tail,               /* Tail of list.             */
        int *list_size,         /* Number of words in list.  */
        char *word_str)         /* Word to add to list.      */
    {
    /* Local Declarations.
       ------------------ */
        lp newlink = 0;

    /* If list is not yet full, allocate new slot.
       ------------------------------------------- */
        if (*list_size < MAX_LINKS) {
            newlink = malloc(sizeof(struct word_link_type));
            (*list_size)++;
        }
    /* Else, recycle the no longer needed tail.
       --------------------------------------- */
        else {
            newlink = *tail;
            *tail = (*tail)->previous;
            (*tail)->next = 0;
        }
    /* Enter information into link.
       --------------------------- */
        strcpy(newlink->word, word_str);
        newlink->noccurs = 1;

    /* If list is empty, treat as special case.
       --------------------------------------- */
        if (!(*head)) {
            *head = *tail = newlink;
            newlink->next = newlink->previous = 0;
            return;
        }
```

```
/* Make the new link the new head.
   ------------------------------- */
   (*head)->previous = newlink;
   newlink->previous = 0;
   newlink->next = *head;
   *head = newlink;
   return;
}
```

2.6   Analysis of Structured Solution

Two justifications are usually touted for a structured approach to programming. The first is code quality. The second is code reusability. Let's look at the **scanner** solution as presented and see how we fare on both counts.

Code quality includes a collection of somewhat related issues. First is code reliability, that is, the probability of the code working as advertised, free from logical flaws and programming errors. Second is maintainability, that is our ability to modify the code to handle unforeseen new requirements. Third, closely associated with each of these, is comprehensibility, or, as Wirth puts it, the intellectual manageability of the code.

In this regard, the structured **scanner** measures well. Each of the pieces is "intellectually manageable." The functionality of each function is well demarcated and easy to follow. The code as presented would be considered good quality by most software houses.

The second justification for structured programming is code reusability, the hope being that if the functionality is broken into small chunks, many of these chunks can be used to solve other problems. Our chunks are reasonably small. The function **check_word_list()**, for example, is only three executable lines long. Even the most complex function, **add_word()**, is only 20 lines of actual code. However, few, if any, of **scanner** functions seem destined for reuse. The only functions with such potential are **get_input_filename()**, **read_word()**, and possibly **display_word()**, three trivial functions.

Why have we failed the reusability test? The problem is that we have a poor separation of application specific and generic functionality. We have code which solves generic problems such as linked list manipulation, but this code is intermingled with highly application specific code such as code which copies word strings. Structured programming methodology, while sympathetic to the separation of the application specific and the generic, gives little guidance as to how this is to be achieved.

In the next chapter, we will see how Object-Oriented Methodology picks up where Structured Programming Methodology leaves off to deal with this issue.

2.7 Exercises

Exercise 2.1 Modify scanner to show over used words only once. The new output file for the advertisement should look like

```
              Overused Words List
              -------- ----- ----
       user (5)      friendly (5)       software (5)
   powerful (5)        object (5)       oriented (5)
        can (2)        easily (2)     completely (5)
        and (2)           the (2)           this (5)
     simply (2)
```

Exercise 2.2 Modify scanner to also check words against a "forbidden" list, which is read from disk before the program runs. Forbidden words are so ugly, they should "never" appear in writing. Candidates for this list include "simple," "powerful," "trivial," and so on.

In the universe the difficult things are done
as if they are easy.
In the universe great acts are made up
of small deeds.
The sage does not attempt anything very big,
And thus achieves greatness.

- Lao Tsu
Tao Te Ching
Translated by Gia-Fu Feng and Jane English

Chapter 3

Object-Oriented Programming In C

In the last chapter we looked at a typical structured program. We found that the use of this methodology improved code quality, but did not result in code reusability. The problem centered around the lack of separation between generic and application specific functionality.

Structured programming methodology gave little guidance as to how such a separation is to be accomplished. This does not mean we should discard the ideas of structured programming methodology, rather we should extend the methodology to address this issue. This extension is called object-oriented programming methodology.

In this chapter and the next we are going to look at object-oriented programming from the perspective of the C programmer. In this chapter we will focus on concepts and use fairly unsophisticated C implementation techniques. In the next chapter we will focus on formalizing and improving these techniques. As we will see, object-oriented methodology has great applicability to standard "procedural" languages such as C. The terminology, the problem solving methodology, even to a large extent the code design process, can be applied with great benefit by C programmers.

Studying object-oriented methodology in C will ease the eventual transition to C++, allowing us to become familiar with the class concept before facing a new language syntax. We can then better understand the issues that C++ is dealing with, and the C limitations C++ addresses. We will also find that the C++ syntax will appear to be a natural extension of the conventions we will be using in the next two chapters.

3.1 Introduction

Object-oriented programming is best understood in contrast to its close cousin, structured programming. Both attempt to deal with the same basic issue, managing the complexity of ever more complex software systems.

Structured programming models a system as a layered set of functional modules. These modules are built up in a pyramid like fashion, each layer representing a higher level view of the system. Structured programming models the system's behavior, but gives little guidance to modeling the system's information.

Object-oriented programming models a system as a set of cooperating objects. Like structured programming, it tries to manage the behavioral complexity of a system. Object-oriented programming, however, goes beyond structured programming in also trying to manage the informational complexity of a system.

Because object-oriented programming models both the behavioral and information complexity of a system, the system tends to be much better organized than if it was simply well "structured." Because systems are better organized, they are easier to understand, debug, maintain, and evolve. Well organized systems also lend themselves to code reuse.

These two views of the universe are by no means irreconcilable. The data manipulation operations of the object-oriented program can, and should, be developed using structured programming techniques. And, when as much of the program as possible has been developed using object-oriented programming methodology, some code may be left to orchestrate the pieces. This code should be developed using standard structured programming techniques.

Well written object-oriented programs are, in fact, also well structured. The procedures are small, well defined, and layered, characteristics we also associate with structured programs. So we see that these two methodologies complement each other nicely.

In this chapter, we resolve the **scanner** problem using object-oriented methodology. We do this entirely in C, demonstrating that object-oriented programming methodology, like structured programming methodology, is a state of mind rather than a byproduct of a programming language. In later chapters we discover some limitations in C and see why C++ was developed to better support object-oriented programming. But one should never be misled into believing either that C++ (or any other language) is necessary for an object-oriented approach to programming, or that object-oriented programming is an automatic result of using C++. Neither of these assertions is true.

We said that object-oriented methodology consists of a series of recursive refinements of organizational units of data. Where do we start with the `scanner` problem?

The hardest part of solving this problem is trying to remember the last 30 unique words in the text. Each new word needs to be checked against the last 30 unique words, and be remembered for future reference. We only need to store 30 words at any given time. For each new word on the list, an old word can be forgotten. That word would be the one which has not been used for the longest time, the thirty-first unique word.

What kind of tools would help? It seems we need some kind of storage structure for words, a Word Box, and in particular, a Word Box with these specifications.

- Words can be inserted into the box.

- The box can hold a maximum of 30 words.

- The box can tell us when a word is inside.

- If we try to insert more words than the box can hold, the box makes room by dumping the least recently referenced words. By "referenced," we mean either inserted or inquired about.

The following diagram shows how the contents of the box change as words are referenced. The right side of the diagram shows the current words in order of future discard. For example, in the series

    horse   cat   dog

the next word available for discard is *dog*. As a word is added to the left, it becomes least available for discard, and all other words move one position closer to discard. When a word needs to be discarded, the last in the series falls off. Figure 3.1 shows this sequence.

Aficionados of data structures will recognize the Word Box as a variation on a cache. The word *cache* is derived from the French word *cacher*, meaning to conceal. In Computer Science, cache has come to describe a storage structure for holding a small number of items, usually a subset of a much larger set. In this specific case the subset is the collection of the 30 most recently used words and the larger set is the set of all words in the text.

Every item in a cache has a unique key, the key is the word itself. Items can be queried and retrieved by key. Each item in a cache has a unique availability for discard which varies with time. When items are displaced, the most "discardable"

Action	*Box Contents*
wb_add(dog)	dog
wb_add(cat)	cat dog
wb_add(horse)	horse cat dog
wb_inquire(cat) returns TRUE	cat horse dog
wb_add(pig)	pig cat horse
wb_inquire(dog) returns FALSE	pig cat horse
wb_add(human)	human pig cat
wb_add(mouse)	mouse human pig
wb_inquire(pig) returns TRUE	pig mouse human
wb_add(fish)	fish pig mouse
wb_inquire(human) returns FALSE	fish pig mouse

Figure 3.1: Word Box Trace For a Three-Word Box

item is the one displaced. Different algorithms are used to determine discardability. A common algorithm, and the one used in this case, considers discardability to be related to time of reference. The longer an item has been in the cache without being referenced, the more discardable it is. This algorithm is often referred to as LRU, for Least Recently Used. Caches are frequently used to speed up I/O processing, but obviously have other applications as well.

Conceptually, a cache can be implemented as a string of items with the position within the string indicating the discard value. Items are added to the front of the string and discarded from the end. This behavior bears a strong resemblance to some of the linked list descriptions we encountered in the previous chapters.

We will thus base our word cache on the linked list. Other valid cache implementations exist, however the implementation details are less important than the data organization. The word cache user, and indirectly, the Word Box user does not care how the cache is implemented as long as it is understandable and dependable.

From this discussion, we can start to see the refinement process as applied to data organizational units. Our Object-Oriented **scanner** will primarily consist of a word box. The word box will be developed from a word cache. The word cache will be developed from a linked list of words. The linked list of words will be developed from a word link. The word link will be developed from a word object. We can diagram this refinement process as follows:

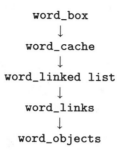

```
word_box
   ↓
word_cache
   ↓
word_linked list
   ↓
word_links
   ↓
word_objects
```

We can now give an overview showing how these pieces fit together. Starting from the bottom, the `word_object` defines the data associated with a word, namely a character string and a word count. It also defines some word specific code, for example, how to overwrite one word with another. The next level will be `word_link`, which will describe a structure that includes a `word_object` and other data that allows one `word_link` to be associated with another. The next level is `word_linked_list`, which will coordinate the activities of many `word_links` into a single linked list of words. The next level will use a `word_linked_list` to form a `word_cache`. The final level will be the `word_box`, which further refines the behavior of the `word_cache`.

In this implementation, there are a large number of `word_objects`, each associated with one `word_link`. There is one `word_linked_list`, which is ultimately defined by the `word_linked_list` level. This restriction will be relaxed in the next chapter.

3.2 Object-Oriented Terminology

Before looking at the implementation, we need to discuss some object-oriented terminology.

A description of a unit of data organization and its associated operations is called a *class*. A *class* describes the form a thing would take, should it come to exist. The concept of a class definition closely parallels the concept of a structure definition. When we see code like

```
struct link {
  struct link *pnext;
  struct link *pprevious;
  int num;
};
```

we see instructions to the compiler describing how a block of memory is to be interpreted, should an instance of it ever be created. The actual creation of such a block of memory requires code like

```
struct link newlink;
```

Similarly, a class description can be thought of as a description to the user and compiler of what a class object looks like, and what behavior can be expected from it. For example, a linked list class would include descriptions of pointers to various link structures, and descriptions of a set of operations which can be used to manipulate the linked list.

The actual occurrence of a class is called an *instance* of that class, or an *object*. A *class* defines operations that can be performed. An *object* gives us an actual target for these operations. Some of the classes described in this chapter, such as the linked list, have only one instance. In C, the code allowing multiple instances per class is more complex, and will be discussed in the next chapter.

Often the term *class* is implied rather than stated. When you see writing such as "the linked list object can be...," or even "a linked list can be...," the implied meaning is "an object of the class linked list can be..." or "an instance of the class linked list can be..." This is confusing to people approaching object-oriented programming for the first time.

The process of creating a specific object of a class is called *instantiation*. The verb form of this is to *instantiate*, thus formally we instantiate an object of class linked list, or informally, we create a linked list. The purpose here is not to confuse relatively simple concepts with big words, but to prepare the reader for terminology often encountered in object-oriented literature.

A class such as a linked list is defined as being a collection of data, much like C's structures, and a set of functions that can be applied to that data. These functions are called *methods*. A *method* is a function, or operation, that can interact with the data of a specific class. C++ programmers usually call methods *member functions*, but the rest of the object-oriented community uses the term *method*, and we will follow suit.

Most data structures such as linked lists and stacks can be implemented as classes. Methods associated with linked lists are `insert()` and `remove()`, whereas methods associated with stacks are `push()` and `pop()`. In C, methods and functions are identical. In C++ there are practical and conceptual differences. In both languages methods, like functions, accept parameters, can return values, and should be strictly prototyped.

We usually say a function is *invoked*, and we will use the same description for methods. The object whose data is to be manipulated by a method we call the *target object*. We say the method is *invoked* on the target object. Other authors sometimes describe the invocation as *sending a message* to an object. They say "a message is sent to the object telling it to perform one of its methods," where we will say "a method is invoked." For the C++ programmers these both mean the same thing.

With the exception of the terms we use for method invocation and inheritance (which we will discuss later) the terminology in this book is consistent with that discussed by Michael L. Nelson [Nelson].

The term *member* refers to either a data item or a method included in a class. We may say that linked list members include data, such as the pointer to the head of the list and the methods `insert()` and `remove()`.

The members of a class may have restricted access. For example, access to data members is typically restricted to class methods, whereas access to class methods is typically unrestricted. For now, we will distinguish two general categories of access: *public access*, which grants access to any client, or user, of the class, and *private access*, which grants access only to class methods. For example, a linked list class might include, as a data item, a pointer to a link structure. But this is an implementation detail that clients of the linked list class should not count on, or even know about. Linked list methods, such as `push()`, need to manipulate this pointer. Therefore, the pointer is considered *private*. The linked list class also includes methods, such as `remove()` which are available to the client. Such methods are considered *public*.

Class access may be more conceptual that actual. Classes implemented in C have no real ability to restrict access. Even C++ does not attempt to prevent the dedicated hacker from breaking access levels. The real point of access control is more contractual. Public members of the class are "guaranteed." Private members are accessed at the peril of the user, and may change without warning at the discretion of the implementor.

Having introduced object-oriented terminology, let's see how this applies to `scanner`. We have identified five classes involved in the solution to `scanner`: `word_box`, `word_cache`, `word_linked_list`, `word_link`, and `word_object`. Most of these classes have no public data members. The one exception is `word_object`, which, in this implementation, contains a character string and a word count. Several of these classes will have private data members, which we will discuss when we examine the implementation details. Each class forms a building block from which other classes may be derived. Later we will discuss inheritance, which is a formalization of one important aspect of class derivation.

Each class has an associated set of methods. For now, we will prefix each method name with a class identifier. Thus, we will identify the linked list `push()` method as `ll_push()`. We can describe a minimal set of methods useful for implementing `scanner`. We will start with the lower level classes (least derived) and work our way back up the derivation hierarchy.

A class is implemented as two C files, a header file, which contains the class definition, and an implementation file. The header file includes whatever information, if any, the client needs to use the class. The implementation file contains the code for the class methods. In the next chapter we will add flexibility (and a little complexity) and the contents of these files will be adapted slightly. However the header file will continue to define the client interface to the class, and the implementation file will continue to contain the method code. We will use this basic class organization even when we move into C++.

Let's consider a trivial example of a class, just to help crystallize these concepts. We want a **counter** class. An object of class **counter** is used to count occurrences. It is like the hand held counters used by ushers in movie theaters to count people entering a theater. An usher's counter has three "methods": the counter can be initialized to zero, it can be incremented, and it can be read. Our counter will also support these methods. We will call them **init()**, **incr()**, and **read()**.

There are many ways we might implement the **counter** class in C. We will consider two here, and stick with the most basic definition of a class and an object. A class is a definition of a set of data and a set of methods to operate on that data. An object is an instance of such a data set. For now, let's say a class implementation is valid if it supports the creation of one or more instances, or objects.

The simplest possible implementation of **counter** consists of an implementation file which contains a static variable to hold the count and the methods, and a header file, which prototypes the methods. The code implementation file is

```
#include "counter.h"
static int count;
void counterInit(void)
{
  count=0;
}
void counterIncr(void)
{
  count++;
}
int counterRead(void)
{
  return count;
}
```

The header file, **counter.h**, is

```
void counterInit(void);
void counterIncr(void);
int counterRead(void);
```

A client program could use a counter object by just invoking the appropriate methods

```
#include <stdio.h>
#include "counter.h"
int main()
{
  int n;
  counterInit();
  for (n=0; n<10; n++){
     counterIncr();
  }
  printf ("counter reads %d\n", counterRead());
  return 0;
}
```

In this implementation, the data for the counter object has been packaged directly into the class code file. This implementation of **counter** supports one instantiation. In this next implementation the instance data is packaged in a structure which becomes part of the user interface, and is, therefore, packaged in the class header file. The class header file becomes

```
#ifndef COUNTER_CLASS
#define COUNTER_CLASS

struct counterType {
  int count;
};
typedef struct counterType counter;

void counterInit(counter *this);
void counterIncr(counter *this);
int counterRead(counter *this);

#endif
```

The class definition is now encased within an **#ifndef** to guard against the possibility of a program inadvertently including the header twice. The double definition of a structure or function prototype is acceptable, but the double definition of a **typedef** is not.

The code for this class is a little different

```
#include "counter.h"
void counterInit(counter *this)
{
  this->count=0;
}
void counterIncr(counter *this)
{
  this->count++;
}
int counterRead(counter *this)
{
  return this->count;
}
```

and our client needs a few modifications

```
#include "counter.h"
#include <stdio.h>
int main()
{
  int n;
  counter myCounter;
  counterInit(&myCounter);
  for (n=0; n<10; n++) {
    counterIncr(&myCounter);
  }
  printf ("counter reads %d\n", counterRead (&myCounter));
  return 0;
}
```

For now we will consider any implementation of classes and objects acceptable, as long as it respects our idea of classes and objects. A class is a description of a set of data and associated behaviors. An object is an instance of some class. The object is made up of the data described by its class, and it responds to the methods defined by the class. In the next chapter we will codify our class concept but for now we want to focus on the object-oriented mindset rather than the development of techniques.

It is possible to have classes with no methods for example, the word_link class. A class has no methods when it is so closely associated with another class, in this case word_linked_list, that the other class subsumes the methods one might otherwise expect to find. When there are no methods, there is nothing to prototype, so there is no header file, and nothing to implement, so no code file. This will change in the next chapter when the concept of C classes is further refined and formalized.

We write `scanner` as a hierarchy of classes. We will implement lower level classes first, and approach each class as a self contained problem which is to be fully analyzed, coded, and tested, before moving on to the next highest level class.

3.3   Overused Words: The Object-Oriented Solution

Now let's see how each of the `scanner` pieces can be developed as a self-contained class.

3.4   The Word Object Class

One of the simplest of our classes is the `word_object`, the class which is, in a sense, the ultimate target of all our other classes. The header file for this class defines the data members of the class packaged together into the structure `object_type` which is then redefined to be an `object`. The next class up the hierarchy will be the link class, and it will be expecting a class of type `object` to exist.

```
#ifndef OBJECT
#define OBJECT

#define MAX_WORD_SIZE 50

struct object_type {
  char word[MAX_WORD_SIZE];
  int noccurs;
};
typedef struct object_type object;

int obj_match(object *this_object, void *lookfor);
void obj_cpy(object *dest, object *src);
#endif
```

The class `object` contains the only application specific information in the class hierarchy. For the purposes of scanner, `object` is a word object. For other applications it will likely contain different information reflecting some other application specific type. The application specific information in `object` contains the word string and number of occurrences count.

The class definition prototypes two class methods: `obj_match()` and `obj_cpy()`. Since none of the other classes will understand the nature of the data they are storing, it is up to the `object` class to define code specific to its class.

Other classes will make use of these methods when they need to accomplish an application specific function such as copying the application data into a link.

These methods defined in the object class represent a contract between the linked list client and the linked list class designer. The client can use the linked list class to store any information, and in return promises to rewrite the definition of the class object, re-implement the required methods, and recompile the linked list module. The linked list is then automatically changed into a new linked list of the desired type.

The code file for object must #include the object header. It then contains the code for the two application specific methods. These methods are written by the same person or group who defined object. The first method is very simple, and depends on little more than understanding the nature of the data members of object. It assumes it has been passed two object pointers, and overwrites the object pointed to by the first by the object pointed to by the second.

```
#include <string.h>
#include "object.h"

void obj_cpy(object *dest, object *src)
{
  strcpy(dest->word, src->word);
  dest->noccurs = src->noccurs;
}
```

The interface to obj_cpy() never changes, regardless of the implementation of the object class. This is part of the contract with the higher level classes, in particular, the link and linked_list class. Thus we know that the name of the function must be obj_cpy(), and it must accept two parameters. The first parameter must be the destination object and the second must be the source. The function must be of type void. There is also a general understanding between link and object about the semantics of obj_cpy(), that obj_cpy() copies objects, although it is left up to obj_cpy() to decide exactly what this means in the context of a particular object class.

The second object method defined is obj_match(), which decides whether a given object matches some criteria. The "criteria" is passed in through the second parameter, which is of type void *.

```
int obj_match(object *o1, void *lookfor)
{
    return (!strcmp(o1->word, lookfor));
}
```

We use a void * rather than an object * because the caller of obj_match(), one of the linked list methods, does not know what the match criteria looks like.

This may seem strange, since the linked list is the client of **object**, but in fact, the linked list methods will only serve as a conduit for the criteria, the definition of which is part of the definition of the object class.

The match criteria may or may not be another instance of the same class. For the case of word objects, the search criteria are simply a character string, which will be checked against the character string contained in a particular instance.

Since the linked list and the object classes can't agree in advance about the type of the second parameter, they agree to disagree. Thus the generic **void ***. If you are unfamiliar with the use of **void *** as a generic pointer, see Section 1.5.

3.5 The Link Class

The next class is the **link** class, the simplest of our classes. It has no methods and is tightly coupled with the linked list code. In fact, there is no difference between this class and a C structure; however we will continue to think of this as a class to help focus our refinement process on class hierarchies. Notice how **link** has no direct knowledge of the object it is storing; it just picks up whatever is currently defined as the object class in **object.h**

```
#ifndef LINKTYPE
#define LINKTYPE

#include "object.h"
struct linktype {
  struct linktype *pnext;
  struct linktype *pprevious;
  object contents;
};
typedef struct linktype link;

#endif
```

3.6 The Linked List Class

Next up the class hierarchy is the linked list class, the first of our more complex classes. Our linked list class supports one linked list object, or, in formal terms, one instance of a linked list class.

The linked list header file defines the linked list public methods. It needs to **#include object.h** to ensure its own references to **object** can be resolved.

```
#ifndef LINKED_LIST
#define LINKED_LIST
#include "object.h"

int ll_size(void);
void ll_head(void);
void ll_tail(void);
int ll_istail(void);
int ll_ishead(void);
void ll_next(void);
void ll_previous(void);
object *ll_retrieve(void);
void ll_addhead(object *newobject);
void ll_promote(void);
void ll_replace(object *newobject);
int ll_find(void *lookfor);
#endif
```

Next is the linked list methods file. The methods file starts by including the needed header files, one of which is link.h, the next lower level class.

```
/* Include files.
   -------------- */
   #include <stdio.h>
   #include "ll.h"
   #include "link.h"
```

Then the methods file declares the data members of the class linked list, and uses the **static** keyword to keep their access private.

```
/* Static pointers to important links.
   ----------------------------------- */
   static link *pcl = NULL;      /* Current Link Pointer */
   static link *phead = NULL;              /* First link */
   static link *ptail = NULL;               /* Last link */

/* Other important information about the list.
   ------------------------------------------- */
   static int listlength = 0;       /* Number of links */
```

The concept of a linked list is different here than the concept as presented in many other books, which do not distinguish between a link and a linked list. Separating these two concepts, however, allows the linked list code to focus on the high level view of the links. The data members of the linked list class, then, are those that give a high level perspective on the links. Two of our data members, **phead** and **ptail**, point to the beginning and end of the list. The data member **pcl** points to the link we think of a current.

The member **pcl** moves relatively freely between **phead** and **ptail**, but none of these pointers are fixed. New links occasionally take over the role of head and tail, and the current link scurries rapidly between these two endpoints.

The last data member, **listlength**, stores the size of the list.

Notice how the methods **ll_next()** and **ll_previous()** methods change the **pcl**

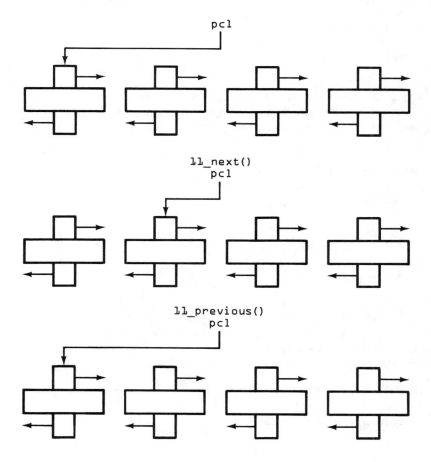

The data members **phead**, **ptail**, and **listlength** are included for convenience only. Any of the linked list methods could be implemented using only `pcl`, although many of them would take substantially longer to execute.

In a perfect object-oriented implementation, the linked list methods would do nothing but provide a user interface to the four linked list data members. Linked list methods would then call link methods to update the link data members. In practice, this is complicated by the fact that many linked list method calls need to update multiple link objects. Such updates require a somewhat detached view of links, and it seems easier to implement this code in the linked list class. This is strictly a judgment call, and either implementation is reasonable.

Next in the linked list methods file is the implementation of the methods. The first is `ll_size()`, which provides read only access to the data member `listlength`.

```
int ll_size(void)
{
    return listlength;
}
```

The next two methods set the current link (i.e., the link pointed to by `pcl`) to either the head or tail of the linked list. They, like many of these methods, take no input and return no information. They simply change the state of the linked list object.

```
void ll_head(void)
{
    pcl = phead;
}

void ll_tail(void)
{
    pcl = ptail;
}
```

The next two methods return information about the state of the object, namely, whether the current link is the head (or tail) of the list. They make use of the logical equality operator's return value, described in Section 1.10. These methods are essentially boolean functions, which are described in Section 1.7.

```
int ll_istail(void)
{
    return (pcl == ptail);
}
```

```
int ll_ishead(void)
{
  return (pcl == phead);
}
```

The next two functions adjust the current link backwards (toward the tail) or forward (toward the head).

```
void ll_next(void)
{
    if (!ll_istail()) pcl = pcl->pnext;
}

void ll_previous(void)
{
    if (!ll_ishead()) pcl = pcl->pprevious;
}
```

As we see here, class methods can call methods of their own class. This is a defensive style of programming, allowing methods to protect themselves against changes to the class implementation. The function `ll_next()`, for example, could have been written

```
void ll_next(void)
{
    if (pcl != ptail) pcl = pcl->pnext;
}
```

but then this is one more piece of code that needs to be changed if the linked list implementation changes, say by removing the private data member **ptail**.

The next method returns the object stored in the current link. This code knows nothing about the nature of linked objects in the link, information which is encapsulated in the **object** class description. This method knows only that some such object exists.

```
object *ll_retrieve(void)
{
    return &(pcl->contents);
}
```

Notice this function returns a pointer to the object embedded in the link. This pointer, then, is pointing inside the link structure. Updates through this pointer will update the interior of the link structure. If the code is well behaved, these updates will be confined to the portion of the link allocated to the embedded object.

The next function is `ll_addhead()` which creates a new link, copies an object instance into the `object` portion of the link, and finally places the new link at the head of the list. This function breaks the problem down into two cases depending on whether or not the list was originally empty. The lines are numbered for later reference.

```
1.    void ll_addhead(object *newobject)
2.    {
3.    /* Set up new link.
4.        ---------------- */
5.        link *newlink;
6.        newlink = (link *) malloc(sizeof(link));
7.        obj_cpy(&(newlink->contents), newobject);
8.        listlength++;

9.    /* Check for special case of first time call.
10.       ------------------------------------------ */
11.       if (listlength == 1) {
12.           phead = ptail = pcl = newlink;
13.           newlink->pnext = newlink->pprevious = 0;
14.           return;
15.       }
16.   /* Handle general case.
17.       -------------------- */
18.       phead->pprevious = newlink;
19.       newlink->pnext = phead;
20.       newlink->pprevious = 0;
21.       phead = pcl = newlink;
22.       return;
23.   }
```

We will now examine this function in detail, diagrammatically, line by line.

```
1.    void ll_addhead(object *newobject)
```

This line declares a parameter of type object pointer, represented as

```
+----------+
|   new    |
|  object  |
+----------+
```

```
5.        link *newlink;
```

This line declares a local pointer to **link**, represented as

```
newlink->??
```

6.   `newlink = (link *) malloc(sizeof(link));`

This line declares a new link with space for an object, and sets **newlink** to its address.

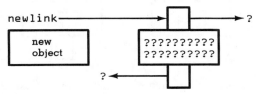

7.   `obj_cpy(&(newlink->contents), newobject);`

This line copies the new object into the object space of the new link.

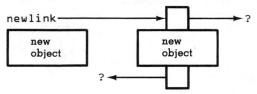

Pay particularly close attention to exactly how line #7 accomplishes the copy into **newlink**. Copying an object is an application specific function, because you must know what an object is before you can figure out what it means to copy one. Since the linked list object has no idea what the object looks like, it defers to the **obj_cpy()** method of the object class. Although the linked list doesn't know much about objects, it does know this

- The object class can be counted on to provide a copying method.

- The name of this method will be **obj_cpy()**.

- This method will accept exactly two parameters.

- These two parameters will be pointers to **objects**, whatever they are.

- The first pointer will contain the location of a destination object.

- The second pointer will contain the location of a source object.

After incrementing the link count (line #8) we branch into one of two mutually exclusive code paths, depending on whether the list is empty or not. If the list is empty, we execute lines 11 to 15. We will simplify the diagrams by ignoring `ptail` and `pcl`.

```
11.       if (listlength == 1) {
12.           phead = ptail = pcl = newlink;
```

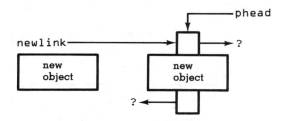

```
13.           newlink->pnext = newlink->pprevious = 0;
14.           return;
```

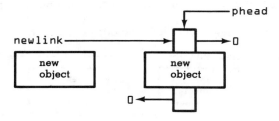

and we have a new linked list with a single link.

The other code path occurs when the list is not empty. In this case, the static global variable `phead` has been pointing all along to the head of the linked list. Adding this to the picture gives

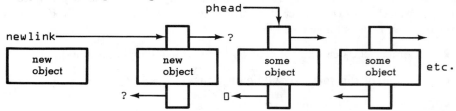

and lines 18 to 22 are executed.

18.   `phead->pprevious = newlink;`

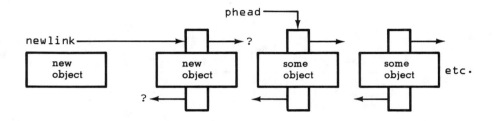

19.   `newlink->pnext = phead;`
20.   `newlink->pprevious = 0;`

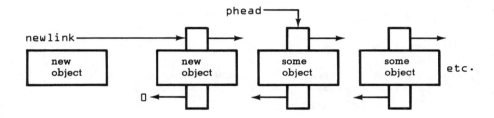

and finally

21.   `phead = pcl = newlink;`

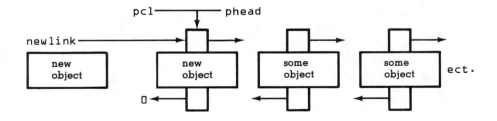

and we have a new head on the linked list. Now that we are finished, **newlink** and **newobject** have completed their roles, and are no longer relevant. From the linked list perspective, the world view is simply

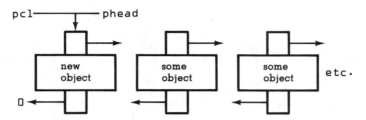

The next method is `ll_promote()`, whose task is to take the current link and move it to the head of the list. First it checks for the special case of a request to promote the head, which means there is nothing to do. Then it checks to see if the tail is being promoted. If the tail is being promoted, then `ptail` will need to be moved back one because what was the tail is about to become the head. Finally it adjusts the necessary link pointers, effectively moving the link forward. The logic of the last phase is almost identical to the series of events depicted in Section 2.5 for `update_list_and_promote()`, and is not repeated here.

```
void ll_promote(void)
{
/* Special case: current link is head, then nothing to do.
   --------------------------------------------------------- */
    if (ll_ishead()) return;

/* If this is the tail, back up the tail to previous link.
   --------------------------------------------------------- */
    if (ll_istail()) ptail = ptail->pprevious;

/* Promote current to head.
   ----------------------- */
    pcl->pprevious->pnext = pcl->pnext;
    pcl->pnext->pprevious = pcl->pprevious;
    pcl->pnext = phead;
    pcl->pprevious = 0;
    phead->pprevious = pcl;
    phead = pcl;
    return;
}
```

The next method replaces the object in the current link by a new object, leaving the link pointers as they were. This method is essentially a subset of `ll_addhead()`.

The only difference is that `ll_addhead()` was "replacing" a null object in a new link, while this method replaces a real object in an existing link. Refer back to the discussion of object copying for `ll_addhead()` if you are not sure what is happening here.

```
void ll_replace(object *newobject)
{
    obj_cpy(&(pcl->contents), newobject);
}
```

The next method runs through the list looking for a particular object, starting with the head, and checking each link in turn. If a link is found which contains the requested object it returns true. If it reaches the tail without finding a link it returns false.

The code that actually decides if a particular object is the one being searched for is application specific. Checking to see if two words match is quite different than checking to see if two employees match. The resolution of application specific matching is similar to the resolution of application specific copying in `ll_replace()`. Refer back to the discussion of `obj_match()` in the class **object** for a discussion on the use of **void** * as an input parameter.

```
int ll_find(void *lookfor)
{
    ll_head();
    for (;;) {
        if (obj_match(&(pcl->contents), lookfor)) return 1;
        if (ll_istail()) return 0;
        ll_next();
    }
}
```

This completes the current version of the linked list class. New methods may be added later as new functionality becomes required. And we will make some changes when we refine our concept of class in the next chapter. But for now, we have a fully implemented linked list class designed to manipulate word objects.

One important advantage of object-oriented programming is that we end up with testable classes. In the structured programming example it is difficult to conduct tests on units of code before all of the coding is complete. In object-oriented programming, we end up with fully implemented and specified classes which can be tested in isolation of how they will eventually be used.

The following program does just this. It populates a list with three words, moves to the head of the list, and looks for the word object matching a particular string. This program can be extended to test the linked list methods under various conditions. It can also be run within a debugger so that various pointers can be monitored as the program progresses. The importance of these test programs in verifying class correctness can hardly be over emphasized. Good programming shops insist on all submitted classes being accompanied by an appropriate test suite.

```c
/* Include files.
   -------------- */
   #include <stdio.h>
   #include <string.h>
   #include "object.h"
   #include "ll.h"

int main()
{
/* Set up local variables.
   ---------------------- */
   object new_word;
   object *wp;
   new_word.noccurs = 0;

/* Populate list.
   -------------- */
   strcpy(new_word.word, "word 1"); ll_addhead(&new_word);
   strcpy(new_word.word, "word 2"); ll_addhead(&new_word);
   strcpy(new_word.word, "word 3"); ll_addhead(&new_word);

/* Try finding an object.
   --------------------- */
   ll_head();
   if (ll_find("word 1")) {
      wp = ll_retrieve();
      printf("%s\n", wp->word);
   }
   else printf ("word not found\n");
   return 0;
}
```

3.7 The Cache Class

We have now written and tested the linked list class and can move up to the next highest class: the cache. Building this cache from a word linked list automatically makes the cache a word cache. Cache acquires this characteristic from linked list just as linked list acquired it from link.

Recall our discussion of caches from earlier in the chapter. Caches typically hold a limited number of items. When a new item is added to a fully populated cache, the cache makes room by discarding an item, in our case the least recently referenced word.

We will use placement on the list to indicate time of reference. The item at the head will be most recently referenced. The item at the tail will be least recently referenced. This implies that items are added to the head of the list, and that queried items, when found, are promoted to the head. When an item is discarded, we discard the tail.

Our admittedly primitive cache class supports three methods

`ca_setsize()`   Sets the maximum number of cache objects.

`ca_examine()`   Looks for an object in the cache.

`ca_add()`   Adds an object to the cache.

We can see how these cache operators manipulate the linked list. The following pictograms show the linked list being updated from the perspective of the cache designer. Remember the data members `phead`, `ptail`, and `pcl` are private to the linked list class, and not a concern to the cache designer.

```
ca_add("shaggy mane");
```

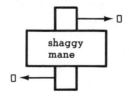

```
ca_add("morel");
```

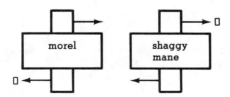

```
ca_add("chanterel");
```

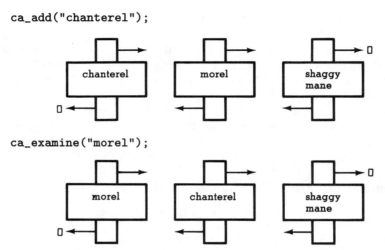

```
ca_examine("morel");
```

The cache class introduces one new data member, `cache_size`, which determines the maximum number of cache objects. This data member is private to cache, just as `listlength` was to linked list, but these two variables should not be confused. Though they seem superficially similar, they have entirely different purposes. `cache_size` stores the *maximum* number of links the linked list can ever contain, while `listlength` stores the *actual* number of links the list does contain. In this implementation, `listlength` will vary between 0, at the start of the program, and `cache_size`, when the cache is fully populated.

First, our header file for the cache object, which prototypes the three public cache methods.

```
#ifndef CACHE
#define CACHE
#include "object.h"

void ca_add(object *newobject);
object *ca_examine(void *lookfor);
void ca_setsize(int newsize);

#endif
```

The start of the code file `#include`s the necessary header files and declares the private data member `cache_size`.

```
#include "object.h"
#include "ll.h"

static int cache_size;
```

Next in the code file is the public method `ca_setsize()`. This function serves as the public update interface to a private data member.

```
void ca_setsize(int newsize)
{
    cache_size = newsize;
}
```

The next method adds a new object to the cache. Like the function `add_word()` of the structured solution, it optimizes memory allocation by recycling the tail when possible.

```
void ca_add(object *newobject)
{
    if (ll_size() >= cache_size) {
        ll_tail();
        ll_replace(newobject);
        ll_promote();
    }
    else {
        ll_addhead(newobject);
    }
}
```

Notice that this method indirectly makes use of the application specific `obj_cpy()` when inserting the new object into either the head or the old tail, but the dependency is buried in lower levels, in the linked list methods.

The last cache method looks for a particular object in the cache. If found, it returns a pointer to the object, otherwise it returns 0, or false. It also promotes any found objects to the head of the list, making them least available for discard.

```
object *ca_examine(void *lookfor)
{
    if (ll_find(lookfor)) {
        ll_promote();
        return ll_retrieve();
    }
    else return 0;
}
```

This method makes use of a sometimes neglected set of facts about C++ and C.

1. When subjected to a boolean test, zero is considered **FALSE**, while any non zero value is considered **TRUE**.

2. The only integer value that can be legally assigned to a pointer is 0.

3. A pointer can be subjected to a boolean test, and will test **TRUE** or **FALSE** according to fact #1.

Therefore, we can see there are two interpretations of this method. We can say it returns **TRUE** or **FALSE** depending on whether a given object is in the cache, or we can say it returns a pointer to an object in the cache if found, 0 otherwise.

The word cache is now complete. The code is remarkably simple, considering the sophistication of the underlying data structures and the amount of work being done.

3.8   The Word Box Class

We are now ready to define our final class, the word box class. The header file defines two simple methods. The first sets the size of the word box and the second queries the word box.

```
#ifndef WORDBOX
#define WORDBOX
#include "ca.h"

void wb_setsize(int newsize);
int wb_query(char *newword);
#endif
```

The code file adds no new data members. Its first method sets the word box size, and is just a front for `ca_setsize()`.

```
#include "ca.h"
#include "object.h"

void wb_setsize(int newsize)
{
    ca_setsize(newsize);
}
```

You may wonder why this method is included at all. Why not have clients call `ca_setsize()` directly, and avoid the overhead of the "unnecessary" method call? The reason is that we want clients to think of a **word box** as a **word box**, and not as a word box implemented on top of a cache. This extra method layer protects clients from any future re-implementations.

There is one code change that avoids the extra method call while still maintaining implementation independence, which is to redefine `wp_setsize()` to be `ca_setsize()` in the header file. With this change the method is no longer needed. The new header file looks like

```
#ifndef WORDBOX
#define WORDBOX
#include "ca.h"

#define wb_setsize ca_setsize
int wb_query(char *newword);

#endif
```

This approach gives slightly less implementation independence than the previous approach. Any changes in the word box implementation will now almost certainly require recompilation of client code. With the original approach changes would have required at most a relink. This tradeoff is reasonable.

With the redefine, the only method code is for `wp_query()` which coordinates the word cache. It adds an occurrence of a word to the cache, either by updating the count of an existing word, or by initializing a new word.

```
int wb_query(char *newword)
{
/* Local Declarations.
   ------------------ */
   object newobject;             /* Temporary object.    */
   object *op;                   /* Found object pointer. */

/* If in cache, update word counter.
   -------------------------------- */
   if ((op = ca_examine(newword))) {
       op->noccurs++;
       return op->noccurs;
   }
/* Otherwise, add word object to cache.
   ----------------------------------- */
   else {
     newobject.noccurs = 1;
     strcpy(newobject.word, newword);
     ca_add(&newobject);
     return 1;
   }
}
```

This completes the word box. This simple method of less than 10 executable lines of code provides a full storage facility for analyzing text files for overused words.

3.9   Object-Oriented Scanner

Having completed all the method implementations needed by our program, let's revisit the higher layer. The very top layer, the main program, is unchanged. We reprint it here for completeness.

```
#define WB_SIZE 30

/* Include files.
   -------------- */
   #include <stdio.h>
   #include "wb.h"

/* Function declarations.
   ---------------------- */
   void get_input_filename(char *file_name);
   int read_word(FILE *input, char *word_str);
   void process_words (FILE *input, int *nwords, int *nowords);
   void display_word(char *word_str, int count);

int main()
{
/* Local Declarations.
   ------------------- */
   int nwords = 0;        /* Number of words processed.      */
   int nowords = 0;       /* Number of overused words found. */
   char filename[100];    /* Name of input file.             */
   FILE *input;

/* Open Input File.
   ---------------- */
   get_input_filename(filename);
   if (!(input = fopen(filename, "r"))) {
      printf("Error - Can't open input file: %s\n", filename);
      return -1;
   }
```

```
/* Process Words.
   -------------- */
   printf("\n");
   printf("%40s\n", "Overused Word List");
   printf("%40s\n", "-------- ---- ----");
   process_words(input, &nwords, &nowords);

/* Close up program.
   ----------------- */
   fclose(input);
   printf("\n\nWords Processed: %d  Overused Words Found: %d\n",
          nwords, nowords);
   printf("Program Complete\n");
   return 0;
}
```

The changes in `process_words()` are fairly subtle. The function is changed only to take advantage of the word box. Compare this version to the version in the previous chapter.

```
void process_words(
FILE *input,              /* File to read from.    */
int *nwords,              /* Words processed.      */
int *nowords)             /* Overused words found. */
{
/* Local declarations
   ------------------ */
   char word_str[MAX_WORD_SIZE];  /* Temporary word. */
   int count;

/* Loop as long as there are words in the file.
   -------------------------------------------- */
   *nwords = 0;
   *nowords = 0;
   wb_setsize(WB_SIZE);
   while (read_word(input, word_str)) {
      (*nwords)++;
      if ((count = wb_query(word_str)) > 1) {
         (*nowords)++;
         display_word(word_str, count);
      }
   }
}
```

The major difference between the structured and object-oriented approach occurs at the layer below `process_words()`. In the structured approach, our work is barely begun. In the object-oriented approach, our work is complete.

You may argue that this comparison is not fair. After all, we did a lot of work for the object-oriented solution, we just did it up front. However the object-oriented solution has some significant side benefits. Even though our methodology is in its infancy, having not yet seen either the run time resolution techniques of the next chapter or the significant advantages of C++, already we can appreciate some of these benefits.

The object-oriented code is simpler. Compare these two sections of code, which accomplish similar objectives. First, the structured code

```
void update_list_and_promote(
    lp *head,          /* Head of list.    */
    lp *tail,          /* Tail of list.    */
    lp found_link)     /* Link to update. */
{
/* Update link.
   ------------ */
    found_link->noccurs++;
    display_word(found_link->word, found_link->noccurs);

/* If this is the head, we are already promoted.
   --------------------------------------------- */
    if (!found_link->previous) return;

/* If this is the tail, back up tail to previous link.
   --------------------------------------------------- */
    if (found_link == (*tail)) (*tail) = (*tail)->previous;

/* Otherwise, update next link.
   ---------------------------- */
    else found_link->next->previous = found_link->previous;

/* Promote found link to head.
   --------------------------- */
    found_link->previous->next = found_link->next;
    found_link->next = *head;
    found_link->previous = 0;
    (*head)->previous = found_link;
```

```
/* Update return variables.
   ----------------------- */
   *head = found_link;
   return ;
}
```

and now the object-oriented version:

```
object *ca_examine(void *lookfor)
{
    if (ll_find(lookfor)) {
        ll_promote();
        return ll_retrieve();
    }
    else return 0;
}
```

The object-oriented code is more reusable. Both the structured and object-oriented solution required a linked list. The "structured" linked list was not reusable, because the linked list concept was completely enmeshed in application specific details. The object-oriented linked list can, with minor work, be reapplied in new programming problems, as can the cache, and perhaps even the word box.

The object-oriented code is more reliable. Partly, this is a byproduct of its decreased complexity as well as increased reusability, but also the style lends itself to developing modules which can be independently tested. We could write a test program to exercise the linked list class before it is ever released for use. The structured solution, in contrast, has very few modules which could be tested in isolation.

3.10 Exercises

Exercise 3.1 Consider a programmer wanting to count the number of times a particular function is called. Write a sample function and main program which uses the counter class to count calls to the functions. Which version of **counter** is easier to use?

Exercise 3.2 Modify **counter** to track not only number of calls, but average time between calls. Try to make your timing unit as small as possible, preferably less than a millisecond (1/1000 second). Use operating system calls appropriate to your system. Decide how you are going to provide read access to this information.

Exercise 3.3 Repeat exercise 1 of the last chapter for the object-oriented **scanner**.

Exercise 3.4 Repeat exercise 2 of the last chapter for the object-oriented **scanner**.

'Tis but thy name that is my enemy.
Thou art thyself, though not a Montague.
What's Montague? It is nor hand, nor foot,
Nor arm, nor face, nor any other part
Belonging to a man. O, be some other name!
What's in a name? That which we call a rose
By any other name would smell as sweet.

- Romeo and Juliet
William Shakespeare

Chapter 4

Run Time Resolution in C

In the last chapter we discussed object-oriented methodology, and used this methodology to solve a reasonably complex programming problem. Object-oriented proponents make two important claims about their style of programming. First, the code is more modular. Second, the code is more reusable.

The benefits of modularity include verifiability through inspection and testing, and maintainability. The benefit of reusability is increased productivity in the future. Modularity pays off today. Reusability pays off tomorrow.

In this chapter we will focus on code reusability. Having discussed the object-oriented thought process, we will now introduce more sophisticated coding techniques which will improve the reusability of our code.

4.1 Introduction

The linked list class in the last chapter had several constraints which were then inherited by the cache class. To understand these constraints, let's consider a new problem.

A Health Maintenance Organization needs a program called HMO to manage a waiting room. This program will coordinate the assignment of physicians and patients. Each physician has a specialty code: "c" for cardiology, "i" for internal medicine, and "g" for general practice. When patients arrive a nurse notes symptoms and decides which specialist needs to be seen. As a physician becomes available, the patient waiting the longest for that specialty will be the next assigned.

There are many physicians in each specialty, and they take turns seeing patients. If a physician becomes free, and no appropriate patient is waiting, the physician rests until needed. When a resting physician is needed, the appropriate specialist who has been resting the longest is called.

In addition to making assignments, the program needs three display options. It must display the resting physicians in the order they will be assigned. It must display the waiting patients in the order they will be assigned. And, it must display current assignments, that is, which physicians are currently seeing which patients.

A few observations are worth noting about this program. Patients can be waiting in spite of resting physicians, as long as none of the resting physicians are of the needed specialty. Physicians get to take breaks fairly, and patients are assigned fairly.

HMO can be implemented with three linked lists, storing three different objects. The first contains information about waiting patients. The second contains information about available physicians. The third contains information about current physicians/patient assignments. A patient can be either on the patient or assignment list but not both. Similarly a physician can be on either the physician or assignment list, but not both.

Most of the HMO code will manipulate linked lists. In the previous chapter we developed a linked list class, and claimed to use a methodology which fostered reusability. If ever a program should be able to use a reusable linked list class, HMO should be that program.

As we attempt to use our linked list class code in HMO, we run into three problems.

Problem 1: Limited Instantiations. The linked list class supports only one linked list. We need three.

Problem 2: Object Data Inflexibility. Even if we find a way to support multiple linked lists, we are limited to one object type in those lists. HMO needs to store a different object type in each of its lists.

Problem 3: Object Method Inflexibility. Even if we find a way to store different data types in the linked lists, we have no way to distinguish between application specific methods, such as `obj_match()`. Each of our three objects will have different application specific methods. For example, when we scan physician list looking for potential assignments, matching will be by specialty. When scanning the assignment list looking for particular physician assignments, matching will be by the physician's employee ID.

These three problems are all related to compile time resolution. Each problem is caused by some characteristic of the class being determined at compile time. In each case, the solution comes from identifying the characteristic causing the limitation, and rewriting the code so that the characteristic is determined at run time.

4.2 Limited Instantiations

The linked list class is now limited to a single instantiation. How can we rewrite the code to allow for an unlimited number of instantiations? The clue is in the code examples of the last chapter.

Notice that of the classes we defined, not all are limited to one instantiation. The link class has no limit to the number of instances. What is the difference between the link class, which allows many instantiations, and the linked list class, which allows only one? The difference lies in how the class data is packaged, and how an instance is instantiated.

The code that instantiates a linked list class is contained in the first section of the linked list methods file. It looks like this

```
/* Static pointers to important links.
   ----------------------------------- */
   static link *pcl = NULL;       /* Current Link Pointer */
   static link *phead = NULL;            /* First link */
   static link *ptail = NULL;            /* Last link */

/* Other important information about the list.
   ------------------------------------------- */
   static int listlength = 0;        /* Number of links */
```

The code that instantiates a link is contained in the linked list method `ll_addhead()`. It looks like this:

```
newlink = malloc(sizeof(link));
```

There is also a difference in how the two classes package their data members. The linked list packages its data members as static variables inside the class method file. The link class packages its data members in a structure defined in the class definition file, `link.h`, which looks like

```
#ifndef LINKTYPE
#define LINKTYPE

#include "object.h"
struct linktype {
  struct linktype *pnext;
  struct linktype *pprevious;
  object contents;
};
typedef struct linktype link;

#endif
```

This packaging is similar to the packaging of the word object, whose data members are defined in object.h.

```
#ifndef OBJECT
#define OBJECT

#define MAX_WORD_SIZE 50

struct object_type {
  char word[MAX_WORD_SIZE];
  int noccurs;
};
typedef struct object_type object;

int obj_match(object *this_object, void *lookfor);
void obj_cpy(object *dest, object *src);
#endif
```

The word object illustrates another important difference between classes of limited and unlimited instantiations: the parameters which are passed to class methods. This does not show up in the link methods, because there are no link methods. But compare the parameters of, say, obj_cpy() and ll_addhead().

```
void ll_addhead(object *newobject);
void obj_cpy(object *dest, object *src);
```

Because there is only one possible instantiation of a linked list object, ll_addhead() is not told which object will receive the operation. obj_cpy(), on the other hand, may be called to modify any one of many possible instantiations. Therefore, it must be passed, as one of its parameters, a pointer to the target object.

This may seem confusing, since both methods have at least one parameter of type `object *`. But in the case of `ll_addhead()`, this parameter is the object which will be inserted into the linked list object, not the linked list object itself. For `obj_cpy()`, the first parameter indicates the object which will be updated as a result of the method call.

We can conclude that there are some basic requirements a class must meet in order to allow unlimited instantiations. First, the responsibility for allocating objects must rest with the client, not the class. Second, the data members must be packaged together into a structure and placed in the class definition header file where it is available to clients. Third, every class method needs to provide a mechanism for identifying the target object of the method call.

The details of instantiating, initializing, and finally, deinstantiating a class object can get rather messy and class specific. Since we are going to require that clients take responsibility for coordinating this activity, it seems only fair that the class itself provide methods for accomplishing this as painlessly as possible. Therefore, we will impose this new requirement on all classes: they must provide **new** and **delete** methods. The first will allocate a new object. The second will deallocate an object, freeing the memory it used.

We will also require classes to package their data members following the example of **link** and **object**. Finally, we require all class methods to provide a way of identifying the target object.

Repackaging the linked list data members gives us the structure:

```
struct linked_list_type {
  link *pcl;
  link *phead;
  link *ptail;
  int listlength;
};
typedef struct linked_list_type linked_list;
```

Notice how these four data members, **pcl**, **phead**, **ptail**, and **listlength** together define the concept of a linked list. To fulfill our packaging requirement, these definitions are removed from the code file and placed in the linked list header file, which now looks like:

```
#ifndef LINKED_LIST
#define LINKED_LIST
#include "link.h"
```

```
struct linked_list_type {
  link *pcl;
  link *phead;
  link *ptail;
  int listlength;
};
typedef struct linked_list_type linked_list;

int ll_size(void);
void ll_head(void);
void ll_tail(void);
int ll_istail(void);
int ll_ishead(void);
void ll_next(void);
void ll_previous(void);
object *ll_retrieve(void);
void ll_addhead(object *newobject);
void ll_promote(void);
void ll_replace(object *newobject);
int ll_find(void *lookfor);
#endif
```

We said classes will provide an allocator and deallocator. We will follow the convention that these methods will be named <class_name>_new() and <class_name>_delete(), respectively. For linked lists, these methods look like

```
void *ll_new(void)
{
  linked_list *this;
  this = malloc(sizeof(linked_list));
  this->pcl = this->phead = this->ptail = 0;
  this->listlength = 0;
  return this;
}
```

and

```
void ll_delete(void *this)
{
  free(this);
}
```

The linked list header file must be updated to include these two declarations

```
void *ll_new(void);
void ll_delete(void *this);
```

Now let's return to the question of how best to inform class methods which object is the target of their actions. There are at least two reasonable ways to handle this, each with advantages and disadvantages.

The first possibility is to use a static structure pointer in the code file. The client then sets or resets the pointer (via a pointer reset method) before calling any other class methods. The beginning of the linked list code file has a static pointer, say pll, added and becomes

```
#include <stdio.h>
#include "ll.h"
static linked_list *pll;

/* ... followed by methods code. */
```

and a reset method is added to update this new variable.

```
void ll_reset(linked_list *new_list)
{
  pll = new_list;
}
```

Each linked list method is then modified to work not on the single static instance of the linked list, but on the linked list to which pll is currently pointing. For example, ll_size() and ll_head() are modified from

```
int ll_size(void)
{
  return listlength;
}

void ll_head(void)
{
  pcl = phead;
}
```

to

```
int ll_size(void)
{
  return pll->listlength;
}
```

```
void ll_head(void)
{
    pll->pcl = pll->phead;
}
```

Notice that `pll` is a static variable, globally available to any method defined in this code file. This is one of the guarantees of C scope rules. If you are unfamiliar with these scope rules, review Section 1.12.

This use of `pll` may seem confusing to many readers. After all, haven't we just finished saying that we need many linked lists, not one? To what is `pll` pointing? No memory has yet been allocated. The answer to these questions lies on the client side.

A client using such a linked list class might look like this, with lines numbered for future reference.

```
1     #include "ll.h"
2     int main()
3.    {
4.        linked_list *llp1;
5.        linked_list *llp2;
6.        object new_word;

7.        llp1 = ll_new();
8.        llp2 = ll_new();

9.        ll_reset(llp1);
10.       strcpy(new_word.word, "abc"); ll_addhead(&new_word);
11.       ll_reset(llp2);

12.       strcpy(new_word.word, "123"); ll_addhead(&new_word);
13.       ll_reset(llp1);

14.       strcpy(new_word.word, "def"); ll_addhead(&new_word);
15.       ll_reset(llp2);

16.       strcpy(new_word.word, "456"); ll_addhead(&new_word);
17.       ll_delete(llp1);
18.       ll_delete(llp2);
19.       return 0;
20. }
```

The next series of pictograms shows the effect of these lines on the linked list side of things. Up until line 6, all we have done is declare two pointers to linked lists, a structure defined in the ll.h file. Lines 7 and 8 then allocate two chunks of memory, each enough for one linked list structure, and sets pointers to these chunks. No links have yet been allocated, only the space necessary to store the linked list instances themselves. The situation now looks like

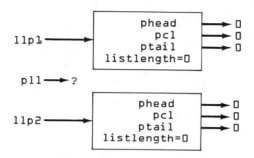

9.   ll_reset(llp1);

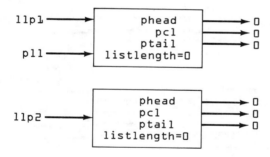

10.   strcpy(new_word.word, "abc"); ll_addhead(&new_word);

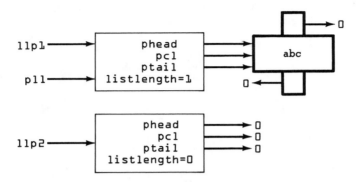

11.   ll_reset(llp2);
12.   strcpy(new_word.word, "123"); ll_addhead(&new_word);

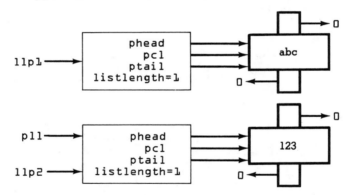

This continues, with pll shifting back and forth between llp1 and llp2, and links being added to whichever list pll is currently pointing. Lines 17 and 18 deallocate both lists.

The use of the static variable pll is one way to let the linked list methods know about the current target. The other option is to include this information as one of the parameters to the methods as we did for obj_cpy(). The header file is the same in either case except for the extra target parameter which is added to each method. The ll_reset() method and the static variable pll are no longer needed. Instead, pll becomes the first parameter to each method. For example, ll_size() and ll_head(), which were

```
int ll_size(void)
{
  return listlength;
}


void ll_head(void)
{
  pcl = phead;
}
```

now look like

```
int ll_size(linked_list *pll)
{
  return pll->listlength;
}


void ll_head(linked_list *pll)
{
  pll->pcl = pll->head;
}
```

and the method declarations in the header file become updated accordingly. Notice that the method code changes are similar using either system, the only difference is in the management of pll. In one case it is a static variable. In the other, a method parameter. Using this second technique the sample program becomes

```
#include "ll.h"
int main()
{
  linked_list *llp1;
  linked_list *llp2;
  object new_word;

  llp1 = ll_new();
  llp2 = ll_new();
  strcpy(new_word.word, "abc"); ll_addhead(llp1, &new_word);

  strcpy(new_word.word, "123"); ll_addhead(llp2, &new_word);
  strcpy(new_word.word, "def"); ll_addhead(llp1, &new_word);
  strcpy(new_word.word, "456"); ll_addhead(llp2, &new_word);
```

```
      ll_delete(llp1);
      ll_delete(llp2);
      return 0;
  }
```

Which of these two techniques is preferred? The first technique eliminates one parameter from all method calls, but requires a reset call whenever the linked list may have changed. The consequence of forgetting a reset is list corruption, which is most likely catastrophic. The second technique eliminates the reset at the expense of an additional parameter for every method.

Readers of *Reusable Data Structures for C* [Sessions] will recall that the first technique was used throughout. Here we will use the second technique because, among other reasons, it is consistent with the approach used by C++. Therefore we will add a target object parameter to each method. By convention, we will use the first parameter for this purpose.

We have now solved the first of our three problems, limited instantiation, and can move onto the second.

4.3   Object Type Inflexibility

We aren't quite ready to solve our HMO problem. We have reached the point where we can multiply instantiate the linked list, but we cannot use them to store different types of objects. With the current methodology, the three linked lists must all contain either physicians, patients, or assignments. We need the three linked lists to manage three different classes of objects.

Let's start by looking at the code causing the problem. The linked list itself is primarily a set of pointers to link objects, and is independent of the class being stored. The problem is not in the linked list class, but in the link class.

The link class contains the object being manipulated, and varies in size as the size of the object varies. When defining a linked list of physicians, the link contains, in addition to the two generic link pointers, space for an employee ID, specialty code, and last name. Links for patients allocate considerably more space, allowing symptom descriptions to be stored. The assignment link is the largest of all, containing the sum of both of the above.

Surprisingly, embedding the object class in the link structure serves only one purpose: letting the compiler know how much space is needed for the object inside the link. This information is needed only during link allocation, inside `link_new()`. This allocation method is one of our new class requirements. This is the only linked list method that cares how big an object is or what it looks like. This size information is important and cannot be ignored. A patient object will not fit in a physician link.

What we need is a general technique for creating links that are independent of the size of the objects they are managing. Such links could contain physicians, patients, or assignments.

The solution is suggested by the link independence of the linked list class. The linked list class is independent of the size of links because it never deals with links. It deals with pointers to links. Though the size of the links changes along with the size of their embedded objects, the size of a link pointer is constant. The suggested solution, then, is to have links manipulate pointers to objects rather than objects. With this change, links always look the same regardless of the type of object they "contain."

This forces us to rethink the memory allocation for objects. Until now, instantiating a link meant automatically allocating space for the embedded object. Now the link will contain only a pointer to the object. Somebody else needs to take over the responsibility for allocating space for the object. We will make this the responsibility of the linked list client.

This changes the sequence of events that occurs when, say, a new object is inserted into the head of a list. Before, the client passed an object pointer to `ll_addhead()` which allocated a new link and copied the object into the link. Now the client will first call `object_new()` to allocate permanent space for the new object and pass that address to `ll_addhead()` which will allocate a new link and set an internal link pointer to that object.

The picture of a linked list changes from this:

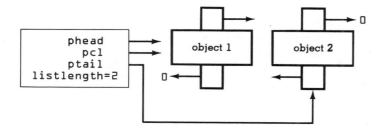

to this

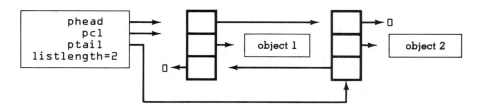

The main problem now is that our code occasionally uses an `object` *, assuming we know what an object looks like. But this is exactly what we are trying to forget. What is needed is a pointer to some generic type, which fortunately is the definition of `void` *.

Therefore, we need to change any code which references an `object` * to reference a `void` *. Again `ll_addhead()` and `ll_replace()`, which had taken an `object` * parameter, now takes a `void` * parameter, and `ll_retrieve()`, which had returned an `object` * will now return a `void` *.

The second change is to the definition of the link structure, which was

```
struct linktype {
  struct linktype *pnext;
  struct linktype *pprevious;
  object contents;
};
typedef struct linktype link;
```

and becomes

```
struct linktype {
  struct linktype *pnext;
  struct linktype *pprevious;
  void *pcontents;
};
typedef struct linktype link;
```

The third change is to the link allocator, which had taken no arguments, and is now passed a pointer to the embedding object. The new version looks like

```
void *link_new(void *pnewcontents)
{
  link *lp;
  lp = malloc(sizeof(link));
  lp->pcontents = pnewcontents;
  return lp;
}
```

By now the actual code for the linked list class must be seeming a bit blurry. Don't worry; we will soon show the new version in its entirety. We are getting close to a linked list class which will support our HMO problem. We still have one remaining issue.

4.4 Object Method Inflexibility

We can now create three different linked lists, each containing objects of different classes. Each of these classes will have its own set of application specific class methods. For example, `obj_match()` for the physician linked list looks for an available specialist, and looks like

```
obj_match(void *this, void *lookfor)
{
  physician *pp = this;
  return (pp->specialty == *lookfor);
}
```

However the `obj_match()` for the assignment is called to locate an assignment by an employee ID:

```
obj_match (void *this, void *lookfor)
{
  assignment *ap = this;
  physician *pp = &(ap->phys);
  return (!strcmp(pp->eid, lookfor));
}
```

The problem is, when we call `obj_match()`, how do we control which of these functions will be called?

There are several techniques available to solve this problem, and each has several variants. All solutions are reminiscent of the solutions to the earlier problems, and can be summarized by this rule: Run time resolution invariably involves indirection, and indirection invariably involves pointers. The only debatable point is how these pointers will be set up.

Before you continue with this section be sure you understand the use of pointers to functions and how indirect calls work. If you are not comfortable with these techniques, refer back to 1.13 for a refresher.

The first possibility is to pass as a parameter the address of an application specific method to any method which invokes the application specific method. Thus, a client calling `ll_addhead()` would pass in, as a parameter, the address of the `obj_cpy()` that goes with the object type it is dealing with.

Since calls to application specific methods would then be indirect, their names would be irrelevant. The three different `obj_match()` functions for the HMO program could be called `physician_match()`, `patient_match()`, and `assignment_match()`.

We have to modify class methods which call such indirect functions. For example, `ll_find()`, which uses the now indirect `obj_match()`, would change from

```
int ll_find (linked_list *this, void *lookfor)
{
  ll_head(this);
  for (;;) {
    if (obj_match(this->pcl->pcontents, lookfor)) return 1;
    if (ll_istail(this)) return 0;
    ll_next(this);
  }
}
```

to

```
int ll_find(linked_list *this, void *lookfor,
            int (*match)())
{
  ll_head(this);
  for (;;) {
    if ((*match)(this->pcl->pcontents, lookfor)) return 1;
    if (ll_istail(this)) return 0;
    ll_next(this);
  }
}
```

Notice the only changes are to the function prototype and the call to the application specific method. The line containing the call looks complex, but it follows a pattern which will reoccur throughout much of this book. This line

```
if ((*match)(this->pcl->pcontents, lookfor)) return 1;
```

says:

> The addresses of a linked list and a match function have been passed in
> as parameters. Call the match function whose address was passed. Pass
> to that match function two things: first, the contents of the current
> link of whatever linked list was passed in, and second, a value being
> looked for. If that match function returns true, return true. Otherwise,
> continue with the next link in that linked list.

The client of such a linked list class is then responsible for setting up the match
functions, which had always been necessary, and for passing in the match function
addresses as parameters to the appropriate functions. *This must be done even when
only one linked list has been instantiated.*

This may seem strange. After all, if there is only one class of objects being
stored in only one instantiated linked list, there is only one way application specific
methods can be resolved. So why does the client have to pass in resolution
information? But the linked list class now has no idea what type of objects are
going to be stored, or how many linked lists, if any, are going to be instantiated.
It is likely that even the client may not know this information. The client may be
using many other generic data structure classes, and some of these may make use
of the linked list class unbeknownst to the client.

The following code shows how a client might set up a linked list of simple strings.
First, a header file for a string class.

```
#ifndef STRING_CLASS
#define STRING_CLASS
struct string_type {
  char str[100];
};
typedef struct string_type string;

void string_copy(void *dest, void *src);
int string_match(void *this, void *lookfor);
void *string_new(char *newstr);
void string_delete(string *this);
#endif
```

Then the code file:

```
#include "str.h"

void string_copy(void *dest, void *src)
{
  strcpy (dest, src);
}
```

```
int string_match (void *this, void *lookfor)
{
  return (!strcmp(this, lookfor));
}

void *string_new(char *newstr)
{
  string *this;
  this = malloc (sizeof(string));
  strcpy(this->str, newstr);
  return this;
}

void string_delete (string *this)
{
  free(this);
}
```

Notice that the string class itself is almost unaffected by the philosophy of the indirect calls. It is defined very much as it would have been before indirect calls, with one exception. Before, these functions would have been given generic names such as obj_match(). Since these names will no longer be the basis for method resolution, we now have the freedom to choose names descriptive of the class.

Next is the client code for string linked lists. This code looks the same as it would without indirect method calls, except for the call to ll_find(), which has been modified to accept the address of the method which knows how to determine a match.

```
#include "str.h"
#include "ll.h"
int main()
{
  linked_list *str_list = ll_new();

  ll_addhead(str_list, string_new("string 1"));
  ll_addhead(str_list, string_new("string 2"));
  ll_addhead(str_list, string_new("string 3"));

  if (ll_find(str_list, "string 3", string_match))
      printf("found\n");
  else printf ("not found\n");
  return 0;
}
```

The concept of indirectly calling an application specific method may seem complicated. But as you can see, the difficulties are more or less localized to the service class (linked list in this case). Clients are largely shielded from the messy details of how this works and need to understand little of the underlying mechanisms. Even to the service class designer, indirect method calls rapidly lose their novelty and soon become just another tool of the trade.

The second technique for resolving class specific methods uses permanent method pointers rather than parameter method pointers. Such pointers are then reset through specialized reset methods. There are four choices as to where such pointers can be located.

First, they can be located statically in the linked list code file, the advantage being that only one set of pointers need be stored for all linked lists. The disadvantage is that reset methods will need to be called whenever a list type is switched from, say, a physician list to a patient list.

Second, they can be located in the linked list structure. The advantage is only one set of pointers is stored regardless of how long the list is. There are two disadvantages. One is that a given list can store only one type of object, and the other is that the solution is not general, since it applies only to linked lists.

Third, pointers can be stored in the link structure. The advantage is that any link can store any type of object. Again, there are two disadvantages: one, that every link object needs a pointer to every application specific method, quite a bit of storage overhead, and two, that the reset functions need to be called every time a new link is created, making calls to methods such as `ll_addhead()` quite messy.

Fourth, the pointers can be stored in the object structure itself, **string** in this case. The advantages are that any object can be stored in any link, and the pointers can be set up in the object allocator, keeping calls to linked list methods relatively simple. The disadvantage is that this makes the instantiators much more difficult to write, and probably beyond the ability of all but advanced C programmers.

There is no clear favorite among these. We will choose number two, storing the pointers in the linked list. For our purposes the limitations are not a problem and we can keep the code relatively simple. This is not in keeping with the C++ approach; we can extrapolate easily enough when we get there.

Only a few code changes are required. The first is to the linked list structure definition which has a function pointer added, becoming

```
struct linked_list_type {
  link *pcl;
  link *phead;
  link *ptail;
  int listlength;
  int (*match)();          /* Pointer to match function */
};
```

```
typedef struct linked_list_type linked_list;
```

The easiest time to initialize this function pointer is when the linked list is instantiated, which happens when ll_new() is invoked. This function now becomes

```
void *ll_new(int (*newmatch)())
{
  linked_list *this;
  this = malloc(sizeof(linked_list));
  this->pcl = this->phead= this->ptail = 0;
  this->listlength = 0;
  this->match = newmatch;    /* Set match function pointer. */
  return this;
}
```

This function makes use of two function pointers. The first is the parameter, which looks much like the declaration of ll_find() after being modified to accept a pointer to the match() function. The second pointer is the class data member match(). The line that initializes the data member,

```
this->match = newmatch;
```

has a certain grace to it. It modestly accomplishes a technically sophisticated goal. Paraphrased, this line says

> Someplace out there lives a function. Set this pointer to the address of that function. From now on, that function can be called indirectly through this pointer.

One more change is needed to ll_find(), the method that actually invokes the match function. The new version is similar to the last version except the pointer is now called as a structure member. The method now looks like

```
int ll_find(linked_list * pll, void *lookfor)
{
   ll_head(pll);
   for (;;) {
     if ((*pll->match)(pll->pcl->pcontents, lookfor)) return 1;
     if (ll_istail(pll)) return 0;
     ll_next(pll);
   }
}
```

Notice the evolution in how ll_find() invokes the match function. It started this chapter as a hard coded function name

```
if (obj_match(this->pcl->pcontents, lookfor)) return 1;
```

It then turned into a indirect call through a parameter

```
if ((*match)(this->pcl->pcontents, lookfor)) return 1;
```

Finally, it has turned into an indirect call through a pointer which is a data member of the linked list class, which is itself passed in as a pointer

```
if ((*pll->match)(pll->pcl->pcontents, lookfor))
    return 1;
```

Our last version of the sample program needs one minor change to work with these newest updates. The setting of **string_match** is moved from **ll_find()** to **ll_new()**.

```
#include "str.h"
#include "ll.h"
int main()
{
  linked_list *str_list = ll_new(string_match);

  ll_addhead(str_list, string_new("string 1"));
  ll_addhead(str_list, string_new("string 2"));
  ll_addhead(str_list, string_new("string 3"));

  if (ll_find(str_list, "string 3")) printf("found\n");
  else printf ("not found\n");
  return 0;
}
```

Now that we have a clearer idea about what it means to instantiate objects, we will define four special types of methods associated with creating and destroying objects.

Creating an object is a two stage effort. First, memory is allocated for the object. Second, memory is initialized. A method which allocates memory for an object is called an **allocator**. A method which initializes memory is called a **constructor**.

Destroying an object is also a two stage effort. First, an object is prepared for destruction, which may or may not be necessary depending on the class definition. Second, the object's memory is released to the system. A method which prepares the object for destruction is called a **destructor**. A method which frees an object's memory is called a **deallocator**.

All of these special methods are optional. The system provides default versions of the allocator and deallocator. In C, **malloc()** and **free()** can be thought of as the default allocator and deallocator. A class can also provide multiple versions of any of these. This is particularly useful for constructors, since a given class may support multiple initialization schemes. For the linked list class, we could imagine one constructor which initializes an empty list and another which assumes we already know the first element.

The state of the art of class development has advanced quite a bit since the end of the last chapter. We now know how to create multiple class instantiations. We know how to create generic data structures, and we know how to resolve class specific methods.

4.5   Current Version of the Linked List Class

Many changes have been discussed in this chapter. Let's see what the linked list class looks like after incorporating these changes. The header file is now

```
#ifndef LINKED_LIST
#define LINKED_LIST
#include "link.h"

struct linked_list_type {
  link *pcl;
  link *phead;
  link *ptail;
  int listlength;
  int (*match)();
};
typedef struct linked_list_type linked_list;
int ll_size(linked_list *pll);
void ll_head(linked_list *pll);
void ll_tail(linked_list *pll);
int ll_istail(linked_list *pll);
int ll_ishead(linked_list *pll);
void ll_next(linked_list *pll);
void ll_previous(linked_list *pll);
void *ll_retrieve(linked_list *pll);
void ll_addhead(linked_list *pll, void *newobject);
void ll_promote(linked_list *pll);
void ll_replace(linked_list *pll, void *newobject);
int ll_find(linked_list *pll, void *lookfor);
void *ll_new(int (*newmatch)());
void ll_delete(void *pll);
#endif
```

The code file now looks like

```
/* Include files.
   -------------- */
   #include <stdio.h>
   #include "ll.h"

int ll_size(linked_list *pll)
{
   return pll->listlength;
}

void ll_head(linked_list *pll)
{
   pll->pcl = pll->phead;
}

void ll_tail(linked_list *pll)
{
   pll->pcl = pll->ptail;
}

int ll_istail(linked_list *pll)
{
   return (pll->pcl == pll->ptail);
}

int ll_ishead(linked_list *pll)
{
  return (pll->pcl == pll->phead);
}

void ll_next(linked_list *pll)
{
   if (!ll_istail(pll)) pll->pcl = pll->pcl->pnext;
}

void ll_previous(linked_list *pll)
{
   if (!ll_ishead(pll)) pll->pcl = pll->pcl->pprevious;
}
```

```
void *ll_retrieve(linked_list *pll)
{
    return &(pll->pcl->pcontents);
}


void ll_addhead(linked_list *pll, void *newobject)
{
/* Set up new link.
   ---------------- */
    link *newlink;
    newlink = link_new(newobject);
    pll->listlength++;

/* Check for special case of first time call.
   ----------------------------------------- */
    if (pll->listlength == 1) {
        pll->phead = pll->ptail = pll->pcl = newlink;
        newlink->pnext = newlink->pprevious = 0;
        return;
    }

/* Handle general case.
   -------------------- */
    pll->phead->pprevious = newlink;
    newlink->pnext = pll->phead;
    newlink->pprevious = 0;
    pll->phead = pll->pcl = newlink;
    return;
}


void ll_promote(linked_list *pll)
{
/* Special case: current link is head, then nothing to do.
   ------------------------------------------------------- */
    if (ll_ishead(pll)) return;

/* If this is the tail, back up the tail to previous link.
   ------------------------------------------------------- */
    if (ll_istail(pll)) pll->ptail = pll->ptail->pprevious;
```

```
/* Promote current to head.
   ----------------------- */
   pll->pcl->pprevious->pnext = pll->pcl->pnext;
   pll->pcl->pnext->pprevious = pll->pcl->pprevious;
   pll->pcl->pnext = pll->phead;
   pll->pcl->pprevious = 0;
   pll->phead->pprevious = pll->pcl;
   pll->phead = pll->pcl;
   return;
}


void ll_replace(linked_list *pll, void *newobject)
{
   pll->pcl->pcontents = newobject;
}


int ll_find(linked_list *pll, void *lookfor)
{
   ll_head(pll);
   for (;;) {
     if ((*pll->match)(pll->pcl->pcontents, lookfor)) return 1;
     if (ll_istail(pll)) return 0;
     ll_next(pll);
   }
}


void *ll_new(int (*newmatch)())
{
  linked_list *this;
  this = malloc(sizeof(linked_list));
  this->pcl = this->phead= this->ptail = 0;
  this->listlength = 0;
  this->match = newmatch;
  return this;
}


void ll_delete(void *this)
{
  free(this);
}
```

4.6   The HMO Problem

Now back to the HMO program. We should be in good shape to solve this problem. The linked list class has been modified to allow multiple instantiations. Each instantiation can contain different classes, and we have techniques for resolving the different class-specific methods.

The following pictograms illustrate how the three linked lists will be coordinated. The character in parentheses is the specialty code, either "C," "I," or "G," for Cardiology, Internal Medicine, or General.

day starts

physician	Kildare(C)	Casey(I)	Pierce(G)	Zhavago(G)

patient

assignment

patients arrive: Romeo(C), Juliet(G)

physician

Casey(I)	Pierce(G)

patient

assignment

Kildare(C) Romeo(C)	Zhavago(G) Juliet(G)

patients arrive: Caesar(G), Hamlet(G)

physician

Casey(I)

patient

Hamlet(G)

assignment

Pierce(G) Caesar(G)	Kildare(C) Romeo(C)	Zhavago(G) Juliet(G)

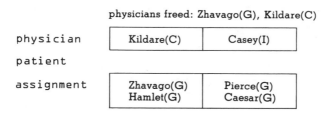

physician patient assignment

There is still one small problem with the linked list class, but one easily solved. HMO assigns both physicians and patients fairly. In practice this means the patient or physician waiting the longest is the next assigned (within the constraints of specialties). The easiest way to implement this is to place elements on one side of the list, and remove them from the other. This means either placing new elements on the head side and removing from the tail side, or visa versa. Currently, both our add method and remove method start at the head side. We need a new version of one of these methods which starts from the tail side.

The following method adds a new link to the tail of the linked list, basically the inverse of `ll_addhead()`.

```
void ll_addtail(linked_list(linked_list *pll, void *newobject)
{
/* Set up new link.
   --------------- */
   link *newlink;
   newlink = link_new(newobject);
   pll->listlength++;

/* Check for special case of first time call.
   ---------------------------------------- */
   if (pll->listlength == 1) {
      pll->phead = pll->ptail = pll->pcl = newlink;
      newlink->pnext = newlink->pprevious = 0;
      return;
   }
```

```
/* Handle general case.
   ------------------- */
   pll->ptail->pnext = newlink;
   newlink->pprevious = pll->ptail;
   newlink->pnext = 0;
   pll->ptail = pll->pcl = newlink;
   return;
}
```

Everything is now in place for solving HMO. HMO introduces three new classes: patient, physician, and assignment. A patient object is either on the patient list or the assignment list, but never both. A physician object is similarly on the physician list or the assignment list, but never both. Let's consider the physician object for a moment.

The physician object is constantly shuffling back and forth between the physician and assignment list. We can implement this in two ways. We can have an assignment class which duplicates the physician information. Placing a physician on assignment then means copying the information from the physician to the assignment object. Or, we can create an assignment class which contains only two pointers, one for a physician and one for a patient object. In this case, placing a physician on assignment means setting the physician pointer in the assignment object to that physician. This second implementation is both faster and more memory efficient, and this is how HMO will be set up.

The next three pictograms represent this HMO state.

- Available Physicians: Two physicians are available to see patients: Honeycut and Casey. Both are Internists. Casey has been free the longest, and will be the next assigned.

- Waiting Patients: Socrates and Hamlet are both waiting for General Practitioners. Hamlet is waiting the longest, and should be seen next.

- Assignments: Zhavago is seeing Juliet, and Pierce is seeing Caesar. Zhavago has been seeing Juliet the longest, though this information is not relevant. Whichever physician becomes available first will be assigned to Hamlet.

A physician list looks like this

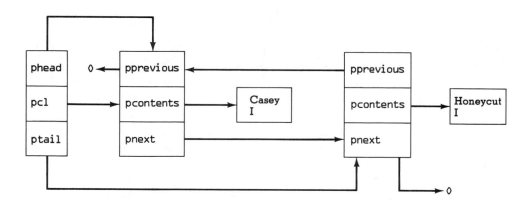

The patient list looks almost identical, except patient objects replace physician objects (the boxes with Casey and Honeycut).

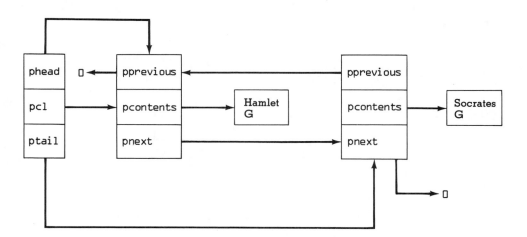

An assignment list is more complex because the objects in the links are more complex. The assignment objects, as we said, contain only pointers, pointing to physicians and patients, the same objects stored in the previous two lists. The *list* part of this list is the same as the last two lists. Only the object being stored is different. The assignment list looks like

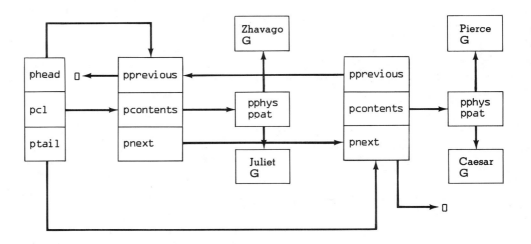

This pictogram looks confusing because we are seeing all of the details at once. One advantage of object-oriented programming is we can focus on the level of detail in which we are interested. For example, from the point of view of assignment managing code, this assignment list looks like

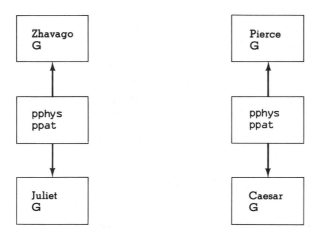

While from the perspective of the linked list managing code, that same data set

looks like

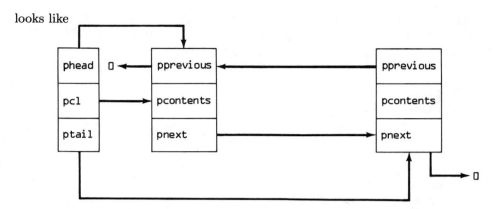

The patient class includes four data members and five methods. The data members are self describing, except possibly **specialty**, which is the specialty code of the physician needed. The class methods provide this functionality

patient_new():	Class constructor.
patient_delete():	Class destructor.
patient_match():	Class equality operator.
patient_print():	Class output method.
patient_get_info():	Method to query user for patient data.

The class description file looks like

```
#ifndef PATIENT_CLASS
#define PATIENT_CLASS
struct patient_type {
  char name[80];
  char ssn[15];
  char symptoms[100];
  char specialty[2];
};
typedef struct patient_type patient;

void *patient_new(void);
void patient_delete(void *this);
void patient_copy(void *dest, void *src);
int patient_match (void *this, void *lookfor);
void patient_print(void *this);
void *patient_get_info(void *this);
#endif
```

The code file for the patient methods includes the necessary headers and then defines the class constructor; no global static variables are needed for this class. The constructor allocates memory for a patient and initializes the data members. The constructor is followed by the class destructor.

```
#include <stdio.h>
#include <stdlib.h>
#include "patient.h"

void *patient_new(void)
{
  patient *pp;
  pp = malloc(sizeof(patient));
  strcpy(pp->name, "");
  strcpy(pp->ssn, "");
  strcpy(pp->symptoms, "");
  strcpy(pp->specialty, "");
  return pp;
}


void patient_delete(void *this)
{
  free (this);
}
```

The match method for patients checks for a patient's name. It could have checked social security number. For this exercise it doesn't really matter. The method is used only when initializing the linked list and is never actually invoked. We include it here only for completeness.

```
int patient_match(void *this, void *lookfor)
{
  patient *pp = this;
  return (!strcmp(pp->name, lookfor));
}
```

The remaining methods are straight forward. The next one prints a patient object. This is followed by a method to query the user for patient information. The latter function calls **get_line()** to read a line of user input. **get_line()** is a regular C function, not a class method, and is not shown.

```
void patient_print(void *this)
{
  patient *pp = (patient *) this;
  printf("-----------------------------------------------\n");
  printf("        Patient Name: %s\n", pp->name);
  printf("         Patient SSN: %s\n", pp->ssn);
  printf("    Patient Symptoms: %s\n", pp->symptoms);
  printf("Assigned Specialty: %s\n", pp->specialty);
}


void *patient_get_info(void *this)
{
  patient *pp = (patient *) this;
  printf("        Patient Name: "); get_line(pp->name);
  printf("         Patient SSN: "); get_line(pp->ssn);
  printf("    Patient Symptoms: "); get_line(pp->symptoms);
  printf("Assigned Specialty: "); get_line(pp->specialty);
  return pp;
}
```

The physician class is similar to the patient class. The class has three data members and six methods. The data members are self explanatory. The methods are

physician_new():	Class constructor.
physician_delete():	Class destructor.
physician_spec_match():	Equality operator to check against physician specialty.
physician_id_match():	Equality operator to check against physician ID.
physician_print():	Class output method.
physician_get_info():	Method to query user for physician data.

The class descriptor header file looks like

```
#ifndef PHYSICIAN_CLASS
#define PHYSICIAN_CLASS
struct physician_type {
  char emp_id[10];
  char name[80];
  char specialty[2];
};
```

```
typedef struct physician_type physician;

void *physician_new(void);
void physician_delete(void *this);
void physician_copy(void *dest, void *src);
int physician_spec_match (void *this, void *lookfor);
int phys_id_match (void *this, void *lookfor);
void physician_print(void *this);
void *physician_get_info(void *this);
#endif
```

The beginning of the code file for the physician methods is highly reminiscent of the patient code file, and most of the physician methods are very close to their patient counterparts. The start of the file looks like

```
#include <stdio.h>
#include "phys.h"
```

The constructor and destructor are identical in concept to those of the patient class, and are left as an exercise.

The physician class has two match methods, one which considers specialty, and one which considers employee ID. This may seem confusing. The last class didn't really need any match methods and this class needs two. The linked list class assumes its client classes will provide one, and only one, match method. How is this reconciled?

The patient class provides its match method to satisfy the linked list constructor. The patient linked list method that would have invoked this, `ll_find()`, is not used by HMO. However, HMO does invoke `ll_find()` when looking for the next available physician of a particular specialty.

Because `ll_find()` uses `physician_spec_match()`, this method is passed into the constructor. The second match method is provided for the benefit of the assignment class. We will see how it is used when we look at `assignment_match()`. These details are not important now. The physician class has no idea how these methods will be used. It is simply making available a set of potentially useful class methods.

```
int physician_spec_match(void *this, void *lookfor)
{
  physician *pp = this;
  return (!strcmp(pp->specialty, lookfor));
}
```

```
int phys_id_match(void *this, void *lookfor)
{
  physician *pp = this;
  return (!strcmp(pp->emp_id, lookfor));
}
```

The remaining physician methods are `physician_print()` and `physician_get_info()`, both of which are similar to their patient counterparts. They are left as exercises.

Next is the assignment class. An assignment contains no data per se, only two pointers: one to a physician object and one to a patient object. An assignment object defines a relationship between two other objects. The class includes two data members, the pointers and four methods. The class methods are these

`asgn_new()`:	Class constructor.
`asgn_delete()`:	Class destructor.
`asgn_match()`:	Class equality operator.
`asgn_print()`:	Class output method.

The class descriptor file looks like this

```
#ifndef ASSIGNMENT_CLASS
#define ASSIGNMENT_CLASS
#include "patient.h"
#include "phys.h"

struct assignment_type {
  physician *pphysician;            /* assigned physician */
  patient *ppatient;               /* assigned patient */
};
typedef struct assignment_type assignment;

void *asgn_new(physician *new_phys, patient *new_patient);
void asgn_delete(void *this);
int asgn_match(void *this, void *lookfor);
void asgn_print(void *this);
#endif
```

Like the physician and patient classes, the assignment methods file contains no static global variables. After including the necessary header files, the constructor and destructor are defined. Notice this constructor does not allocate space for either a patient or physician object. These objects are assumed to be already instantiated.

```
#include <stdio.h>
#include <stdlib.h>
#include "assign.h"

void *asgn_new(physician *new_phys, patient *new_patient)
{
  assignment *pa;
  pa = malloc(sizeof(assignment));
  pa->pphysician = new_phys;
  pa->ppatient = new_patient;
  return pa;
}


void asgn_delete(void *this)
{
  free (this);
}
```

The assignment match function will be called by `ll_match()`. The HMO code uses `ll_match()` to free an assignment, once a physician has finished seeing a patient. HMO asks for a physician ID, and then searches the assignments looking for that physician, or more precisely, the correct assignment containing a pointer to a physician whose ID matches.

```
int asgn_match(void *this, void *lookfor)
{
  assignment *pa = this;
  return (phys_id_match(pa->pphysician, lookfor));
}
```

Notice how `asgn_match()` tries to protect itself from the details of how IDs are actually stored in physician objects. It does this by calling `phys_id_match()` to determine if the ID matches, rather than making that determination itself. This protects `asgn_match()` from any unexpected implementation changes in physician object definitions. The method is dependent only on the concept of a physician ID, not the details of how that ID is implemented.

Finally, we have the class print method, which is implemented as a pass through function to the print methods of the two objects to which the assignment points.

```
void asgn_print(void *this)
{
  assignment *pa = this;
  physician_print(pa->pphysician);
  patient_print(pa->ppatient);
}
```

Our classes are fully defined and we move on to HMO. At the highest level, HMO is just a loop, pseudocoded as

```
main()
{
  set up program;
  initialize linked lists;
  done = FALSE;
  while (!done) {
    display option;
    process option;
  }
  prepare to quit program;
  exit;
}
```

Recalling the HMO specifications, we need to support these options.

1. Terminate or free an assignment,

2. Add a newly arrived patient,

3. Display list of waiting patients,

4. Display list of available physicians,

5. Display list of current assignments,

6. Terminate program.

Notice that half of the program's options involve displaying the contents of a list. Since this seems a general requirement of lists, we add a new method to the linked list class, `ll_print()`, which prints the contents of each item on the list.

There are two different aspects of printing items on the list. The first is the mechanics of iterating through the list. The second is the process of printing the contents of a particular link. Iterating is accomplished easily enough using existing linked list methods, such as `ll_head()`, `ll_next()`, and `ll_istail()`. The printing, however, requires knowledge of the application specific nature of the object in the link.

The solution to printing is the same as the solution to matching. `ll_print()` needs to make indirect method calls just as `ll_find()`. The code for `ll_print()`, and other necessary changes to the linked list are left as a reader exercise, and the example of `ll_find()` and application specific matching should be closely followed. The remainder of this chapter assumes these changes have been made.

The programming details of **process option** are the guts of HMO. The code for each option will be encapsulated into a separate function. To simplify the code, we will include all HMO functions in the same file, **hmo.c**, which starts with global information and continues with the main body.

```
/*
Include files.
-------------- */
#include <stdio.h>
#include "ll.h"
#include "assign.h"
#include "patient.h"
#include "phys.h"

/*
Local constants.
---------------- */
#define FREE_ASSIGNMENT 1
#define NEW_PATIENT 2
#define SHOW_WAITING_PATIENTS 3
#define SHOW_FREE_DOCTORS 4
#define SHOW_ASSIGNMENTS 5
#define EXIT_PROGRAM 6
#define LAST_OPTION EXIT_PROGRAM
/*
Function declarations.
---------------------- */
void init_doctor_list(void);
void display_options(void);
int get_option(void);
void free_assignment(void);
void new_patient(void);
void show_wait(void);
void show_free(void);
void show_assign(void);
int check_status(void);
```

```
/*
Global Declarations.
-------------------- */
linked_list *phys_list, *pat_list, *asgn_list;

int main()
{
/* Local variable declarations.
   --------------------------- */
   int done = 0;

/* Instantiate linked lists.
   ------------------------ */
   phys_list = ll_new(physician_spec_match, physician_print);
   pat_list =  ll_new(patient_match, patient_print);
   asgn_list = ll_new(asgn_match, asgn_print);

/* Initialize system.
   ----------------- */
   init_doctor_list();

/* Main program loop.
   ----------------- */
   while (!done) {
     display_options();
     switch (get_option()) {
       case FREE_ASSIGNMENT:
          free_assignment();
          break;
       case NEW_PATIENT:
          new_patient();
          break;
       case SHOW_WAITING_PATIENTS:
          show_wait();
          break;
       case SHOW_FREE_DOCTORS:
          show_free();
          break;
       case SHOW_ASSIGNMENTS:
          show_assign();
          break;
```

```
        case EXIT_PROGRAM:
            done = 1;
            break;
    }
  }
  /* Free memory.
     ------------ */
  ll_delete(phys_list);
  ll_delete(pat_list);
  ll_delete(asgn_list);
  return 0;
}
```

The first function called is `init_doctor_list()`. The program presumably runs at the start of each day, and this function is called once to initialize the list of available physicians (`phys_list`). This function might consist of a loop, whose pseudocode could look like

```
init_physician_list()
{
  ask user how many physicians;
  for (that many physicians) {
    instantiate a new physician object;
    invoke physician get_info on that object;
    add the new object to the physician list;
  }
}
```

or this function could assume that physicians are usually the same, and read them from a text file. In either case, the result is a list consisting of all of the physicians available for assignment. The function `init_doctor_list()` is left as an exercise.

The next two invoked functions are `display_options()` and `get_option()`. The former displays a menu of HMO choices. The latter returns the choice as one of the defined constants between the values of `FREE_ASSIGNMENT` and `LAST_OPTION`. Neither of these trivial functions is shown.

The next function is `free_assignment()`, called to process assignment completion. It asks for the ID of the now available physician. It then looks in the assignment list for the assignment containing that physician. This checking is done through `ll_find()`, which indirectly invokes `asgn_match()` which *directly* invokes `physician_id_match()`. How can we be so sure `ll_find()` will invoke `asgn_match()` rather than, for example, `patient_match()`? This is assured at linked list instantiation time, by the line

```
asgn_list = ll_new(asgn_match, asgn_print);
```

Once `free_assignment()` has set the current link of the `asgn_list` to the link containing the desired physician, it retrieves the assignment, then deletes the patient, and places the now available physician object back on the `phys_list`. Then an interesting function, `check_status()`, is called. But before getting into this function, let's examine the rest of `free_assignment()`.

```c
void free_assignment(void)
{
/* Local declarations.
   ------------------- */
   char free_id[100];
   assignment *pa;
   int found;

/* Ask for information.
   -------------------- */
   printf("Physician ID: ");
   get_line(free_id);

/* Locate assignment.
   ------------------ */
   found = ll_find(asgn_list, free_id);

/* If found, free assignment.
   -------------------------- */
   if (found) {
       pa = ll_retrieve(asgn_list);
       ll_remove(asgn_list);
       patient_delete(pa->ppatient);
       ll_addtail(phys_list, pa->pphysician);
       printf("physician %s freed\n", free_id);
       check_status();
   }
/* Otherwise, tell 'em about the error.
   ------------------------------------ */
   else {
     printf("Sorry...\n");
     printf("Can't find physician %s in assigned list\n",
            free_id);
   }
}
```

Now let's look at `check_status()`. This function is called whenever an event

has occurred that may have changed either the physician list or the patient list.
The function checks the current system status to see if any new assignments can
be made; that is, if any of the waiting patients need specialties represented by one
of the available physicians. If check_status() finds such a patient/physician pair,
it creates a new assignment and notifies the human operator.

There are two times when the system status changes so that an assignment
might have just become possible. The first is when an assignment is completed,
and a physician with a possibly not previously available specialty becomes available.
The second is when a new patient checks into the HMO. If the new patient requires
a specialty not required by any other of the waiting patients, and an appropriate
physician is already available with that specialty, then a new assignment can be
made.

```c
int check_status(void)
{
/* Allocate variables and initialize system.
   --------------------------------------- */
    int n, nend;
    int updated = 0;
    patient *pp;
    physician *pph;
    assignment *pa;
    ll_head(pat_list);
    nend = ll_listlength(pat_list);

/* Loop through waiting patients.
   ---------------------------- */
    for (n=0; n<nend; n++) {
        pp = ll_retrieve(pat_list);

/*      If physician is available, assign.
        --------------------------------- */
        if (ll_find(phys_list, pp->specialty)) {
            pa = asgn_new(ll_retrieve(phys_list), pp);
            ll_addtail(asgn_list, pa);
            ll_remove(phys_list);
            ll_remove(pat_list);
            printf("New Assignment\n");
            asgn_print(pa);
            updated = 1;
        }
```

```
        ll_next(pat_list);
    }
    return updated;
}
```

The function **new_patient()** is called to instantiate a new patient object, get data for that object, and add the patient to the waiting patient list. HMO then checks to see if an assignment is possible via **check_status()**.

```
void new_patient(void)\index{new_patient(void)}
{
    patient *pp;
    pp = patient_new();
    patient_get_info(pp);
    ll_addtail(pat_list, pp);
    check_status();
}
```

The functions **show_wait()**, **show_free()**, and **show_assign()** dump the contents of the waiting patient, the available physician, and the assignment lists respectively. All three act as fronts for the appropriate calls to **ll_print()**.

```
void show_wait(void)
{
    if (ll_listlength(pat_list)) {
      printf("Waiting Patients\n");
      ll_print(pat_list);
    }
    else printf("No Waiting Patients\n");
}


void show_free(void)
{
    if (ll_listlength(phys_list)) {
      printf("Free Physicians\n");
      ll_print(phys_list);
    }
    else printf("No Free Physicians\n");
}
```

```
void show_assign(void)
{
  if (ll_listlength(asgn_list)) {
    printf("Assignments\n");
    ll_print(asgn_list);
  }
  else printf("No Assignments Being Processed\n");
}
```

Now let's see what it looks like to run HMO. The options menu looks like this.

```
1. Free Doctor From Assignment
2. New Patient Arrival
3. Show Waiting Patients
4. Show Available Doctors
5. Show Assignments
6. Exit Program
Enter Choice:
```

Since our list is initialized with four physicians, Pierce (Generalist), Casey (Internist), Zhavago (Generalist), and Honeycut (Internist), choosing option 4 from the menu causes this display

```
Free Physicians
-------------------------------------------------
        Physician ID: 1111
      Physician Name: Pierce
Assigned Specialty: G
-------------------------------------------------
        Physician ID: 2222
      Physician Name: Casey
Assigned Specialty: I
-------------------------------------------------
        Physician ID: 3333
      Physician Name: Zhavago
Assigned Specialty: G
-------------------------------------------------
        Physician ID: 4444
      Physician Name: Honeycut
Assigned Specialty: I
```

No patients have arrived yet, so option 3 displays

```
No Waiting Patients
```

A new patient arrives, so option 2 is chosen and the operator is prompted for patient information:

```
        Patient Name: Hamlet
         Patient SSN: 1234
    Patient Symptoms: Stab Wound
   Assigned Specialty: G
```

We are now under the control of **new_patient()**, which always invokes **check_status()**. **check_status()** will see that Pierce has the needed specialty, and immediately makes the assignment. The operator is notified of this fact by this display

```
New Assignment
------------------------------------------------
         Physician ID: 1111
       Physician Name: Pierce
   Assigned Specialty: G
------------------------------------------------
         Patient Name: Hamlet
          Patient SSN: 1234
     Patient Symptoms: Stab Wound
   Assigned Specialty: G
```

Another patient arrives. Again, the operator is prompted for patient information, and **check_status()** finds an available physician.

```
         Patient Name: Socrates
          Patient SSN: 2345
     Patient Symptoms: Seems to have drunk too much of something.
   Assigned Specialty: G
```

```
New Assignment
------------------------------------------------
         Physician ID: 3333
       Physician Name: Zhavago
   Assigned Specialty: G
------------------------------------------------
         Patient Name: Socrates
          Patient SSN: 2345
     Patient Symptoms: Seems to have drunk too much of something.
   Assigned Specialty: G
```

If the operator chooses option 5 the current assignments are displayed

```
Assignments
-------------------------------------------------
        Physician ID: 1111
      Physician Name: Pierce
   Assigned Specialty: G
-------------------------------------------------
        Patient Name: Hamlet
         Patient SSN: 1234
    Patient Symptoms: Stab Wound
   Assigned Specialty: G
-------------------------------------------------
        Physician ID: 3333
      Physician Name: Zhavago
   Assigned Specialty: G
-------------------------------------------------
        Patient Name: Socrates
         Patient SSN: 2345
    Patient Symptoms: Seems to have drunk too much of something.
   Assigned Specialty: G
```

A new patient arrives, but this time no physicians are available and no assignment is made.

```
        Patient Name: Juliet
         Patient SSN: 3456
    Patient Symptoms: No sign of movement.
   Assigned Specialty: G
```

Again a new patient arrives, and again no physicians are available.

```
        Patient Name: Caesar
         Patient SSN: 4567
    Patient Symptoms: Feels rejected by friends.
   Assigned Specialty: G
```

If we show waiting patients, both Juliet and Caesar are on the list

```
Waiting Patients
-------------------------------------------------
        Patient Name: Juliet
         Patient SSN: 3456
    Patient Symptoms: No sign of movement.
   Assigned Specialty: G
-------------------------------------------------
```

```
        Patient Name: Caesar
         Patient SSN: 4567
     Patient Symptoms: Feels rejected by friends.
  Assigned Specialty: G
```

If we show free physicians, we see

```
Free Physicians
-------------------------------------------------
        Physician ID: 2222
      Physician Name: Casey
  Assigned Specialty: I
-------------------------------------------------
        Physician ID: 4444
      Physician Name: Honeycut
  Assigned Specialty: I
```

Now Pierce finishes seeing Hamlet. The operator chooses option 1 to free the doctor from the assignment. This transfers control to **free_assignment()**, which starts by asking which physician is finished:

```
Physician ID: 1111
physician 1111 freed
```

and then calls **check_status()**, which decides this physician is needed for another assignment

```
New Assignment
-------------------------------------------------
        Physician ID: 1111
      Physician Name: Pierce
  Assigned Specialty: G
-------------------------------------------------
        Patient Name: Juliet
         Patient SSN: 3456
     Patient Symptoms: No sign of movement.
  Assigned Specialty: G
```

If we now show waiting patients, only Caesar appears:

```
Waiting Patients
-------------------------------------------------
        Patient Name: Caesar
         Patient SSN: 4567
     Patient Symptoms: Feels rejected by friends.
  Assigned Specialty: G
```

If we show waiting physicians, we see the usual two:

```
Free Physicians
-------------------------------------------------
        Physician ID: 2222
      Physician Name: Casey
   Assigned Specialty: I
-------------------------------------------------
        Physician ID: 4444
      Physician Name: Honeycut
   Assigned Specialty: I
```

And showing the current assignments gives

```
Assignments
-------------------------------------------------
        Physician ID: 3333
      Physician Name: Zhavago
   Assigned Specialty: G
-------------------------------------------------
       Patient Name: Socrates
        Patient SSN: 2345
   Patient Symptoms: Seems to have drunk too much of something.
   Assigned Specialty: G
-------------------------------------------------
        Physician ID: 1111
      Physician Name: Pierce
   Assigned Specialty: G
-------------------------------------------------
       Patient Name: Juliet
        Patient SSN: 3456
   Patient Symptoms: No sign of movement.
   Assigned Specialty: G
```

This can continue indefinitely.

4.7 Summary

This chapter has investigated three classes of problems related to resolution: class resolution, instance resolution, and method resolution.

Class resolution is concerned with keeping classes as general as possible. Our link objects, for example, should be able to contain many different classes so we can decide at run time the class object needed by the link.

Instance resolution is concerned with the ability to instantiate a class many times, and choose at run time the particular instance on which a method operates. Our HMO program instantiates three lists, one of which is manipulated with each linked list method call.

Method resolution is concerned with the ability to leave code holes which are filled in at the last moment. These code holes are necessary when we have application specific code that may be called upon to manipulate instances of different classes. Such code is closely tied to particular classes. The class resolution may not occur until run time, and the code holes cannot be filled in until the class resolution is complete. Therefore we need run time method resolution ability, or what is often called dynamic binding or late binding.

The process of generating classes is primarily a process of moving from compile time resolution to run time resolution. At the end of the last chapter many of our classes were limited by compile time resolution. The contents of the link were determined at compile time, so only one category of link list could be created. The linked list instance was determined at compile time so only one linked list could be instantiated. The methods were all resolved at compile time, so only one set of application specific methods could be used.

Run time resolution invariably consists of packaging and indirection. First we create a package of information that is resolved as a group. A class instance is packaged as a structure. A set of application specific code is packaged in a method. Second, we apply indirection. Indirection invariably means pointers. Methods receive pointers to their target objects. Application specific code is called through pointers to methods.

These techniques allow us to create classes of objects that are well defined, quite generic, and therefore useful in a wide variety of situations. This is the historical starting point for C++. As this technology was pushed harder and harder, it became clear that language extensions were needed to improve and extend the process. We will investigate these issues and C++ extensions over the next several chapters.

4.8   Exercises

Exercise 4.1 Write constructor and destructor functions for the physician class in the HMO program.

Exercise 4.2 Write `physician_print()` and `physician_get_info()` for the physician class in the HMO program.

Exercise 4.3 Write the `ll_print()` program prototyped in the linked list class. Use `ll_match()` as a guideline.

Exercise 4.4 Write `init_doctor_list()`, whose pseudo code appears in this chapter.

Exercise 4.5 The function `show_wait()` prints the waiting patient list by calling `ll_print()`, the same function used by `show_assign()` to print the assignment list. The format needed to print a waiting patient list is quite different than the format needed to print an assignment list. Yet neither `show_wait()` nor `show_assign()` give any formatting information to `ll_print()`. How does `ll_print()` know which printing format to associate with which list?

Exercise 4.6 When Juliet arrives as a new patient, no assignment is made although both Casey and Honeycut are available. Why is this?

The fault, dear Brutus, is not in our stars,
But in ourselves.

- Julius Caesar, I, i, 1
William Shakespeare

Chapter 5

C Limitations

We have seen how to apply object-oriented programming methodology. We saw how to create application specific classes such as physicians, and application independent object managers such as linked lists. The techniques discussed could be applied to many generic object managers, including caches, queues, and tree structures, to name a few.

The linked list code was very flexible by the end of the last chapter. A program could create hundreds of linked list objects, each manipulating different classes. The linked list class could be used as a building block for other object managers such as stacks.

We also discussed application specific classes. The examples were physicians, patients, assignments, and words. These classes encapsulated application specific information, including both data and code.

5.1 Introduction

It should be clear by now that object-oriented methodology is not the exclusive domain of a so called object-oriented language such as C++. It is a natural extension of structured programming. It is a way of thinking about programming, not a language for writing programs. It is just as possible to write object-oriented programs using nonobject-oriented languages as it is to write nonobject-oriented programs using object-oriented languages.

However C is limited in its ability to support object-oriented programming, although few C programmers push the language even close to these limits. In this chapter we will explore these limits, and see why the development of C++ was considered necessary.

5.2   Method Resolution by Name

Method resolution in C is strictly by method name, and the resolution occurs at the time the program is loaded, or bound, into an executable file. Consider, for example, an invocation of `ll_add()`. One or more source files may invoke the method `ll_add()`. These source files are compiled into object files. Each of these object files is flagged as containing a call to a method `ll_add()`. The linker examines all of the object files, looking for one that contains the code for `ll_add()`. When the code is found, the calls to `ll_add()` are replaced by calls to the address of the object version of `ll_add()`. If more than one version of `ll_add()` is found, an error occurs, since the linker doesn't know which to use. This error message often appears as something like "`multiple defines of ll_add`."

To see where this can cause problems, let's return to the HMO program which tracked physicians and patients. Suppose this office also has a lab which wants a program to keep track of incoming lab test requests. The specifications for this program are slightly different than those of HMO. A lab request is received and logged into the computer. Requests are processed strictly in the order they are received. Once processed, the results are returned to the physician and the computer is no longer involved.

The programmer assigned to this project decides to use a linked list to track lab requests, with each link containing a particular lab test request. New requests are added to the tail of the list and processed from the head. The closer a request is to the head of the list, the longer it has been waiting.

The programmer considers the existing linked list class, but realizes there is a significant difference between the existing and desired classes. In the former, items are removed from the interior of the list. In the latter, items are removed only from the head. The linked list class needed to manage requests is therefore much simpler than the existing linked list class.

The lab program had no need for backwards pointers in its links. There are only two reasons for backwards pointers in links. The first is to process the `ll_previous()` method. The second is to glue the list back together after an interior link is either promoted (by `ll_promote()`) or removed (by `ll_remove()`).

The request manager doesn't use either `ll_previous()` or `ll_promote()` and can make do with a simpler version of `ll_remove()`, one which only removes from the head of the list. This version of `ll_remove()` doesn't need to worry about backwards pointers or interior or tail deletes. The current version of `ll_remove()` looks like this:

```
1.    void ll_remove(linked_list *pll)
2.    {
3.    /* General activity.
4.       ----------------- */
5.        link *plink = pll->pcl;
6.        if (ll_listlength(pll) < 1) return;
7.        pll->listlength--;

8.    /* Special case: only one link.
9.       --------------------------- */
10.       if (ll_listlength(pll) == 0) {
11.           pll->pcl = pll->phead = pll->ptail = 0;
12.       }
13.   /* If this is the tail, back up to previous link.
14.      ---------------------------------------------- */
15.       if (ll_istail(pll)) pll->ptail = pll->ptail->pprevious;

16.   /* If this is the head, move head up to next link.
17.      ----------------------------------------------- */
18.       if (ll_ishead(pll)) pll->phead = pll->phead->pnext;

19.   /* Excise current link.
20.      -------------------- */
21.       if (pll->pcl->pprevious)
22.           pll->pcl->pprevious->pnext = pll->pcl->pnext;
23.       if (pll->pcl->pnext)
24.           pll->pcl->pnext->pprevious = pll->pcl->pprevious;

25.   /* Reset current link and delete.
26.      ---------------------------- */
27.       if (pll->pcl->pnext) pll->pcl = pll->pcl->pnext;
28.       else pll->pcl = pll->pcl->pprevious;
29.       link_delete((void *) plink);
30.       return;
31.   }
```

Notice how much of this is unnecessary for the lab program. Line 15 can be removed, since we never delete a tail. Line 18 can become unconditional, since we will always be deleting the head. Lines 21 through 28, whose purpose is to properly handle interior and tail deletes can be removed. The method turns into this:

```
void ll_remove(linked_list *pll)
{
/* General activity.
   ----------------- */
   link *plink = pll->pcl;
   if (ll_listlength(pll) < 1) return;
   pll->listlength--;

/* Special case: only one link.
   --------------------------- */
   if (ll_listlength(pll) == 0) {
       pll->pcl = pll->phead = pll->ptail = 0;
   }
/* Normal case.
   ------------ */
   pll->phead = pll->phead->pnext;
   link_delete((void *) plink);
   return;
}
```

The Lab Request Programmer decides to create a new version of the linked list class using the existing class as a base. The previous pointer is removed from the link class. ll_remove() is modified as shown. ll_promote() and ll_previous() are removed entirely. Any code dealing with the previous pointer is deleted. The result of this is a new linked list class composed of less complex and faster code with simpler data structures.

The programmer then completes the Lab Request Manager, and all is well and fine. The problem occurs much later, when the decision is made to integrate the two systems, the physician/patient manager, and the request manager. Both functions will now be coordinated by one program, running on one computer.

This change should be straight forward. The request manager has been well structured with two high level routines, one for adding and one for removing tests. All that should be necessary is to add two more options to the HMO program to call these two routines, and link these routines into the HMO executable.

Unfortunately, we quickly run into name conflicts. The request manager wants one set of linked list methods called, and the HMO program wants another. The lab test programmer now faces some difficult choices. The programmer can switch over to using the two-way linked list class. This will decrease performance, make data structures unnecessarily large, and may even require some code changes. Or the programmer can remove the name conflicts. This requires significant code changes to both the one-way linked list class and the client code.

We could use some help here from the language. Suppose the programmer could simply modify the class name of the one way linked list, change the declaration of the list, and let the programming language choose the appropriate method. This should be possible, since between the compiler and the linker the necessary information is available.

With this kind of language support, we could have two similar linked list header files. The two-way list header would be unchanged. The one-way header would need only two changes: the name of the link class would change, say to `link1` and the name of the linked list class would change, say to `linked_list1`. The main HMO program would then look like

```
int main()
{
  linked_list *phys_list = (linked_list *)
     ll_new(physician_match, physician_copy);
  linked_list *pnt_list = (linked_list *)
     ll_new(patient_match, patient_copy);
  linked_list *asgn_list = (linked_list *)
     ll_new(asgn_match, asgn_copy);
  linked_list1 *lab_list =(linked_list1 *)
     ll_new (lab_copy);
  ...
```

We would expect our programming language to realize that the last line is calling a different `ll_new()`, the one designed for one-way lists. This would require the language to resolve methods based on context, rather than name. But this is an idle speculation. Since C resolves methods based solely on method name, it has no way to distinguish these two calls. Similarly it cannot tell that

```
ll_addtail(lab_list, newtest);
```

should invoke a different `ll_addtail()` than

```
ll_addtail(phys_list, pp);
```

and that the latter call should invoke the same `ll_addtail()` as

```
ll_addtail(pnt_list, newpatient);
```

The inability of C to resolve methods based on anything other than name often causes obscure problems as software systems are pieced together. Subsystems are usually developed independently, often with little planning for function naming conventions on any but the client visible level. Unexpected name conflicts can occur as these subsystems are pieced together, and there may be little warning when this occurs. The result is unexpected method calls, usually followed by disaster.

Naming conflicts are avoided only through tedious naming conventions. It is not uncommon for a large software system to devote the first five characters of the function names to some uniqueness scheme, a burden on both the writer and maintainer.

Even with the relatively simple code examples shown in this book, it has been necessary to incorporate a name conflict avoidance scheme. We have been prefacing each method by a class code. Without this, we could end up with `ca_add()` and `ll_add()` both called `add()`, and no way to tell them apart.

Method resolution by name not only creates problems at software development time, but also at software refinement time.

Suppose we wanted a variation of the overused words program, say a unique words program. This program is to keep track of every unique word in the input file, and keep count of the number of times it was used. The word object, with its character string and word count is a good starting point.

For a quick and dirty prototype we decide to use the linked list. The algorithm looks like

```
unique_words()
{
  initialize_word_structure
  while (there_are_more_words) {
    read_word;
    see_if_word_is_in_structure;
    if (in_structure) increment_word_count;
    else add_to_structure;
  }
}
```

This prototype will call many linked list methods, including `ll_new()`, `ll_addhead()`, and `ll_find()`. But once the prototype is complete, we realize we have performance problems when large text files are used. We can't afford the overhead associated with constantly scanning the large linked lists this program creates.

So we change our implementation to use a tree structure instead of a linked list. This greatly reduces the amount of time it takes to find a word in our storage structure. But this requires major changes to the code. Every instance of, say, `ll_new()` must be located and changed to `tree_new()`. Every `ll_addhead()` must change to `tree_add()`, and every `ll_find()` to `tree_find()`.

With a different method resolution process, this could have been easier. We could have used similar names for both linked lists and trees, say `new()`, `add()`, and `find()`. We then change the declaration of the word box from a linked list to a tree, and our hypothetical language would then automatically resolve a completely different set of methods.

With languages that can resolve by context as well as name, such as C++, programmers start to reorient their thinking about naming conventions for methods. Suddenly it becomes not only possible to use similar names for different classes, but even desirable. Many storage classes have analogous patterns for placing and retrieving data, like the linked list and the tree. If the method names are kept similar, class types can be switched easily.

5.3 Flat Classes

Many proponents of C++ will tout as its major feature its support for classes, support they claim is lacking in C. Of course, this is not true. But it is fair to say that C++ offers much better support for classes than C. Method name resolution is one important area in which C++ offers improvements. Another is class hierarchies.

C is more or less limited to flat classes, classes that are nonhierarchical. To see what a hierarchical class might look like, consider the patient class of HMO. The patient header looked like

```
#ifndef PATIENT_CLASS
#define PATIENT_CLASS
struct patient_type {
  char name[80];
  char ssn[15];
  char symptoms[100];
  char specialty[2];
};
typedef struct patient_type patient;

void *patient_new(void);
void patient_delete(void *this);
void patient_copy(void *dest, void *src);
int patient_match (void *this, void *lookfor);
void patient_print(void *this);
void *patient_get_info(void *this);
#endif
```

Suppose, in addition to regular patients, the HMO also takes referrals. A referral patient is exactly like a regular patient with one additional piece of information: the name of the referring physician. The header for a referral patient looks like

```
#ifndef RPATIENT_CLASS
#define RPATIENT_CLASS
struct rpatient_type {
  char name[80];
  char ssn[15];
  char rphys[80];      /* Doesn't exist for patient class. */
  char symptoms[100];
  char specialty[2];
};
typedef struct rpatient_type rpatient;

void *rpatient_new(void);
void rpatient_delete(void *this);
void rpatient_copy(void *dest, void *src);
int rpatient_match (void *this, void *lookfor);
void rpatient_print(void *this);
void *rpatient_get_info(void *this);
#endif
```

We can just reimplement the methods for this new patient class, but wouldn't it be easier to say that a referral patient is like a regular patient, but with a little more information and a few method substitutions?

In most cases, these two classes can be treated as interchangeable. An rpatient, for example, can be placed on the waiting patient list. The rpatient can participate in assignments just like patients. An rpatient is freed from an assignment and disposed of using the same algorithms as a patient. The rpatient can even use some of the patient methods unchanged. The match method, patient_match(), works exactly the same for both patient and rpatient.

In a few cases, we do need to substitute revised versions of methods such as for patient_print(). However, even when we need revised methods, the new methods will, in most cases, look like the old methods. The high-level description will remain unchanged. The parameters will probably be unchanged. The return values, both in meaning and in type, will be unchanged. Usually, the change will be limited to adding a little more code to deal with the additional information, in this case, the referring physician field.

Object-oriented programming languages call rpatient a *subclass*, or *derived class* of patient. Similarities are said to be *inherited*. This can be implemented in the C programming language only with difficulty for both programmers and maintainers.

Hierarchical classes are often described as *is a* relationships. One class *is* another class, with a few additions. For example, an rpatient *is a* patient with the addition of a referring physician field. Hierarchies are helpful for defining classes, defining classes, although their lack does not eliminate C as a language for realizing object-oriented designs.

Lack of hierarchical classes in C does not prevent classes from being built from other classes. We have already seen word boxes created from caches, and caches from linked lists. It is easier in C to work with a *has a* relationship than an *is a* relationship. For example, it is easier in C to think of a cache as *having a* linked list than *being a* linked list.

Nevertheless, hierarchies are an important tool for creating reusable, object-oriented code, and the serious object-oriented programmer will sorely feel their lack.

5.4 Lack of Privacy

We have discussed class privacy, that is, hiding data members and methods. The fact is, however, that C offers few tools for implementing this, and even those it does offer must often be abandoned for programming considerations.

Data members can be stored in only two places: in the object data structure, or in the code file. For example, in the linked list example, the variable containing the total number of links in the list, `listlength`, is stored in the linked list structure defined in the class definition file:

```
struct linked_list_type {
  link *pcl;
  link *phead;
  link *ptail;
  int listlength;  /* Number of links. */
  int (*match)();
};
typedef struct linked_list_type linked_list;
```

However, if we wanted a variable to keep track of the total number of instantiated linked lists, say `nlists`, we would probably declare the variable statically in the header for the linked list code

```
/* Include files.
   -------------- */
  #include <stdio.h>
  #include "ll.h"

/* Static variables.
   ----------------- */
  static int nlists = 0;  /* Number of lists. */
```

```
int ll_size(linked_list * pll)
{
    return pll->listlength;
}
/* ... */
```

Data in the structures is unprotectable. You may protest, but there is no way to prevent client written code such as

```
/* ... */
linked_list *ll = ll_new(my_match);
int HiBob = 10;
ll->phead = (link *) HiBob;
```

Your only recourse is an "I told you so" when they complain about your code crashing their system.

The only truly private data is data declared static in the method code file, such as **nlists** above. However, this data cannot be duplicated for each instantiated object without using specialized programming techniques. So this technique works fine for **nlists**, which should only exist once, but would not work for **listlength**. We need a **listlength** in every instantiated list. If we have 500 instantiated linked lists, we will have 500 copies of **listlength**, but only one copy of **nlists** (whose value will be 500).

Privacy is a problem for C even without considering object-oriented methodology. It is often desirable to make variables available to a set of functions without allowing access to the whole world. C allows this only if the entire set of routines is placed in a single code file. The private variables can then be declared static in the global definition section of the file, before any of the routines are coded. The variable **nlists** would be available to any method in the linked list methods file, but would be unavailable to code outside this file.

There are several reasons why declaring private variables globally static might not be practical.

A code file starts becoming unwieldy after reaching a few hundred lines, or more than 5 to 10 methods. If your set of methods is large or the size of the methods is large, you would be better off to split the file into separate files, say one for each method. If these different methods must then access the same variable, that variable cannot be declared static. For the **nlists** example, the first file might contain the code for **ll_size()**, and look like

```
#include <stdio.h>
#include "ll.h"
int nlists = 0;   /* Number of lists. */

int ll_size(linked_list\index{ll_size(linked_list} *pll)
{
    return pll->listlength;
}
```

The second file might contain code for `ll_head()` and a few other methods, and look like:

```
#include <stdio.h>
#include "ll.h"
extern int nlists;   /* Cannot have been declared static. */

void ll_head(linked_list\index{ll_head(linked_list} *pll)
{
    pll->pcl = pll->phead;
}
...
```

Once we remove the static attribute from the first declaration of `nlists`, we are free to access it from the other linked list method files simply by declaring it to be an external variable. Unfortunately, there is no way to limit this declaration to the linked list method files, and our errant programmer is free once again to create code such as

```
extern int nlists;
int HiBob = 10;
...
nlists = HiBob;
```

which again corrupts our class.

Thus, we are in an unresolvable quandary. We either give up our ability to intelligently organize code methods into separate files. Or we give up privacy.

C++ solves these problems by allowing much better access control. For example, variables can be set up with class access, giving access to any class method regardless of the file the method happens to live in, while denying access to nonclass code. C++ also allows a class to grant special access to selected methods or classes which are not part of the class implementation.

5.5   Small Annoyances

We have covered what many consider the major object-oriented limitations of C. There are other problems which, though they can be worked around, require too much effort.

For example, one finds oneself rewriting the same basic methods, such as allocators, over and over. For many classes, a perfectly acceptable allocator looks like

```
void *class_name_new()
{
  class_name *ptemp;
  ptemp = malloc(sizeof(class));
  ptemp.member1 = 0;
  ptemp.member2 = 0;
  /* etc. */
  return ptemp;
}
```

Many of the class allocators in this book follow this pattern, and many others are only minor variants. Why can't the compiler automatically generate this default allocator, and trouble the programmer only for special cases?

While we're at it, there are other default methods that would be useful. A default assignment operator method could overwrite one object by another of the same class. A default deallocator could free memory used by an object.

Another area requiring too much work, or at least too much thought, is application specific method resolution. This is the resolution that occurs when the linked list class invokes an application specific match method. Any solution C has to offer involves pointers to functions. Function pointers are a relatively advanced programming technique, and only a small minority of programmers use them on any regular basis. Ideally, an object-oriented programming language should not require advanced techniques to solve common problems. Application specific method resolution is a common problem in object-oriented methodology.

The last area is *operator overloading*. A language supports *operator overloading* if the meaning of operators, such as =, can be redefined to have new meanings when used with new classes. The assignment operator, =, is well defined for basic data types, but what does it mean to assign a physician to a linked list, as in

```
#include "ll.h"
#include "patient.h"
int main()
{
  linked_list *ll = (linked_list *) ll_new();
  physician *p = (physician *) physician_new();
  /* ... */
  ll = p;
  /* ... */
}
```

C offers no tools for defining these semantics. C++, on the other hand, allows any of the standard operators to be redefined according to their arguments. In this example, we might decide that assignment means list initialization followed by object insertion. We can define the semantics of assignment differently when a list is assigned another list, and differently again when it is assigned a link.

This technique is called *operator overloading*. Many consider operator overloading to be an important feature. Others consider it to be a frill, since the same functionality is available through methods.

5.6 Summary

This chapter highlights some of the functionality C would need to fully support object-oriented programming. C is of course a popular language, one which has proven itself well adapted for a great range of programming areas, and a language for which the author has great fondness. This chapter does not seek to discredit C, but only to discuss some of the background against which C++ was developed.

5.7 Exercises

Exercise 5.1 Write a one-way version of the linked list class.

Exercise 5.2 Consider writing a preprocessor for C that would solve some of the problems discussed above. Our approach will be as follows: we extend the syntax of C as little as possible, then our preprocessor will read source files written in our extended syntax, and will create source files of valid C. You don't need to write the preprocessor, but design the syntax and discuss the transformation into C that you use to solve as many of the problems discussed in this chapter as possible, and any others that occur to you.

Chapter 6

Introduction to C++ Classes

The method resolution of C is limited to match by method name, a situation which often causes name clashes. This occurred in the last chapter when we tried to integrate a package based on a one-way linked list into a system already using a two-way linked list. It seemed that the compiler should decide which linked list method to call based on the class of the object on which the method was invoked. If, say, `ll_addhead(ll)` is called, and `ll` is a pointer to a one-way linked list, then the one-way `ll_addhead()` should be invoked. If `ll` is a pointer to a two-way list, the two-way `ll_addhead()` should be invoked.

6.1 Introduction

In order to accomplish class based method resolution, C++ needs a formal mechanism for connecting methods with classes. For C, we have been doing this informally in the class header. The class header included a structure definition which defined the class data members and a set of function prototypes. This set of function prototypes was understood to be the class methods. This works fine as long as we take responsibility for associating these methods with the class. If we want the compiler to take over this responsibility, we need to tell the compiler that these function prototypes aren't just any function prototypes, they are class method prototypes. And not just any class method prototypes, but ones specific for this class.

Once the compiler has been told of this connection, there is no problem having
`ll_addhead()` prototyped in both the one-way and two-way class header files, and
the type of problems we see in this C code

```
#include "linked_list.h"
#include "linked_list1.h"
int main()
{
  linked_list *ll;
  linked_list1 *lll;
  /* ... */
  ll_previous(ll);
  ll_previous(lll);
  /* ... */
```

can be dealt with by recognizing that the first invocation of `ll_previous()` is
associated with a pointer to a two-way linked list class, and therefore, resolves to
a `linked_list` method, and the second invocation resolves to a `linked_list1`
method.

Let's reexamine the `ll.h` file for the `linked_list` class.

```
#ifndef LINKED_LIST
#define LINKED_LIST
#include "link.h"

struct linked_list_type {
  link *pcl;
  link *phead;
  link *ptail;
  int listlength;
  int (*match)();
};
typedef struct linked_list_type linked_list;

int ll_size(linked_list *pll);
void ll_head(linked_list *pll);
void ll_tail(linked_list *pll);

/* ... */
```

As you can see, the **struct** construct *almost* works to define classes. Although
it ties together the data elements of the class, it stops short before associating the
methods. In our minds, the fact that the function prototypes are in the same header

file as the structure definition defines them as class methods. The C compiler, however, attaches no special significance to header file organization. So we need a new construct that serves to tie a particular collection of methods together with a particular collection of data. The C++ construct that does this is the `class`.

6.2 Building a Simple Class

To see how classes are constructed in C++, we will compare a simple class written in C and C++. First the C version.

Our class describes dogs. Dogs have three characteristics. They have a name. They have a certain type of bark. They bark for a certain number of times. We will store the name, bark type and number of barks in private instance variables. We will have three dog methods: an allocator, a constructor, and a bark method. These methods will be named, respectively, `newDog()`, `describe()`, and `bark()`.

The C version of the dog header file describes a dog structure, which includes the private instance variables and prototypes for the three methods. The header file looks like

```
struct dogType {
  char myName[100];
  char myBark[100];
  int nBarks;
};
typedef struct dogType dog;

dog *newDog(void);
void describe(dog *this, char *newName, int newN, char *newBark);
void bark(dog *this);
```

The C version of the method code file for `dog` is straight forward. It looks like

```
#include <stdio.h>
#include <stdlib.h>
#include <string.h>
#include "dog.h"


dog *newDog(void)
{
  return malloc(sizeof(dog));
}
```

```
void describe(dog *this, char *newName, int newN, char *newBark)
{
  this->nBarks = newN;
  strcpy(this->myName, newName);
  strcpy(this->myBark, newBark);
}


void bark(dog *this)
{
  int n;
  printf("%s goes\n", this->myName);
  for (n=0; n<this->nBarks; n++) printf("  %s\n", this->myBark);
}
```

We can create a small program to instantiate, initialize, and manipulate dogs

```
#include <stdio.h>
#include "dog.h"

int main()
{
  dog *littleDog = newDog();
  dog *bigDog = newDog();

  describe(littleDog, "Little dog", 2, "bow wow");
  describe(bigDog, "Big dog", 5, "BOW WOW");

  bark(littleDog);
  bark(bigDog);
  return 0;
}
```

The output from this program looks like

```
Little dog goes
  bow wow
  bow wow
Big dog goes
  BOW WOW
  BOW WOW
  BOW WOW
  BOW WOW
  BOW WOW
```

6.3 C is C++

Before discussing the enhancements offered by C++, it is important to point out that C++ is a superset of ANSI C. There are a few minor exceptions to this rule, but generally C code can be used by C++ program without change. C functions can be called by C++ clients, even by C++ classes. C++ classes can even be defined following our C conventions, although this would be pointless. When C++ code is not dealing with classes the code is C.

C++ does offer general language enhancements beyond those that are class related, so you cannot expect a program written in C++ to compile under C, even programs which are not using classes. However C programs, if they are strictly ANSI compliant (particularly in the area of function prototypes) will generally compile as C++.

This places the C programmer at an advantage in learning C++. Syntax does not have to be relearned. All of your favorite bit operators, cast operations, and pointer arithmetic operations work just as you expect.

The biggest hurdle most C programmers face in learning C++ is not the syntax. It is learning to think in the object-oriented paradigm. However, as this book points out, the object oriented paradigm is as relevant to C programmers as to C++ programmers. Once you understand, appreciate, and know how to apply the concepts of object-oriented programming, you will find the transition to C++ to be painless and the new syntax a relief rather than a strain.

6.4 The Class Construct

The C++ `class` construct replaces the C `struct` construct for defining classes. A `class` is similar to a `struct` in that both package data together into a unified structure. However, a `class` goes further, by associating a set of methods with the set of data.

We will use the `.hpp` extension to differentiate C++ header files from C header files. The C++ header file for the dog class looks like this

```
class dog {
  char myName[100];
  char myBark[100];
  int nBarks;

  void describe(char *newName, int newN, char *newBark);
  void bark();
};
```

Notice that in the **dog** class, there are two general categories of things described.

One is data. The other is methods. Compare the C++ and C description of dog, and you see three main differences. First, the key word class replaces the key word struct. Second, the C++ methods are defined *inside* the class definition, as opposed to *outside* the C struct. Third, the typedef defining dog is missing. The C++ class automatically incorporates this function.

One of the few areas where C and C++ syntax differ is in the declaration of functions and methods with no parameters. C uses the keyword void to specify no parameters, as in

```
int ll_istail(void);
```

C++, on the other hand, assumes that a function or method declared without parameters does not take parameters. The declaration

```
void bark();
```

is taken to mean that bark() has no parameters. The equivalent declaration in C would be

```
void bark(void);
```

The class definition gives the compiler all the information needed to associate methods with classes. Conceptually, there is no reason the compiler couldn't deal with another class, say bird, which also contains a describe() method. If the bird class is described as

```
class bird {
  int nTweets;
  describe(int newN);
};
```

we should be able to deal with a hypothetical code situation like

```
#include "dog.h"
#include "bird.h"
int main()
{
  dog *myDog = newDog();
  bird *myBird = newBird();
  describe(myDog, "My dog", 2, "bow wow");
  describe(myBird, 3);
  /* ... */
```

The class definition ties a specific describe() method to a specific class. When the C++ compiler sees the describe() method invoked on something pointing to a **dog**, it knows to invoke the **describe()** associated with **dog** classes. Experienced C++ programmers will realize that the invocation of **describe()** is not really valid C++ code, but it will do for illustration until we discuss the correct invocation syntax.

6.5 Default Instantiation

The C++ class definition does not include a prototype for **newDog()**. This is because C++ automatically generates a default allocator for every class. The default allocator behaves much like the C version of **newDog()**, that is, it allocates memory necessary for the class, but makes few other guarantees. Often this is inadequate, and later we will see how this functionality can be extended when needed.

6.6 Class Member Accessibility

One of our complaints about C was the lack of privacy. There is no way to prevent client code from accessing data that should be private to the class. C will be perfectly happy with client code like

```
#include "dog.h"
int main()
{
  int n;
  dog *myDog = newDog();
  describe(myDog, "Rover", 2, "Woof");
  for (n=0; n<1000; n++) myDog->myBark[n] = 0;
  /* ... */
```

which will overwrite the **nBarks** variable and beyond.

C++ provides keywords to describe member accessibility. Two of these keywords are **private** and **public**. Members which are **private** can be accessed *only* by methods of the class. **private** members can include both data and methods. A **private** method cannot be invoked by clients of the class. Members which are **public** can be accessed by anybody, either methods of the class or clients of the class.

Class members default to private. Classes with exclusively private members are unusual; most C++ classes have a public declaration.

These access specifiers act as toggles. Once a keyword is encountered in the class definition, further members take that access attribute until another access specifier is encountered. The syntax for an access specifier is the keyword followed by ":".

Modifying the **dog** class to incorporate access specifiers gives us this new class definition:

```
class dog {
public:
  void describe(char *newName, int newN, char *newBark);
  void bark();
private:
  char myName[100];
  char myBark[100];
  int nBarks;
};
```

The class has been rearranged to conform with the C++ convention of listing public members first.

This class definition says that the **dog** class includes two public methods, **describe()** and **bark()**, and three private data elements, **myName**, **myBark** and **nBarks**. The three data elements can be accessed only by **describe()** and **bark()**. The class definition also implies that the C++ default constructor will be used for the **dog** class.

Notice how in the **dog** class, the data has all been declared private, and the methods have all been declared public.   This is typical of most classes. Data is generally considered an implementation detail of the class, of interest to the class designer, but no one else. The methods generally represent the public contract of the class. The **dog** designer guarantees to support a **describe()** and **bark()** method with prescribed parameters. The details of how these methods are implemented, including the private data they may or may not use, may change without notice.

A class is said to be well *encapsulated* when the implementation details are not exposed to clients of the class. One of the two goals of encapsulation is to give the class implementor freedom to reimplement without having to worry about breaking client code. The other goal is to prevent clients from changing the internal state, or data, of an object without going through approved channels, or methods. Direct access to internal data is an open invitation to object corruption.

6.7   New Syntax in Class Method Code

C++ class methods are implemented much like their C counterparts, with two important enhancements. The first has to do with the specification of the method's class. The second has to do with how the method accesses other class members.

A C++ class is typically made up of two files, much like our C classes. The first file is a class definition header file, which describes the data members, the methods, and the accessibility of the class components. The second file is the class implementation file, which includes the actual code for the methods. The implementation can be dispersed over several files, if the size becomes unwieldy.

We defined our **dog** class to include methods for **describe()** and **bark()**. We discussed the possibility of another class, say **bird**, that also defines a **describe()** method. We noted that the compiler has the information needed to resolve the **describe()** invocation, based on the class on which it is invoked.

If there are two versions of **describe()**, one for dogs and one for birds, then someplace there must exist two source files, one containing the code for the **dog** **describe()**, and one for the **bird** **describe()**. This brings up a problem for the compiler. How does it know which **describe()** is associated with which class?

C++ requires that each method explicitly tell the compiler the class to which it belongs. The syntax for this is a slight extension of our standard C method declaration. Each method name is immediately prefaced by the class name followed by double colon. The declaration of the **dog::describe()** looks like this

```
void dog::describe(char *newName, int newN, char *newBark)
{
  nBarks = newN;
  strcpy(myName, newName);
  strcpy(myBark, newBark);
}
```

which, as you can see, looks similar to its C counterpart

```
void describe(dog *this, char *newName, int newN,
              char *newBark)
{
  this->nBarks = newN;
  strcpy(this->myName, newName);
  strcpy(this->myBark, newBark);
}
```

The second C++ method code enhancement has to do with class member access. The C version of **describe()** explicitly passes in a pointer to the target object. Member data such as **nBarks** are elements of the class structure pointed to by the target object parameter **this**. The C++ version does not have a target object parameter, and looking at the code, there is no obvious reference to a class structure. How does the C++ version know what variable to update when it sees the line

```
nBarks = newN;
```

In both C and C++, every method invocation is associated with some target object, which is some instantiation of the class for which that method is defined. For example, in C

```
dog *littleDog = newDog();
describe(littleDog, "Little dog", 2, "bow wow");
```

first instantiates a object `littleDog` of class `dog`, and then invokes the method
`describe()` on that object. We say `littleDog` is the target object for the method
`describe()`. Since every object of class `dog` has three associated variables, `myName`,
`nBarks` and `myBark`, we know that any updates `describe()` does to, say, `nBarks`,
will be done to the specific `nBarks` belonging to `littleDog`.

The syntax used to specify the target object is different in C++. In C the
target object is explicitly specified as the first parameter of the method. In C++,
the target object is implicitly passed to the method, and any class members referred
to are assumed to belong to the target object. When the C++ compiler sees a line
in `describe()` like

```
nBarks = newN;
```

it checks the `dog` class definition for a data member named `nBarks`. `describe()`
knows it is a member of the `dog` class because of its declaration

```
void dog::describe(char *newName, int newN, char *newBark)
```

`nBarks` is declared private to `dog`, but that is acceptable, because `describe()` is a
method of the `dog` class, and class methods can access private data.

Since the compiler knows the method is associated with the `dog` class, and it
knows the target object will be of class `dog`, it knows which `nBarks` to update. It
updates the `nBarks` of its target object.

We can now look at the full implementation of the C++ `dog` class. First, we
see `#include` files for standard C functions. Second, we see an `#include` for the
class definition file. Finally, we have the code for the `dog` methods.

```
#include <stdio.h>
#include <string.h>
#include "dog1.hpp"

void dog::describe(char *newName, int newN, char *newBark)
{
  nBarks = newN;
  strcpy(myName, newName);
  strcpy(myBark, newBark);
}
```

```
void dog::bark()
{
  int n;
  printf("%s goes\n", myName);
  for (n=0; n<nBarks; n++) printf("   %s\n", myBark);
}
```

When necessary, it is possible to refer to the target object directly. Every class method has access to its target object through the predefined variable **this**, which is defined to be a pointer to an object of the class to which the method belongs. It is not an error to refer to the target object directly, but it is rarely necessary. The following version of **bark** is also valid, but unnecessarily complicated:

```
void dog::bark()
{
  int n;
  printf("%s goes\n", this->myName);
  for (n=0; n<this->nBarks; n++) printf("   %s\n", this->myBark);
}
```

The ability to access target object members directly is valid for class methods as well. If a **dog** method had this line:

```
bark();
```

the method would invoke the **dog::bark()** method, since **bark()** is a member of the target object. The target for **bark()** would be the same target as for the method invoking **bark()**. It would also be valid (but unnecessary) to use this syntax

```
this->bark();
```

Later we will see some situations where we must refer to **this**, but in the great majority of cases its use is unnecessary and undesirable.

6.8 New Syntax for Method Invocation

We have discussed invocation from the method's perspective. Now we will examine method invocation from the client's perspective.

One goal of C++ is to provide an integrated syntax for accessing all class members, both data and method members. Let's review for a moment the syntax in C for accessing a class data member.

Our C class client can instantiate a class in one of two ways. First, and probably most common, is by declaring a pointer to the class and then setting the pointer to memory returned by the allocator. Once this is done, we can refer to data members using the C -> operator. So, for example, once we have declared and initialized the littleDog pointer by

```
dog *littleDog = newDog();
```

we can write code which references the data members, like

```
if (littleDog->nBarks > 100)
  printf("This is a BIG littleDog!!!\n");
```

The second way to instantiate an object in C is to declare a structure of type dog. Such an instantiation looks like

```
dog littleDog;
```

Data members are now referred to with the . syntax, like

```
if (littleDog.nBarks < 0)
  printf("Are you SURE this is a dog?\n");
```

The problem in C is that the syntax which refers to *method* members is inconsistent with the syntax which refers to *data* members. Method members are referred to by the older syntax of regular C function calls, with class conventions enforced on a strictly voluntary basis.

The instantiation of an object looks identical in C++ as in C. Thus, if we had written a **dog** method **newDog()**, which we didn't, we could then instantiate a new dog either with

```
dog littleDog;
```

or

```
dog *littleDog = newDog();
```

C++ data members are then accessed exactly like the C data members. But, unlike C, C++ accesses methods using a consistent syntax. Therefore, if we used the instantiation

```
dog *littleDog = newDog();
```

we invoke the **bark()** method on **littleDog** by

```
littleDog->bark();
```

On the other hand, if the instantiation was of the form

```
dog littleDog;
```

then the invocation looks like

```
littleDog.bark();
```

In either case, the compiler invokes a class method on a specific object. The target object is either the object pointed to by littleDog, as in the first example, or littleDog itself, as in the second example. And when the code inside the method refers to a data member, say nBarks, the compiler knows that the specific nBarks we are talking about is that associated with the target object littleDog.

Methods such as dog::describe() often accept parameters. The parameters are added into the method call, just as they would be in C. So we might have, in C++,

```
dog littleDog;
littleDog.describe("Little dog", 1, "bow wow");
```

or

```
dog *littleDog = dogNew();
littleDog->describe("Little dog", 1, "bow wow");
```

But notice the difference between passing in data as parameters and passing in data as target object data members. The latter is automatically taken care of by the C++ compiler. The former is managed by the programmer, and is used when a method needs data beyond that which is associated with the target object. describe(), for example, needs to know what data should be used for initializing the target object, and this data is passed in as standard parameters.

6.9 Default Allocators

The C version of the dog class includes an allocator, newDog(). The C++ version does not. In C++, classes do not need to provide an allocator. C++ automatically provides a default allocator for every class. For simple classes such as dog the default allocator is acceptable.

The default instantiator is called new. It is defined as returning a pointer to the class on which it is invoked. The syntax for invoking it looks like

```
className *classPointer = new className;
```

The method new is equivalent to a malloc() call of the form

```
return (className *) malloc (sizeof(className));
```

that is, it returns a block of memory large enough to hold an object of the requested class, cast appropriately.

There are several actions new() does *not* take:

- it does not initialize the block of memory,

- it does not allocate any indirect memory requirements of the class.

So, for example, the default **new** cannot incorporate the function of
dog::describe() since that would involve initializing the data members **myName**,
nBarks and **myBark**. Nor can it allocate memory needed indirectly by the class.
This would be a problem if the **dog** class is rewritten as

```
class dog {
public:
  describe(char * myName, int newN, char *newBark);
  void bark();
private:
  char *myName;
  char *myBark;
  int nBarks;
};
```

myName and **myBark** are character pointers which should be set to a block of
memory large enough to hold their respective strings. **new** will dynamically allocate
memory for the **dog** class with enough memory for two character pointers. With
this redefinition of **dog**, **dog::describe()** can no longer be as simple as

```
void dog::describe(char *newName, int newN, char *newBark)
{
  nBarks = newN;
  strcpy(myName, newName);
  strcpy(myBark, newBark);
}
```

because the memory pointed to by **myName** and **myBark** has not been allocated.
Something must change to allocate memory for these strings. The most likely
change is the addition of two memory allocation calls within the body of
dog::describe(), although adding a class constructor, which will be covered later,
is also an option.

This concludes the introductory tour of C++. We now have enough information
to examine the **dog** class in its full glory.

One more time, the **dog** header file, which defines the class

```
class dog {
public:
  void describe(char *newName, int newN, char *newBark);
  void bark();
private:
  char myName[100];
  char myBark[100];
  int nBarks;
};
```

Next, the class implementation file. Notice a couple of interesting points. First, the implementation file **#include**s the class definition file. It needs this file to know what is meant by a **dog** class. Second, the method code file knows nothing about the accessibility of the methods it implements, since the person writing the **dog** methods does not need to know which methods are public and which are private.

```
#include <stdio.h>
#include <string.h>
#include "dog1.hpp"

void dog::describe(char *newName, int newN, char *newBark)
{
  nBarks = newN;
  strcpy(myName, newName);
  strcpy(myBark, newBark);
}


void dog::bark()
{
  int n;
  printf("%s goes\n", myName);
  for (n=0; n<nBarks; n++) printf("  %s\n", myBark);
}
```

And finally, we have the client program which creates and manipulates **dog** objects. Notice the client program has a very limited knowledge of the **dog** class. It does not know about private data; such data is never directly manipulated. The program deals only with the allocator and the public methods. Notice also that the client includes the class description file.

```
#include "dog1.hpp"
int main()
{
  dog *littleDog = new dog;
  dog *bigDog = new dog;

  littleDog->describe("Little dog", 2, "bow wow");
  bigDog->describe("Big dog", 5, "BOW WOW");

  littleDog->bark();
  bigDog->bark();
  return 0;
}
```

And once again, the output from this program

```
Little dog goes
   bow wow
   bow wow
Big dog goes
   BOW WOW
   BOW WOW
   BOW WOW
   BOW WOW
   BOW WOW
```

The **new** operator can be used as a general memory allocator. The function **malloc()** is still available in C++, but is used infrequently. Most authors recommend use of **new** instead of **malloc()** for two reasons. First, the syntax for dynamic memory usage is consistent throughout a program. Second, all system memory allocation and deallocation is guaranteed to flow through identical channels.

Any memory allocated by **new** should be freed by the **delete** operator. We will discuss the use of **delete** on class objects later.

The **new** operator is typically used for allocating class instances, structures, and arrays. We have already seen its use in allocating class instances. The following program shows its use in allocating structures and arrays:

```
#include <stdio.h>
#include <stdlib.h>
#include <string.h>

struct doubleStringType {
  char *str1;
  char *str2;
};
typedef struct doubleStringType doubleString;

void setup(doubleString *dest, char *str1, char *str2);

int main()
{
  doubleString *myStrings = new doubleString; /* Structure
                                                 Allocation */
  setup(myStrings, "String 1", "String 2");

  printf("%s\n", myStrings->str1);
  printf("%s\n", myStrings->str2);

  delete myStrings->str1;
  delete myStrings->str2;
  delete myStrings;

  return 0;
}
void setup(doubleString *dest, char *src1, char *src2)
{
  /* Array Allocation */
  dest->str1 = new char[strlen(src1)+1];
  /* Ditto */
  dest->str2 = new char[strlen(src2)+1];

  strcpy(dest->str1, src1);
  strcpy(dest->str2, src2);
}
```

The output from this program is

```
String 1
String 2
```

The `malloc()` version of this program looks like

```
/* Same prelude as before. */
main()
{
  doubleString *myStrings = malloc(sizeof(doubleString));
                              /* Structure Allocation */
  setup(myStrings, "String 1", "String 2");

  printf("%s\n", myStrings->str1);
  printf("%s\n", myStrings->str2);

  delete myStrings->str1;
  delete myStrings->str2;
  delete myStrings;

  return 0;
}
void setup(doubleString *dest, char *src1, char *src2)
{
  /* Array Allocation */
  dest->str1 = malloc(strlen(src1)+1);
  /* Ditto */
  dest->str2 = malloc(strlen(src2)+1);

  strcpy(dest->str1, src1);
  strcpy(dest->str2, src2);
}
```

6.10 Comments

One final C++ enhancement deserves mention at this time. C++ recognizes two types of comments. One is the traditional C style of comments. The other is the token //. When C++ sees the token //, the remainder of the line is taken to be a comment. This facility is used most frequently in class definitions, as in

```
class dog {
public:
  void describe(char *newName, int newN, char *newBark);
  void bark();
private:
  char myName[100];      // String identifier of this object.
  char myBark[100];      // Sound this dog makes.
  int nBarks;            // Number of times it makes sound.
};
```

6.11 Building a Complex C++ Class

Classes may be built out of other classes in a process called *construction*. We have defined a **dog** class. Let's now construct a **dogHouse** class which will be a collection of dogs.

Our **dogHouse** class has three public methods: **init()**, which initializes a new dogHouse object, **addDog()**, which adds a new dog to the **dogHouse**, and **wakeUp()**, which has each dog in the **dogHouse** make its appropriate noise.

From the client's perspective, a **dogHouse** is a collection of dogs each with a name, bark, and bark count. Clients have no interest in how the **dogHouse** stores or accesses this information.

Our **dogHouse** class will be implemented as an array of pointers to **dog** objects. Since this is an implementation detail, the array will be declared **private**.

The **dogHouse** definition file looks this

```
#include "dog1.hpp"

class dogHouse {
public:
  void init();
  void addDog(char *newName, int newN, char *newBark);
  void wakeUp();

private:
  int nDogs;             // Total dogs in this dogHouse.
  dog *dogBunch[100];    // Pointers to dog objects.
};
```

Notice that **dogBunch** is declared as an array of pointers to **dog** class objects. Because this class makes use of the **dog** class, the **dog** class description file, **dog1.hpp**, is included in this file.

Next comes the **doghouse** implementation file. This file starts by including the class descriptor file, as usual. Next comes the first method, the class constructor, whose sole responsibility is the initialization of the **dog** array index variable.

```
#include "dogh.hpp"
void dogHouse::init()
{
  nDogs = 0;
}
```

The second method adds a new **dog** to the **dogHouse**.

```
void dogHouse::addDog(char *newName, int newN, char *newBark)
{
  dogBunch[nDogs] = new dog;
  dogBunch[nDogs]->describe(newName, newN, newBark);
  nDogs++;
}
```

The first line of **addDog()** is straight forward. It simply sets the array element to point to a newly allocated **dog** object. The next line,

```
dogBunch[nDogs]->describe(newName, newN, newBark);
```

looks more confusing, but there are only two aspects which are unusual. The first is invocation of a method via a pointer to an object of the class. But this is really no different than code we have seen before, say

```
littleDog->describe("Little dog", 2, "bow wow");
```

The second unusual aspect is that the pointer invoking the method is now one element of an array, as opposed to a simple pointer as in the **littleDog** example. If it helps in understanding, you can break up the code, as in

```
dog *tempDog = new dog;
tempDog->describe(newName, newN, newBark);
dogBunch[nDogs] = tempDog;
nDogs++;
```

If you understand the **addDog()** method, then **wakeUp()** is just more of the same:

```
void dogHouse::wakeUp()
{
  int n;
  for (n=0; n<nDogs; n++) dogBunch[n]->bark();
}
```

The `dogHouse` client `#includes` the `dogHouse` header description, initializes a `dogHouse` object, adds some dogs, and invokes `wakeUp()`:

```
#include "dogh.hpp"

int main()
{
  dogHouse *myDogHouse = new dogHouse;

  myDogHouse->init();
  myDogHouse->addDog("Frenchie", 1, "woof");
  myDogHouse->addDog("Rover", 2, "bow wow");
  myDogHouse->addDog("Rex", 5, "BOW WOW");

  myDogHouse->wakeUp();
  return 0;
}
```

The output from this program looks like:

```
Frenchie goes
  woof
Rover goes
  bow wow
  bow wow
Rex goes
  BOW WOW
  BOW WOW
  BOW WOW
  BOW WOW
  BOW WOW
```

A class must be defined before it is referenced. This means, for example, that in this definition of `dogHouse`

```
#include "dog1.hpp"
class dogHouse {
  /* ... */
  dog *dogBunch[100];      /* dog is a valid type. */
};
```

`dog` must be defined before it is referenced as a type. Fortunately, this is effectively done by the inclusion of `dog1.hpp`. Our code segment is treated by the compiler as if it is

```
class dog {
  /* ... */
};

class dogHouse {
  /* ... */
  dog *dogBunch[100];
};
```

There are times when this way of defining a class will not work. Suppose this is our definition of dog:

```
class dog {
  dogHouse *myHouse;
  /* ... */
};
```

Now we are in a bind. This same code is now treated by the compiler as if it is

```
class dog {
  dogHouse *myHouse;       /* Error: dogHouse not yet defined. */
  /* ... */
};
class dogHouse {
  /* ... */
  dog *dogBunch[100];
};
```

Since **dogHouse** is not defined when encountered in the **dog** definition we get a compile error. Switching the class definitions around only changes which class gives the error.

C++ solves this problem by allowing a class to be declared without being defined. This tells the compiler that the class is a valid type, but its actual definition is deferred until later. The syntax for this is

```
class classname;
```

We can use this capability to solve our circular dependency:

```
class dogHouse;          /* Predeclare dogHouse. */

class dog {
  dogHouse *myHouse;   /* Now dogHouse is a valid type. */
  /* ... */
};
```

```
class dogHouse {
  /* ... */
  dog *dogBunch[100]; /* dog is also a valid type. */
};
```

6.12 Another C++ Example: Order Entry

Now let's apply these fundamentals to a slightly more complex problem. Let's consider building an order entry application for a bookstore. Here is a high level pseudocode version of **bookstore**

```
bookstore()
{
  GetCustomerName;
  GetCustomerAddress;
  while(MoreBooks) {
    GetBookTitle;
    GetQuantityPurchased;
    GetCostPerBook;
  }
  CalculateTotalCostOfLineItems;
  AddInSalesTax;
  DisplayOrderAndTotalCost;
  EnterPaymentAmount;
  PrintOrder;
  PrintPaymentAmount;
  PrintChangeDueCustomer;
}
```

We will use two related classes to manage this information. One, the **Order** class, will contain the order information, that is, the customer name, address and total purchase price, and will define methods related to this information. The other, the **LineItem** class, will contain information on a particular line item, that is, a particular book sale, the quantity and price per book, and methods related to this data. An **Order** will include an array of pointers to **LineItem**. This array will have an arbitrary maximum size of 100. Pictorially, the data for these classes can be

represented as

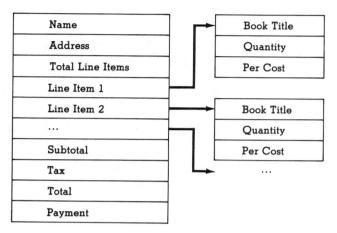

If Alice Brown places an order for two copies of *Mushrooms of North America* and three copies of *Zen of Programming*, and pays with a 100 dollar bill, the data members for her order look like

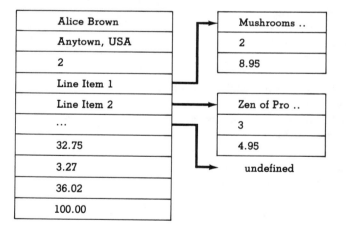

6.13   Helper Functions

We'll start with some helper functions written in standard C. They are not tied to any class. They do not make use of the C++ extensions. We will maintain the prototypes for these functions in a single header file, `helper.hpp`, which looks like:

```
void getLine(char *string);
void PromptForString(char *prompt, char *response);
void PromptForInt(char *prompt, int *response);
char *CentsToDollars(int totalCents);
int DollarsToCents(char *dollars);
```

We will briefly go through the code file. The C code should be straight forward for most C programmers. The code file starts by including necessary header files, and then defines the function **getLine()**, a function which reads characters from **stdin** until reaching the end of the line.

```
#include <stdio.h>
#include <stdlib.h>
#include <string.h>
#include "helper.hpp"
void getLine(char *c)
{
  for (;;) {
     *c = getc(stdin);
     if (*c == '\n') break;
     c++;
  }
  *c = '\0';
}
```

Next, a few prompting functions, one of which returns an integer, and the other which returns a string.

```
void PromptForInt(char *prompt, int *response)
{
  char tempstr[100];
  printf("%s ", prompt);
  getLine(tempstr);
  *response = atoi(tempstr);
}

void PromptForString(char *prompt, char *response)
{
  printf("%s ", prompt);
  getLine(response);
}
```

The most interesting of these helper functions have to do with money. We will store all money as cents to simplify the arithmetic. One hundred dollars is stored as the integer 10000. Regardless of how money is stored, it needs to be presented in the familiar form. One hundred dollars should be presented as the string "100.00." We need functions to translate in each direction. Thus we have

$$
\begin{array}{c}
\text{CentsToDollars} \\
10000 \quad \overrightarrow{\underleftarrow{}} \quad 100.00 \\
\text{DollarsToCents}
\end{array}
$$

The first of these makes use of a standard C library function called `sprintf()`. This function is less well known than some. Basically, it does exactly what `printf()` does, except that the resulting ASCII characters are placed in a string buffer instead of an output device.

```c
char *CentsToDollars(int totalCents)
{
    static char temp[20];
    char *zero = "0";
    int length;

/* Prepare dollar figures.
   ---------------------- */
    int ndollars = totalCents/100;
    int ncents = totalCents - (ndollars * 100);
    sprintf(temp, "%d.", ndollars);

/* Prepare cents, with leading zero if less than 10.
   ------------------------------------------------- */
    if (ncents < 10) strcat (temp, zero);
    length = strlen(temp);
    sprintf(&temp[length], "%d", ncents);
    return temp;
}
```

The second function uses the standard C function `atoi()` to turn a character string into an integer. The function `atoi()` can be thought of as doing the reverse of `sprintf()`.

```
int DollarsToCents(char *dollars)
{
   char *dot, *dollarsPart, *centsPart;
   int ndollars, ncents, totalCents;

/* See where the string breaks.
   --------------------------- */
   dot = strchr(dollars, '.');
   dollarsPart = dollars;
   centsPart = dot + 1;

/* Calculate amounts.
   ------------------ */
   ndollars = atoi(dollarsPart);
   ncents = atoi(centsPart);
   totalCents = (ndollars * 100) + ncents;

   return totalCents;
}
```

6.14   The LineItem Class

This program uses two classes. We start by looking at the simpler of the two, the
LineItem class. This class contains the data and methods that manipulate a single
line item of the order. This class is similar in complexity to the dog class. The
class definition file, lineItem.hpp, looks like

```
#ifndef LineItemClass
#define LineItemClass
class LineItem {
public:
   void InitLineItem();
   int  EnterLineItem();
   void DisplayLineItem();
   int  GetLineItemPrice();
private:
   char BookTitle[100];
   int BookQuantity;
   int BookPrice;                    // In cents
};
   void DisplayLineItemHeading();
#endif
```

The class defines four public methods. Notice that there is one oddball function thrown in, `DisplayLineItemHeading()`, which is prototyped in this header file, but is not part of the class.

`DisplayLineItemHeading()` is provided to display an appropriate heading to line items. `DisplayLineItem()` can then be called within a loop to display the data from an individual line item. Code like this

```
DisplayLineItemHeading();
for (n=0; n<nItems; n++) {
  Item[n]->DisplayLineItem();
}
```

might produce output like this

```
Book                                   Qty  Price   Total
------------------------------------   ---  ------  -----
Mushrooms of North America               2    8.95  17.90
Zen of Programming                       3    4.95  14.85
```

It's a little hard to know what to do with the function `DisplayLineItemHeading()`. On the one hand, it is intimately tied to a knowledge of how the method `DisplayLineItem()` works. This would seem to make it a `LineItem` method. One the other hand, it is not clear what it means to invoke this method on a `LineItem` object.

The other `LineItem` methods are all conceptually associated with particular objects. For example, we invoke `DisplayLineItem()` on a `LineItem` object which contains real data. We invoke `EnterLineItem()` on an allocated `LineItem` object which stands ready to accept data. However, it is quite possible to invoke `DisplayLineItemHeading()` before any `LineItem` objects have ever been instantiated.

This could be an argument for making `DisplayLineItemHeading()` part of the `Order` class, since surely it does not make sense to invoke this function without an associated instantiated order. But this belies its close association with other `LineItem` methods. We will use the compromise approach of defining `DisplayLineItemHeading()` as a function, but one whose association with a particular class is underscored both by its prototype being included in the class definition, and its code being included in the class implementation file.

The code file for the `LineItem` class starts by including standard and class definition headers

```
#include <stdio.h>
#include <string.h>

#include "l_item.hpp"
#include "helper.hpp"
```

and then continues with method implementations. The first is InitLineItem(),
which is analogous to dog::describe().

```
void LineItem::InitLineItem()
{
  BookTitle[0] = '\0';
  BookQuantity = 0;
  BookPrice = 0;
}
```

The next method is used to query for LineItem data. It returns 1 if the user enters
LineItem data, 0 if the user hits <return> to indicate they have no data to enter.

```
int LineItem::EnterLineItem()
{
  char price[20];
  printf(".........................\n");
  PromptForString("      Book Title: ", BookTitle);
  if (!strlen(BookTitle)) return 0;
  PromptForInt   (" Number of Books: ", &BookQuantity);
  PromptForString("   Price of Book: ", price);
  BookPrice = DollarsToCents(price);
  return 1;
}
```

DisplayLineItem() displays a line item object. It converts dollar figures from
cents to a string dollar format, as we discussed earlier when looking at the helper
functions.

```
void LineItem::DisplayLineItem()
{
  printf("%-35s ", BookTitle);
  printf("  %3d ", BookQuantity);
  printf("%6s ", CentsToDollars(BookPrice));
  printf("%7s ", CentsToDollars(GetLineItemPrice()));
  printf("\n");
}
```

If you are approaching C++ for the first time you may be surprised by the following method, which appears, at first, to be manipulating global variables. In fact, the method is just operating on data private to the target object.

```
int LineItem::GetLineItemPrice()
{
  return BookPrice * BookQuantity;
}
```

Nothing more complicated is occurring than in

```
void dog::bark()
{
  int n;
  printf("%s goes\n", myName);
  for (n=0; n<nBarks; n++) printf("   %s\n", myBark);
}
```

with the variables BookPrice and BookQuantity playing a similar role as nBarks and myBark.

Finally, we have the function DisplayLineItemHeading(). As we discussed, this is not a method of the LineItem class, but is so closely associated that we have prototyped it in the class definition file, and implemented it along with the class methods.

```
void DisplayLineItemHeading()
{
  printf ("\n");
  printf (
"Book                                        Qty   Price   Total\n");
  printf (
"----------------------------------------    ---   ------   -----\n");
}
```

6.15   The Order Class

Next is the Order class. Like the dogHouse class, it contains an array of pointers to objects of another class. Despite the surfeit of private data, conceptually this class is no more complex than dogHouse. The class definition file looks like

```
#ifndef OrderClass
#define OrderClass
#include "l_item.hpp"
```

```
class Order {
public:
  void InitOrder();
  void EnterOrder();
  void DisplayOrder();
  int CostOfOrder();
  float TaxRate();
private:
  char name[100];
  char address[100];
  int nItems;              // Number of line items
  LineItem *Item[100];     // Line Items
  int subtotal;            // Total Cost, not including tax.
  int tax;
  int total;               // Total, including tax.
  int payment;             // In cents
};
#endif
```

The class implementation file starts out just like dogHouse, with InitOrder() playing a similar role to dogHouse::init().

```
#include <stdio.h>
#include "order.hpp"
#include "helper.hpp"

void Order::InitOrder()
{
  nItems = 0;
  subtotal = 0;
  tax = 0;
  total = 0;
}
```

The next method requests data for an Order, and invokes LineItem methods to get LineItem data. Notice how the return value of EnterLineItem() indicates when the user is finished entering line items on the order.

```
void Order::EnterOrder()
{
/* Local Declarations.
   ------------------ */
   LineItem *lip;      // Line Item Pointer
   int done;
   char dollars[10];

/* Get Name and Address.
   -------------------- */
   PromptForString("   Name: ", name);
   PromptForString("Address: ", address);

/* Get Line Items.
   -------------- */
   done = 0;
   nItems = 0;
   while (!done) {
     lip = new LineItem();
     if (lip->EnterLineItem()) {
        Item[nItems++] = lip;
        subtotal += lip->GetLineItemPrice();
     }
     else {
        done = 1;
     }
   }
/* Display cost of order.
   -------------------- */
   tax = TaxRate() * subtotal;
   total = subtotal + tax;
   printf (".......................................\n");
   printf ("Subtotal: %10s\n", CentsToDollars(subtotal));
   printf ("     Tax: %10s\n", CentsToDollars(tax));
   printf ("   Total: %10s\n", CentsToDollars(total));
   printf (".......................................\n");

/* Get Payment and convert to cents.
   -------------------------------- */
   PromptForString(" Payment: ", dollars);
   payment = DollarsToCents(dollars);
}
```

DisplayOrder() is the inverse of EnterOrder().

```
void Order::DisplayOrder()
{
/* Local Declarations.
   ------------------ */
   int n;
   LineItem *lip;    // Line Item Pointer.
   int change;

/* Print name and address.
   --------------------- */
   printf("\n********************************\n");
   printf("%s\n", name);
   printf("%s\n", address);

/* Print Line Items.
   ---------------- */
   DisplayLineItemHeading();
   for (n=0; n<nItems; n++) {
     lip = Item[n];
     lip->DisplayLineItem();
   }
/* Display Payment Information.
   -------------------------- */
   printf("\n*******************************************\n");
   printf(" Subtotal: %10s\n", CentsToDollars(subtotal));
   printf("      Tax: %10s\n", CentsToDollars(tax));
   printf("    Total: %10s\n", CentsToDollars(total));
   printf("*******************************************\n");
   printf("  Payment: %10s\n", CentsToDollars(payment));
   change = (payment - total);
   printf("Change Due: %10s\n", CentsToDollars(change));
}
```

The next method is provided to determine the cost of an order. We never
actually use this, since within the order entry method we can calculate the cost
more efficiently as we go along, but it seems like it might come in handy someday.

```
int Order::CostOfOrder()
{
  int n;
  int total = 0;

  for (n=0; n<nItems; n++ ) {
    total += Item[n]->GetLineItemPrice();
  }
  return total;
}
```

The next method returns the tax rate. Its functionality could have been subsumed by another private data member. We have used a method so that it can easily be changed into a virtual method, a technique we will discuss later.

```
float Order::TaxRate()
{
  return .100;
}
```

Given all this, how much work is now involved in writing a program to enter a book order? Here it is

```
#include "order.hpp"
int main()
{
  Order *op = new Order();
  op->InitOrder();
  op->EnterOrder();
  op->DisplayOrder();
  return 0;
}
```

Running this program gives the following user interaction, with user input shown in slanted font:

```
    Name:  Merlin
 Address:  c/o King Arthur, Camelot, Britain
 . . . . . . . . . . . . . . . . . . . . . . . . .
     Book Title:  100 Card Tricks U Can Do
 Number of Books:  2
   Price of Book:  8.95
 . . . . . . . . . . . . . . . . . . . . . . . . .
     Book Title:  Complete Horoscopes for 543 A.D.
 Number of Books:  1
   Price of Book:  3.50
 . . . . . . . . . . . . . . . . . . . . . . . . .
     Book Title:
 . . . . . . . . . . . . . . . . . . . . . . . . .
 Subtotal:       21.40
     Tax:         2.14
   Total:        23.54
 . . . . . . . . . . . . . . . . . . . . . . . . .
  Payment:  100.00
 ********************************
```

The last line of the program invokes `DisplayOrder()`, which prints the following on the terminal:

```
    Merlin
    c/o King Arthur, Camelot, Britain

    Book                                Qty  Price  Total
    ----------------------------------  ---  -----  -----
    100 Card Tricks U Can Do              2   8.95  17.90
    Complete Horoscopes for 543 A.D.      1   3.50   3.50

    ********************************************
       Subtotal:       21.40
           Tax:         2.14
         Total:        23.54
    ********************************************
       Payment:       100.00
    Change Due:        76.46
```

6.16 Exercises

Exercise 6.1 Modify the C version of the `dog` class so that the allocator also serves as a constructor. In other words, merge the functionality of `describe()` into `newDog()`.

Exercise 6.2 Write another class similar to `dog` called `littleDog`. Have `littleDog` do everything `dog` does, and in addition, support `setTrick()` and `trick()`. The first method is passed an arbitrary character string. The second method prints:

```
My trick is <string passed into setTrick()>.
```

Write a main program which declares and uses a `littleDog` object. Try having your program declare both a `littleDog` and a `dog` object.

Exercise 6.3 Create a class named **money**. Redefine the various classes of the order entry class to use this class for dealing with money issues.

Exercise 6.4 Modify the order entry program as follows: Create a **salesperson** class. Have the main program declare an array of objects of type **salesperson**. Modify the **main** program to follow this logic:

```
int main()
{
  initialize salesperson array;
  while (more orders) {
    get order;
    update appropriate salesperson giving credit for sale;
  }
  display summaries of all salesperson activity;
}
```

Ay, in the catalogue ye go for men,
As hounds and greyhounds, mongrels, spaniels, curs,
Shoughs, water-rugs, and demi-wolves are clipt
All by the name of dogs. The valued file
Distinguishes the swift, the slow, the subtle,
The housekeeper, the hunter, every one
According to the gift which bounteous nature
Hath in him clos'd; whereby he does receive
Particular addition, from the bill
That writes them all alike; and so of men.

- Macbeth III.1
William Shakespeare

Chapter 7

Inheritance

In the last chapter we looked at how classes are defined in C++, how objects are instantiated, and how methods are invoked. In this chapter, we are going to look at an important tool for reusing class code, inheritance.

7.1   Introduction

Class derivation, or inheritance, are synonyms. These terms describe the ability of one class to be used as a starting point for another class.

Earlier in this book we discussed a program for managing a Health Maintenance Organization, and created a `patient` class. Later we discussed the possibility of needing another class, referral patient class. A referral patient has everything a regular patient has, plus new data for the referring physician and new methods for manipulating this data. We might also have a surgical patient, which again is a patient but with information and methods specific for planned surgery.

Let's start by considering the three patient classes as independent classes. Our three patient class definitions might look like this. First, the patient class

```
class patient {
public:
  void init(              // Initialize a patient with a
    char *newName,        //    name, and
    char *newSSN);        //    social security number.
  char *nameIs();         // Return the name of this patient.
  char *SSNis();          // Return the Social Security Number.
private:
  char name[80];          // Storage for name.
  char ssn[15];           // Storage for Social Security Number.
};
```

Next, our referral patient

```
class referralPatient {
public:
  void init(              // Initialize a patient with a
    char *newName,        //    name, and
    char *newSSN);        //    social security number.
  char *nameIs();         // Return the name of this patient.
  char *SSNis();          // Return the Social Security Number.
  void setPhysician(      // Set name of referring physician.
    char *newPhysician);
  char *physicianIs();    // Return name of referring physician.
private:
  char name[80];          // Storage for name.
  char ssn[15];           // Storage for Social Security Number.
  char rphys[80];         // Storage referring physician name.
};
```

Finally, our surgical patient

```
class surgicalPatient {
public:
  void init(              // Initialize a patient with a
    char *newName,        //    name, and
    char *newSSN);        //    social security number.
  char *nameIs();         // Return the name of this patient.
  char *SSNis();          // Return the Social Security Number.
  void setSurgery(        // Set the surgery for this patient.
    char *newSurgery);
```

```
      char *surgeryIs();       // Return surgery for this patient.
    private:
      char name[80];           // Storage for name.
      char ssn[15];            // Storage for Social Security Number.
      char surgery[100];       // Storage for surgery description.
    };
```

We can illustrate the overlap in these three classes with Venn diagrams.

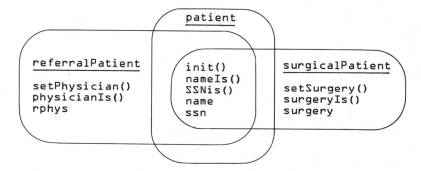

In C++, the class designer attempts to find in an existing class some subset of the functionality needed by a new class. The designer of the **referralPatient** class, for example, should notice that a subset of the **referralPatient** class already exists in the **patient** class, which contains three out of five of the necessary methods and two out of three of the necessary data items. Rather than start a new class from scratch, the **referralPatient** can be created as an extension of the **patient** class.

We often hear this process described as creating a subclass, **referralPatient**, from a parent class, **patient**. **referralPatient** is said to inherit the traits of its parent. This whole process is termed *inheritance*.

The terminology is confusing, and differs from one author to another. Some authors discuss inheritance, with parents and children classes. Others discuss derived classes, with super and subclasses. Or inheritance with super and sub classes. Or derivation with parents and children. All of these are misleading in one way or another.

The word *inheritance* is a particularly poor choice to describe this process, since it does little to elucidate the underlying concept of class derivation. Some of us would agree with Niklaus Wirth [Wirth, 90], who, in the April 1990 issue of *Microprocessors and Microsystems*, writes

> Some programmers find it attractive to view computer systems like humans. An object-oriented system is then compared with a human society. A symptom of this anthropomorphic view — which the author

finds misleading rather than useful — is the notion that a subclass inherits the properties of its superclass. Thus the subject of inheritance has found its entry into the programmers' technical jargon.

To see the problems this language causes, let's return to the HMO problem. C++ allows us to derive classes from other classes. In this example, `referralPatient` can be derived from `patient`. We say we create `referralPatient` as a subclass of `patient` and that `referralPatient` then inherits the characteristics of `patient`, including both methods and data. When one class is derived from another, as `referralPatient` from `patient`, the subclass `referralPatient`, has automatically defined for it all methods defined for the superclass or `patient`. If the superclass has an `init()` method, so does the subclass.

Now we can see some of the problems the inheritance terminology creates.

Describing the `patient` class as a parent implies participation and awareness on the part of the `patient` class. After all, parents are certainly aware of their children. However, when a class becomes the parent of some other class, it is not impacted, at least in theory, by the process.

Describing the `referralPatient` as a child class implies some degree of independence. After all, at some point children become independent of their parents, and decisions made by parents no longer have impact on their children. This, also, is very misleading. The `referralPatient` is forever tied to its roots. A `referralPatient` is an extension of a `patient`, and this extension occurs at compile time, not definition time. Should the `patient` class decide, for example, that the `init()` would be better named `describe()`, `referralPatient` client code which depended on the inherited `init()` would suddenly find that the method no longer exists.

The superclass/subclass terminology has as many problems as the parent/child terminology. As can be seen from the diagram, the so-called superclass (`patient`) actually contains a subset of the functionality of the subclass, whereas the so-called subclass contains a superset of the superclass's functionality.

It's no wonder that so many people have so much difficulty understanding this simple concept: that C++ allows one or more classes to be used as a starting point for developing new classes. We can use a `patient` class as a starting point for a `referralPatient` class. We can similarly use a `patient` class as a starting point for a `surgicalPatient` class.

We will follow the language conventions used by Ellis and Stroustrup [Ellis and Stroustrup]. The `patient` class is called the *base* class. The `referralPatient` is the *derived* class. The derived class *inherits* methods and data members from its base class. Unfortunately, we are still stuck with the inheritance concept.

Although in theory derived classes are created from base classes, often in practice it is the base classes that are created from the derived classes. Typically the class designer has created some useful class, say **referralPatient**. The class designer then creates a similar class, say **surgicalPatient**, and realizes that there is significant overlap between these two classes, as shown here

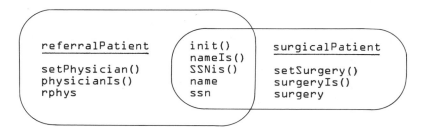

The proper response to this discovery is to create a new class which is the intersection of **referralPatient** and **surgicalPatient**. This new class, **patient**, becomes a base class, and the two other classes are rewritten to be derived classes. Thus, in a practical sense, the base class is often created from the derived class. Technically speaking, we end up with a base class, **patient**, and two derived classes, **referralPatient** and **surgicalPatient**.

Now let's look at this process of class derivation in more detail. We will create a relatively complex hierarchy of relatively simple classes to demonstrate the process.

In the last chapter we created a **dog** class. We have now decided that dogs are good, but too specific. We want to create many different kind of animal objects, not just dogs.

Therefore, we create an **animal** class which generalizes many of the **dog** concepts. The method **bark()** is changed to **says()**. The member variables **myBark** and **nBarks** are changed to **mySound** and **nSound**, respectively. The header file for **animal** looks like this

```
#ifndef ANIMAL_CLASS
#define ANIMAL_CLASS 1
class animal {
public:
  void init(char *newName, int newN, char *mySound);
  void says();
private:
  char myName[100];
  int nSound;
  char mySound[100];
};
#endif
```

And the `animal` code looks like this

```
#include <stdio.h>
#include <string.h>
#include "animal.hpp"


void animal::init(char *newName, int newN, char *newSound)
{
  nSound = newN;
  strcpy(mySound, newSound);
  strcpy(myName, newName);
}


void animal::says()
{
  int n;
  printf("%s goes\n", myName);
  for (n=0; n<nSound; n++) printf("   %s\n", mySound);
}
```

We can now create animal objects much like we created dog objects. For example, this program

```
#include <stdio.h>
#include "animal.hpp"

int main()
{
  animal *BugsBunny = new animal;
  BugsBunny->init("Bugs Bunny", 1, "What's up Doc?");
  BugsBunny->says();
}
```

gives this output

```
Bugs Bunny goes
   What's up Doc?
```

Now we have an `animal` class. An animal has two associated methods. The first describes the name of the animal, the noise the animal makes, and the number of times the animal makes that noise. Now let's consider a `dog` to be a further refinement of `animal`. Let's say that a dog can do anything an animal can do, plus scratch itself. We can define such a `dog` class with the following header:

```
#ifndef DOG_CLASS
#define DOG_CLASS 1
#include "animal.hpp"

class dog : public animal {
public:
  void scratch();
};


#endif
```

dog is now a derived class and we have some new syntax for describing the derivation. The syntax for defining a *nonderived* class looks like

```
class className {
/* ... */
};
```

and the syntax for defining a *derived* class looks like

```
class className : accessSpecifier baseClassName {
/* ... */
};
```

In this example, the className is dog, the accessSpecifier is public, and the baseClassName is animal. We will return to the access specifier, but for now the public keyword, used in this context, means that any public methods or data inherited from the base class are also public in this class.

Notice that the dog header file #includes the animal header file. Whenever a class refers to another class as a base class, the base class must be predefined. The typical way to "predefine" the base class is to #include its header file within the header file defining the derived class, just as we have done.

The implementation file for the dog class looks like

```
#include <stdio.h>
#include "dog.hpp"

void dog::scratch()
{
  printf("   Ooooh... what an itch.\n");
}
```

Although the programmer writes only one method for the dog class, by virtue of its definition as a derived class from animal, dog inherits two additional methods,

init() and says(). From the dog client's perspective, there is no difference
between the methods specifically defined for dog, and those inherited from animal.
In fact, the dog client has no reason to know that a dog is an animal (at least in
these simple examples). This can be seen from the following dog client program:

```
#include <stdio.h>
#include "dog.hpp"

int main()
{
  dog *Snoopy = new dog;
  Snoopy->init("Snoopy", 1, "Good Grief, Charlie Brown!");
  Snoopy->says();
  Snoopy->scratch();
}
```

which gives the following output:

```
Snoopy goes
    Good Grief, Charlie Brown!
    Ooooh... what an itch.
```

7.2   More on Access Specifiers

The time has come to look at the access specifiers in a little more detail. An access
specifier can be one of three keywords: public, private, or protected. An access
specifier can occur in one of two contexts, and we have seen examples of both. The
meaning is different, depending on the context in which it appears.

The first context is within a class declaration, as in

```
class animal {
public:                   // Within the class declaration
  void init(char *newName, int newN, char *mySound);
  void says();
private:                  // Also within the class declaration
  char myName[100];
  int nSound;
  char mySound[100];
};
```

The second context for an access specifier is within a base class list, as in

```
class dog : public animal {  // Within the base class list
public:
  void scratch();
};
```

Access specifiers determine which categories of code can access which class members. Potential accessors are divided into three categories: methods of this class, methods of classes derived from this class, and everybody else. A *public* class member can be accessed by anybody. A *protected* class member can be accessed by either member methods or derived member methods. A *private* class member can be accessed only by member methods.

Within a class definition, access specifiers act as toggles. If we look at the class definition of **animal**, we see

```
class animal {
public:
  void init(char *newName, int newN, char *mySound);
  void says();
private:
  char myName[100];
  int nSound;
  char mySound[100];
};
```

and the toggle effect is to define init() and says() as public, and myName, nSound, and mySound as private. Since init() is public, it can be invoked from anyplace, either within another animal method, from a method in a class derived from animal, or from client code. On the other hand, myName is private, and can be accessed only within one of the two animal methods.

Any code not respecting this accessibility will receive a compiler error. So, for example, since init() is public, this code is legal

```
#include "animal.hpp"
int main()
{
  animal *BugsBunny = new animal;
  BugsBunny->init("Bugs Bunny", 1, "What's up Doc?");
  /* ... */
```

But since myName is private, and main() is not one of the animal member methods, this code generates a compiler error

```
#include <string.h>
#include "animal.hpp"
int main()
{
  animal *BugsBunny = new animal;
  strcpy(BugsBunny->myName, "Bugs Bunny");  // Illegal!
  /* ... */
```

Notice this error has nothing to do with syntax. Within the `init()` routine we have functionally equivalent code

```
void animal::init(char *newName, int newN, char *newSound)
{
  nSound = newN;
  strcpy(mySound, newSound);
  strcpy(myName, newName);          // Legal here!
}
```

but, as a member function of `animal`, `init()` has access privileges to `myName` whereas `main()` does not.

The second way to use access specifiers is as a modifier on a base class. In this context, the access specifier appears within the base class list, as in

```
class dog : public animal {   // Within base class list
/* ... */
};
```

Only two of the access specifiers can be used as a base class modifier: `public` and `private`. Here they determine access to inherited members of the base class. The specifier `public` says inherited members retain their original access control. The specifier `private` says inherited members have `private` access, that is, they are accessible only within member functions of the derived class. A base class is by default `private`.

To get a better feeling for how this works, let's look again at the `animal`/`dog` classes. Let's consider `dog` from the perspective of the `dog` client. The `dog` class may have some private data and/or methods. The client is not interested in these. The `dog` class may have some public data and methods, in which the client is interested.

Some of the public members may have been defined in the `dog` class itself, and some may have been defined in base class(es) of `dog`. Again, this is no concern of the client. The client only cares about what the public members are, not where they came from.

While the actual definition of `dog` looks like

```
class animal {
public:
  void init(char *newName, int newN, char *mySound);
  void says();
private:
  char myName[100];
  int nSound;
  char mySound[100];
};

class dog : public animal {
public:
  void scratch();
};
```

from the client's perspective, **dog** really looks like

```
class dog {
public:
  void init(char *newName, int newN, char *mySound);
  void says();
  void scratch();
};
```

The private data is irrelevant, and the fact that `init()` and `says()` are inherited is strictly an implementation detail.

Now it becomes easier to see the effect of using access modifiers on the base class. If we change the **dog** declaration so that **animal** is a **private** base class, as

```
class dog : private animal {
public:
  void scratch();
};
```

our client view of **dog** becomes

```
class dog {
public:
  void scratch();
};
```

and client code such as

```
dog *Snoopy = new dog;
Snoopy->init("Snoopy", 1, "Good Grief, Charlie Brown!");
```

gives a compiler error on access of the now private method `init()`.

7.3 More Derivations

A derived class can itself serve as a base class for another derived class. **dog** is derived from **animal**. We can now derive more specific types of dogs from **dog**, say **littleDogs**. We know that any dog can **scratch()**, and can make a noise (by virtue of being an animal). Let's says a **littleDog** can do anything a **dog** can do, plus do a trick. **littleDog** is derived from **dog**, just as **dog** was from **animal**. The header file looks like

```
#ifndef LITTLE_DOG_CLASS
#define LITTLE_DOG_CLASS 1
#include "dog.hpp"

class littleDog : public dog {
public:
  void trick();
};
#endif
```

and the code for the new **littleDog** method looks like

```
#include <stdio.h>
#include "litdog.hpp"

void littleDog::trick()
{
  printf("   Watch my trick: I can roll over\n");
}
```

A **littleDog** cannot only do a **trick()**, it can also do anything a regular **dog** can do, including those things that dogs do because they are animals. Therefore, we can have client code such as

```
#include <stdio.h>
#include "litdog.hpp"

int main()
{
  littleDog *Toto = new littleDog;
  Toto->init("Toto", 1, "woof woof");
  Toto->says();
  Toto->scratch();
  Toto->trick();
}
```

which gives this output

```
Toto goes
   woof woof
   Ooooh... what an itch.
   Watch my trick: I can roll over
```

Notice that Toto can do a trick because he is a `littleDog`, can `scratch()` because he is a `dog`, and can `says()` because all `dogs`, including `littleDogs`, are `animals`.

A class can serve as a base class for any number of derived classes. Thus, `bigDogs` as well as `littleDogs` can be derived from `dogs`.

```
#ifndef BIG_DOG_CLASS
#define BIG_DOG_CLASS 1
#include "dog.hpp"

class bigDog : public dog {
public:
  void trick();
};
#endif
```

The code file:

```
#include <stdio.h>
#include "bigdog.hpp"

void bigDog::trick()
{
  printf("   Watch my trick: I can fetch the letter carrier\n");
}
```

Notice that both `bigDogs` and `littleDogs` have a `trick()` method, but the method is different. The `littleDog` trick is to roll over. The `bigDog` trick is to fetch the mail carrier. How does C++ know which `trick()` to invoke for an object? It decides based on the type of the target object. If `trick()` is invoked on a `littleDog`, then `littleDog::trick()` is invoked. If `trick()` is invoked on a `bigDog`, then `bigDog::trick()` is invoked. Consider this program

```
#include <stdio.h>
#include "bigdog.hpp"

int main()
{
  bigDog *Lassie = new bigDog;
  Lassie->init("Lassie", 1, "BOW WOW");
  Lassie->says();
  Lassie->scratch();
  Lassie->trick();
}
```

which gives this output:

```
Lassie goes
   BOW WOW
   Ooooh... what an itch.
   Watch my trick: I can fetch the letter carrier
```

When the compiler hits

```
Lassie->trick();
```

The compiler must figure out what kind of an object `Lassie` is. Since `Lassie` is a `bigDog`, `bigDog::trick()` is invoked.

Our class derivations are starting to get a little complicated, and a graphical representation would be handy. In English, we have `bigDog` and `littleDog` derived from `dog` derived from `animal`. To represent this graphically, we will follow the lead of Ellis and Stroustrup [Ellis and Stroustrup], who use a directed acyclic graph (DAG) for representing what they call the class lattice.

In general, a DAG shows a collection of nodes and arrows. In the case of a class lattice, a node represents a class and an arrow represents the relationship "derived from." Thus the class lattice DAG

$$dog \longrightarrow animal$$

can be read "dog is an animal," "dog is derived from animal," or "animal is a base class for dog," all of which say the same thing. By the way, spatial organization has no meaning in a DAG, so this class lattice could also be shown as

$$animal \longleftarrow dog$$

or even

$$animal$$
$$\uparrow$$
$$dog$$

The only significance in a DAG is the name of the nodes and the relationships implied by the arrows. A DAG is called "directed" because the relationship implied by an arrow connecting two nodes is not bidirectional. The relationship

$$\text{dog} \quad \longrightarrow \quad \text{animal}$$

is not the same as the relationship

$$\text{animal} \quad \longrightarrow \quad \text{dog}$$

A directed graph is said to be "acyclic" when it represents a situation in which cycles cannot occur, as in the case of a class lattice. In other words, there is no node in the graph such that you can start from that node, follow a sequence of paths, and end up back at the same node. A class lattice is certainly acyclic, since no class can indirectly be derived from itself.

The acyclic nature of our class lattice is clear. Starting from the node `littleDog` we can go to `dog`, and from there to `animal`, but there we are stuck. There is no path leading back to `littleDog`.

When you consider the nature of class derivations, it becomes clear that *any* class lattice will be acyclic. A cyclic class lattice, if it were possible, might look like

$$\text{animal} \quad \overset{\longrightarrow}{\longleftarrow} \quad \text{dog}$$

which says that an `animal` is a `dog`, and a `dog` is an `animal`. From an inheritance point of view, this says that `animal` has all of the methods available to `dog`. What are the methods available to `dog`? The `dog` has available all the methods of `animal`. This does not fit in with our concept of class derivation, which has us continuously building from a well defined base class.

7.4 Multiple Inheritance

A class can be derived from more than one base class. Such a class becomes the composite of all the data and methods of the base classes combined with any new data and methods defined in the derived class. As usual, the client of the derived class has little interest in the origins of the derived class methods and data.

To see how this works, let's start by defining a new base class, `performer`. This class describes objects which get paid for doing a performance. The class has one data element which describes the lowest payment the performer will accept for performing, one method for setting this data element, and one method, `bargain()`, which, when invoked, prints a line saying what the performer would like to get paid. The class definition looks like

```
#ifndef PERFORMER_CLASS
#define PERFORMER_CLASS 1
```

```
class performer {
public:
  void setMinimumSalary(int newMin);
  void bargain();
private:
  int min_salary;    // Absolute rock bottom acceptable
                     // pay for a performance.
};
```

```
#endif
```

The class implementation file looks like

```
#include <stdio.h>
#include "perform.hpp"


void performer::setMinimumSalary(int newMin)
{
  min_salary = newMin;
}


void performer::bargain()
{
  printf("   I get %d dollars a performance\n", 2 * min_salary);
}
```

Finally, a sample program which demonstrates a **performer** object:

```
#include "perform.hpp"
#include <stdio.h>

int main()
{
  performer *JohnnyCarson = new performer;
  JohnnyCarson->setMinimumSalary(10000);
  JohnnyCarson->bargain();
}
```

The output from this program

```
I get 20000 dollars a performance
```

Now let's reconsider the **dog** class. **dog** had been defined as an **animal** with the additional **scratch()** method. We say that **dog** is derived from a single base class **animal**. The definition had looked like

```
#ifndef DOG_CLASS
#define DOG_CLASS 1
#include "animal.hpp"

class dog : public animal {
public:
  void scratch();
};


#endif
```

Now let's redefine a **dog** to be derived from two base classes, **animal** and **performer**. The new definition looks like

```
#ifndef DOG_CLASS
#define DOG_CLASS 1
#include "animal.hpp"
#include "perform.hpp"

class dog : public animal, public performer {
public:
  void scratch();
};


#endif
```

Notice the **dog** definition has only two small changes. First, the class definition file for **performer** is #included. Second, **performer** is added to the list of base classes from which this class is derived. These are the *only* changes made to the **dog** class. We have neither added to nor changed any of the code in the implementation file.

This seemingly minor change has fundamentally altered the definition of **dog**, **littleDog,** and **bigDog**. Now, in addition to all its previous abilities, any dog can, by virtue of being a **performer**, have a minimum salary and **bargain()**.

Not only has this change affected **dog**s, but any class derived from **dog**. Our class lattice has changed from

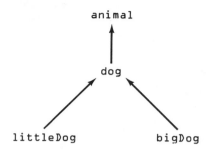

to

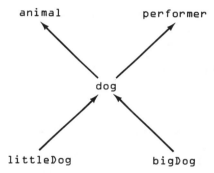

which says `littleDog` and `bigDog` are derived from the single base class `dog`, which is derived from the two base classes `animal` and `performer`. So both `littleDogs` and `bigDogs` now have `performer` characteristics.

If we look at the "new" class definition for, say, `littleDog`, we see no change

```
#ifndef LITTLE_DOG_CLASS
#define LITTLE_DOG_CLASS 1
#include "dog.hpp"

class littleDog : public dog {
public:
  void trick();
};
#endif
```

The class `littleDog` is derived from `dog` as it always was. But although the `dog` changes are removed from the `littleDog` definition, these changes profoundly affect the characteristics of `littleDogs`. They have suddenly inherited all of the abilities of `performer`. We can now write code like

```
#include "litdog.hpp"
#include "bigdog.hpp"

int main()
{
  littleDog *Fifi = new littleDog;
  bigDog *Rex = new bigDog;

  Fifi->init("Fifi", 2, "bow wow");
  Fifi->setMinimumSalary(20);

  Rex->init("Rex", 4, "BOW WOW");
  Rex->setMinimumSalary(25);

  Fifi->says();        // Because Fifi is an animal
  Fifi->trick();       // Because Fifi is a littleDog
  Fifi->bargain();     // Because Fifi is a performer

  Rex->says();         // Because Rex is an animal
  Rex->trick();        // Because Rex is a bigDog
  Rex->bargain();      // Because Rex is a performer
  return 0;
}
```

The output from this program looks like

```
Fifi goes
   bow wow
   bow wow
   Watch my trick: I can roll over
   I get 40 dollars a performance
Rex goes
   BOW WOW
   BOW WOW
   BOW WOW
   BOW WOW
   Watch my trick: I can fetch the letter carrier
   I get 50 dollars a performance
```

A class can serve as a base class for any number of derived classes. For example, just as `dogs` are `animals`, we can define a new class to be derived from `animal`, say

usedCarDealer. We will define this class to do everything an **animal** does, plus **makeSale()**. The class lattice now looks like

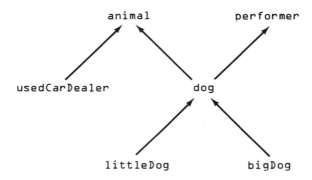

Our class definition file for **usedCarDealer** looks much like the class definition file for **dog**:

```
#include <stdio.h>
#include "animal.hpp"

#ifndef USED_CAR_DEALER_CLASS
#define USED_CAR_DEALER_CLASS 1

class usedCarDealer : public animal {
public:
  void makeSale();
};

#endif
```

The implementation file contains only one method

```
#include <stdio.h>
#include "ucd.hpp"

void usedCarDealer::makeSale()
{
  printf("   ... and only $500 more if you want the wheels!\n");
}
```

Any or all of the classes in our class lattice can be used in a single program, as long as the appropriate class definition files are #included. For example, this program

```
#include "animal.hpp"
#include "dog.hpp"
#include "ucd.hpp"
#include "litdog.hpp"
#include "bigdog.hpp"

int main()
{
  animal          *Frenchie   = new animal;
  dog             *Rover      = new dog;
  littleDog       *Fifi       = new littleDog;
  bigDog          *Rex        = new bigDog;
  usedCarDealer *HonestBob  = new usedCarDealer;

  Frenchie-> init("Frenchie", 1, "Grrrrr");
  Rover->    init("Rover", 1, "Woof");
  Fifi->     init("Fifi", 2, "bow wow");
  Rex->      init("Rex", 4, "BOW WOW");
  HonestBob->init(
    "Honest Bob", 1, "Buy This Car... What A Deal!!!");

  Frenchie->says();
  Rover->says();

  Fifi->says();
  Fifi->trick();

  Rex->says();
  Rex->trick();

  HonestBob->says();
  HonestBob->makeSale();
  return 0;
}
```

gives this output

```
Frenchie goes
   Grrrrr
Rover goes
   Woof
Fifi goes
   bow wow
   bow wow
   Watch my trick: I can roll over
Rex goes
   BOW WOW
   BOW WOW
   BOW WOW
   BOW WOW
   Watch my trick: I can fetch the letter carrier
Honest Bob goes
   Buy This Car... What A Deal!!!
   ... and only $500 more if you want the wheels!
```

Notice that `usedCarDealer` shares only those characteristics with `dog` that are mutually inherited from `animal`. So both `usedCarDealer` and `dog` can make a noise using the mutually inherited `says()`, but only a `dog` can `scratch()`.

7.5   Reuse Through Inheritance

One of the most important uses of inheritance is in reducing the amount of new code necessary to complete projects. In the beginning of this chapter, we discussed three variants on patients, and looked at the code overlap between them. Now we are in a position to see how inheritance can be used to reduce the overall amount of code required to code these three patient types.

There are many ways we might "discover" inheritance patterns among classes. Here we will use an informal methodology where we look for intersections between classes.

First, look again at the three patient classes. We described three patient classes, a regular patient, a referral patient, and a surgical patient. A regular patient has name and social security data, an `init()` method to set these two data items, and two access methods, `nameIs()` and `SSSis()`. A referral patient has all of this plus an additional data element to store the name of the referring physician, and a set and get access method for this new data item. A surgical patient also has everything a regular patient has, plus an additional data element to store the name of the surgical procedure and associated set and get methods for its new data item.

Graphically, we can represent our three patient types as

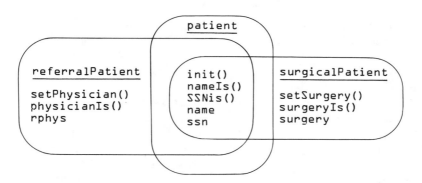

```
referralPatient              patient              surgicalPatient

init()                       init()               init()
nameIs()                     nameIs()             nameIs()
SSNis()                      SSNis()              SSNis()
setPhysician()               name                 setSurgery()
physicianIs()                ssn                  surgeryIs()
name                                              name
ssn                                               ssn
rphys                                             surgery
```

Next we find the intersection (overlap) between these two classes, giving the Venn diagram we saw earlier in this chapter.

```
                          patient

referralPatient         init()            surgicalPatient
                        nameIs()
setPhysician()          SSNis()           setSurgery()
physicianIs()           name              surgeryIs()
rphys                   ssn               surgery
```

Next we pull out the intersection, and make this a base class. We also redefine each derived class as its old self minus the intersection, turning this Venn diagram into a class lattice:

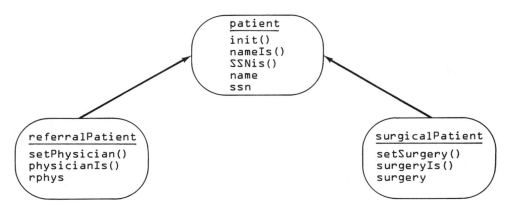

Often the class intersections are not this easy to determine. Different people may have written the specs for the different classes. Similar methods may have been given different names. Analogous code requirements may have been split up into different methods. Essentially similar data may have been named and/or defined differently. This just means that the search for class intersection needs to focus more on content than on form. The process is still much like that described here.

Assuming we are successful in this analysis, let's see what benefit we receive. In our highly simplified patient classes, our patient class definition looks like

```
#ifndef PATIENT_CLASS
#define PATIENT_CLASS 1

class patient {
public:
  void init(              // Initialize a patient with a
    char *newName,        //    name, and
    char *newSSN);        //    social security number.
  char *nameIs();         // Return the name of this patient.
  char *SSNis();          // Return the Social Security Number.
private:
  char name[80];          // Storage for name.
  char ssn[15];           // Storage for Social Security Number.
};

#endif
```

and our surgical patient class definition looks like

```
#ifndef SURGICAL_PATIENT_CLASS
#define SURGICAL_PATIENT_CLASS 1

#include "patient.hpp"

class surgicalPatient : public patient {
public:
  void setSurgery(        // Set the surgery for this patient.
    char *newSurgery);
  char *surgeryIs();      // Return the surgery for this patient.
private:
  char surgery[100];      // Storage for surgery description.
};
#endif
```

and finally, our referral patient class definition

```
#ifndef REFERRAL_PATIENT_CLASS
#define REFERRAL_PATIENT_CLASS 1

#include "patient.hpp"

class referralPatient : public patient {
public:
  void setPhysician(      // Set name of referring physician.
    char *newPhysician);
  char *physicianIs();    // Return name of referring physician.
private:
  char rphys[80];         // Storage referring physician name.
};

#endif
```

Then our patient implementation file

```
#include "patient.hpp"
#include <string.h>

void patient::init(char *newName, char *newSSN)
{
  strcpy(name, newName);
  strcpy(ssn, newSSN);
}
```

```
char *patient::nameIs()
{
  return name;
}


char *patient::SSNis()
{
  return ssn;
}
```

and our surgical patient implementation file

```
#include "spatient.hpp"
#include <string.h>


void surgicalPatient::setSurgery(char *newSurgery)
{
  strcpy(surgery, newSurgery);
}


char *surgicalPatient::surgeryIs()
{
  return surgery;
}
```

and our referral patient implementation file

```
#include "rpatient.hpp"
#include <string.h>


void referralPatient::setPhysician(char *newPhysician)
{
  strcpy(rphys, newPhysician);
}


char *referralPatient::physicianIs()
{
  return rphys;
}
```

Now let's try to quantify our code savings through use of class derivation. Counting the number of code lines needed to create the three classes, including both class definition and implementation, but excluding comments, `#include` lines, and blank lines, we get

Lines of Code Using Class Derivation

```
        patient: 24
referralPatient: 16
surgicalPatient: 16
                 ------
                   56
```

How would this have looked if we had not used class derivation? In this case we would have rewritten our intersection methods for each class. We can approximate the amount of code we would have needed by adding the number of lines for the patient class back into the other two classes, giving

Lines of Code Using Class Derivation

```
        patient: 24 + 0  = 24
referralPatient: 16 + 24 = 40
surgicalPatient: 16 + 24 = 40
                         ------
                          104
```

This shows that we have achieved almost a 50 percent reduction in the amount of source code by using class derivation. One might argue that we have actually saved only 48 lines of code, but this ignores the fact that we have oversimplified the classes for the purposes of showing complete code. In a real programming situation, each of these classes might be ten times the size we have shown, or even larger. Assuming these percent reductions hold steady, a reasonable assumption, we now see the 60 line savings increase to 500 or more. This is still with a very simple class lattice. These savings increase dramatically as we add nodes to the class lattice.

Say we have the following class lattice, where each letter represents a class, and the number in parenthesis shows the number of lines necessary to code the class

using class derivation

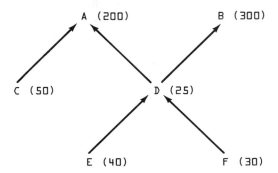

For each node in the lattice, the cost of development using derivation is just the cost of development of that node. The cost of development without using derivation is the cost of development of that node *plus* the cost of development without derivation of all base classes for that node.

For nonderived classes, **A** and **B**, the cost of development is the same regardless of whether hierarchies are used. We can say

```
CWOD(A) = CWD(A) = 200
CWOD(B) = CWD(B) = 300
```

where

```
CWOD(X) = Cost with out derivation (X)
CWD(X) = Cost with derivation (X)
```

For a derived class, calculating the cost without derivation means recursively calculating the cost without derivation of each of its base classes. This is relatively easy if we start with the nonderived classes and work our way out. For C, we have

```
CWD(C) = 50
CWOD(C) = 50 + CWOD(A) = 50 + 200 = 250
```

Continuing, we get

```
CWD(D) = 25
CWOD(D) = 25 + CWOD(A) + CWOD(B) = 25 + 200 + 300 = 525
```

```
CWD(E) = 40
CWOD(E) = 40 + CWOD(D) = 40 + 525 = 565

CWD(F) = 30
CWOD(F) = 30 + CWOD(D) = 30 + 525 = 555
```

Now we can calculate the cost of writing this whole class lattice with and without derivation.

```
CWD(CL) = CWD(A) + CWD(B) + CWD(C) +
          CWD(D) + CWD(E) + CWD(F)
        = 200 + 300 + 50 + 25 + 40 + 30
        = 645
CWOD(CL) = CWOD(A) + CWOD(B) + CWOD(C) + CWOD(D) +
           CWOD(E) + CWOD(F)
         = 200 + 300 + 250 + 525 + 565 + 555
         = 2395
```

Overall, the code size using derivation compared to not using derivation is

```
645/2395 = .27
```

showing that we have achieved a 73 per cent reduction in code size using class derivation.

It is certainly true that class derivation is not the only way to achieve code reuse. Many would argue, fairly, that even non object-oriented programming languages can be subjected to a rigorous design process resulting in a great amount of code reuse. See, for example, *Reusable Data Structures For C* [Sessions].

It is also true that many simplifying assumptions have been made here, such as every line in the base classes is needed in each of the derived classes. You can't assume a 73 percent code reduction can be achieved in every case. Many class lattices will achieve more reduction. Many will achieve less. The important point is this: class derivation is an important technique in the programmer's workbench for accomplishing more work of better quality in less time with fewer lines of code.

7.6 Base Classes As Generic Classes

Since a base class is a subset of a derived class, we say that the derived class has an *is a* relationship with its base class. If a `littleDog` is derived from a `dog`, we say `littleDog` *is a* dog. If a `surgicalPatient` is derived from a `patient`, we say `surgicalPatient` *is a* `patient`.

One implication of the *is a* relationship is that anything that can be done with a base class can also be done with a derived class. If the **dog** class supports a **bark** method so does `littleDog`. If the `patient` class has a private data item **name**, then so does `surgicalPatient`.

Therefore, a base class can be thought of as a generic version of any classes derived from it. We might think of this as either a result of derivation or a result of the *is a* relationship. These are really two different ways of saying the same thing.

Class hierarchies are fully equivalent to the *is a* relationship. If we prefer thinking of hierarchies, we say that the `dog` supports `bark()` and since `littleDog` class is derived from `dog`, `littleDog` supports `bark()`. If we prefer *is a*, we say that `dog` supports `bark()`, and `littleDog` *is a* `dog`, and therefore supports `bark()`. Both lead to the same conclusion — any instance of `littleDog` is a valid instance of `dog`.

The inverse is not the case. Thinking of hierarchies, a `dog` is not derived from `littleDog`, and therefore, does not necessarily support all `littleDog` methods. Thinking of *is a*, a `dog` isn't (necessarily) a `littleDog`.

Since a `littleDog` *is a* `dog`, anything we can do to a `dog` we can also do to a `littleDog`. For example, in Chapter 6 we implemented a `dogHouse` class as an array of `dog` pointers. It is perfectly valid to set any of these pointers to `littleDogs` as well as `bigDogs`.

But remember, neither a `dog` nor a `bigDog` *is a* `littleDog`. If `dogHouse` had been defined as an array of `littleDog` pointers, it would not be valid to use them to point to either `dogs` or `bigDogs`.

7.7   Reuse Through Libraries

We have discussed class hierarchies as set intersections of class functionality. This search process typically occurs during the early design process. In this section, we will look at a different process of discovering hierarchies, through use of class libraries.

The *library* concept is well known to C programmers. Libraries are a well established methodology for achieving code reuse. Of all programming languages, C has probably the largest set of commercially produced libraries ranging in topics from communications to advanced mathematical tools.

The concept of producing commercial libraries of C++ classes is relatively new. A consensus has not yet been reached on exactly what a C++ class library should look like. Many issues are under active debate. For example, does a library ship as source code or as a set of binary files and header files? What does it mean to guarantee upward compatibility? We will return to some of these issues in the chapter on C++ problems.

There are two objectives for C++ libraries which are widely accepted and differ from those of a nonobject-oriented language library. The first is to make available a set of class definitions from which the client can directly instantiate and manipulate.

The second is to make available a set of class definitions which can be used as a base for further derived classes.

Simply providing class definitions for instantiation is achievable even in C, as we saw in the first several chapters of this book. This functionality is rarely provided by C libraries. C programmers still tend to see the world as collections of functions, rather than as a collection of data abstractions. This will most likely change over the next few years, as the object paradigm becomes more pervasive.

We will now take a look at the second purpose of the C++ library, the provision of base classes as a way of achieving code reuse. It is a little early to discuss this topic fully, since the material in the next few chapters is very important in achieving code reuse through class derivation, but we can at least get a preview of this topic.

In the last chapter we discussed an order entry program. This program used two classes: an order and a line item. If this program were to be distributed commercially we can imagine two approaches the developers might follow.

The first is to distribute the **main()** program as a stand alone system, which would be installed and run at customer sites. The advantage of this is that clients need have no knowledge of programming. They simply install the software and start running. The disadvantage is that clients cannot modify the package.

The second approach is to distribute the class definition and implementation files. This allows clients to customize the package as necessary, most likely by deriving classes from the order class which are more suited to their needs. The disadvantage is that clients need to know and have access to C++.

The definition of the **order** class looked like this

```
#ifndef OrderClass
#define OrderClass 1
#include "l_item.hpp"

class Order {
public:
  void InitOrder();
  void EnterOrder();
  void DisplayOrder();
  int CostOfOrder();
  float TaxRate();
```

```
private:
  char name[100];
  char address[100];
  int nItems;             // Number of line items
  LineItem *Item[100];    // Line Items
  int subtotal;           // Total Cost, not including tax.
  int tax;
  int total;              // Total, including tax.
  int payment;            // In cents
};
#endif
```

The method `DisplayOrder()` produced the following output

```
Merlin
c/o King Arthur, Camelot, Britain

Book                                    Qty  Price   Total
------------------------------------    ---  ------  -----
100 Card Tricks U Can Do                  2   8.95   17.90
Complete Horoscopes for 543 A.D.          1   3.50    3.50

**********************************************
    Subtotal:      21.40
         Tax:       2.14
       Total:      23.54
**********************************************
    Payment:     100.00
  Change Due:      76.46
```

Let's say the client wants to make two changes: first, they want to print the name of the salesperson on the receipt, and second, they want a footer printed on each page that gives a little advertisement for the store. These changes are easily made, assuming they have the class definition files, the source code for the `main()` program, and a suitable C++ programming environment. They don't even need the class implementation files, as long as binary (compiled) versions are available.

First, they derive a new class from `Order`, say `Order2`. This class inherits all the public methods from `order` and adds a new private data member to track the salesperson. It adds two new public methods, one to set the salesperson and one to print the footer. The class definition looks like

```
#ifndef ORDER2_CLASS
#define ORDER2_CLASS 1
#include "order.hpp"

class Order2 : public Order {
private:
  char salesPerson[100];
public:
  void SetSalesPerson();
  void DisplayFooter();
};
#endif
```

Next, a class method code file is created for these newly added methods.

```
#include "order2.hpp"
#include "helper.hpp"
#include <stdio.h>


void Order2::SetSalesPerson()
{
  PromptForString("What is your name? ", salesPerson);
}


void Order2::DisplayFooter()
{
  printf("\n\n");
  printf("Your sales person was %s, ", salesPerson);
  printf("and we appreciate your business\n");
  printf("***********************************************\n");
  printf("Have you seen the latest work, Romeo and Juliet\n");
  printf("by that new playwrite William Shakespeare?\n\n");
  printf("The New York Times has praised this play as\n");
  printf(
    "\"...an interesting concept ... engaging dialogue\"\n\n");
  printf(
    "Please stop by our drama section and examine this work.\n");
}
```

Finally, the **main()** program is modified. The **op** pointer is changed to point to an **order2** class rather than an **order** and the two new method invocations are added.

```
#include "order2.hpp"
#include <stdio.h>

int main()
{
  Order2 *op = new Order2();
  op->InitOrder();
  op->SetSalesPerson();      // Added at site
  op->EnterOrder();
  op->DisplayOrder();
  op->DisplayFooter();       // Added at site
  return 0;
}
```

The final order display with these modification now looks like

```
Merlin
c/o King Arthur, Camelot, Britain

Book                                 Qty  Price  Total
------------------------------------ ---  ------ -----
100 Card Tricks U Can Do               2   8.95  17.90
Complete Horoscopes for 543 A.D.       1   3.50   3.50

***********************************************
    Subtotal:      21.40
        Tax:       2.14
      Total:      23.54
***********************************************
    Payment:     100.00
Change Due:      76.46
```

Your sales person was Roger, and we appreciate your business
****
Have you seen the latest work, Romeo and Juliet
by that new playwrite William Shakespeare?

The New York Times has praised this play as
"...an interesting concept ... engaging dialogue"

Please stop by our drama section and examine this work.

7.8 Exercises

Exercise 7.1 The class `dog` was defined to be derived from the public base class `animal`. Change the class derivation to be derived from the private base class `animal`. Recompile the code for `dog`, `animal`, and the main program. What differences do you observe? Explain what you notice.

Exercise 7.2 In the `animal` definition, change `init()` and `says()` to be private. Recompile `animal`, `dog` and the test program, and explain any observations.

Exercise 7.3 Write full definitions and implementations for the various `patient` classes. Write a test program which demonstrates their use.

Exercise 7.4 We showed a client's view of the `dog` class as

```
class dog {
public:
  void init(char *newName, int newN, char *mySound);
  void says();
  void scratch();
};
```

Show a client's view of `animal`, `performer`, `littleDog`, `bigDog` and `usedCarDealer`. Also show a client's view of `dog` as derived from both `animal` and `performer`.

Though this be madness, yet there is method in't.

- Hamlet II.i
William Shakespeare

Chapter 8

Method Resolution in C++

When we looked at how classes are constructed in C, we found that method resolution is by name. So when we find code like

```
strcpy(new_word.word, "abc");
ll_addhead(llp1, &new_word);

strcpy(new_word.word, "123");
ll_addhead(llp2, &new_word);
```

we know that `ll_addhead()` is one of the linked list methods. There is no question about which `ll_addhead()` is going to be invoked. The nature of C ensures that only one can exist.

In Chapter 5 we showed the kind of problems this causes. Integrating two sets of code, one using a one-way and one using a two-way linked list, was greatly complicated by overlapping method names. In this chapter, we will look at the tools C++ offers to resolve these issues.

8.1 Introduction

Although we have not discussed method resolution in C++ in detail, we have already seen that C++ resolves methods differently than C. In our `dog` classes, for example, we have seen method names multiply defined within a single program's name space. Recall how the method `trick()` was defined for both `littleDogs` and `bigDogs`. The lines

217

```
littleDog *Fifi = new littleDog;
/* ... */
Fifi->trick();
```

resulted in this method being invoked

```
void littleDog::trick()
{
  printf("Watch my trick: I can roll over\n");
}
```

while the lines

```
bigDog *Rex = new bigDog;
/* ... */
Rex->trick();
```

resulted in an entirely different method being invoked

```
void bigDog::trick()
{
  printf("Watch my trick: I can fetch the letter carrier\n");
}
```

If this program had been coded in C, we would have had to use different method names, say `littleDogTrick()` and `bigDogTrick()`. Our clients would then look like

```
littleDog *Fifi = littleDogNew();
bigDog *Rex = bigDogNew();
littleDogTrick(Fifi);
bigDogTrick(Rex);
```

If we then decided `Rex` is really a `littleDog`, and changed the declaration appropriately

```
littleDog *Fifi = littleDogNew();
littleDog *Rex = littleDogNew();/* Rex is now a littleDog */
```

but left the calling code as before

```
littleDogTrick(Fifi);
bigDogTrick(Rex);        /* Rex tries to do a bigDog trick */
```

then `Rex` is not going to do what he should. In fact, if `bigDogTrick()` requires private data which only `bigDog`s have, then `Rex` may do something *very* bad (like crash the system).

C++ does not have this problem. We can change `Rex` from a `bigDog` to a `littleDog` by changing nothing but the declaration

```
littleDog *Fifi = new littleDog;
littleDog *Rex = new littleDog;/* Rex is now a littleDog. */
Fifi->trick();
Rex->trick();                   /* Rex does littleDog tricks. */
```

In this chapter, we are going to look in more detail at how C++ resolves methods.

8.2   Resolution by Signature

Every function, including class methods, has an associated *signature*. A signature is composed of three parts: the method name, the type of the target object (for class methods), and the number and type of its parameters. `littleDog::trick()`, for example, looks like

```
void littleDog::trick()
{
  printf("Watch my trick: I can roll over\n");
}
```

and has a signature which can be thought of as

```
          method name: trick
        target object: littleDog
  number of arguments: 0
```

`bigDog::trick()` looks slightly different

```
void bigDog::trick()
{
  printf("Watch my trick: I can fetch the letter carrier\n");
}
```

and has a slightly different signature

```
          method name: trick
        target object: bigDog
  number of arguments: 0
```

The fundamental difference between C and C++ method resolution is that C resolves by name and C++ resolves by signature. So when the C++ compiler sees this code

```
bigDog *Rex = new bigDog;
Rex->trick();
```

it doesn't look at the name of the method `trick()`, it looks at the signature of the method `trick()`. C++ determines that the line

```
Rex->trick();
```

is invoking a method whose signature is

```
        method name: trick
      target object: bigDog
number of arguments: 0
```

C++ knows the target object is a `bigDog`, because of the type of the pointer `Rex`, as defined in the line

```
bigDog *Rex = new bigDog;
```

For every method (or function) invocation, C++ determines the signature of the method being invoked. For every method declaration, C++ likewise determines a method signature. Then at link time the signatures are resolved, much like for C the method names are resolved.

This means that at link time

```
Rex->trick();
```

will resolve to an invocation of `bigDog::trick()`, because the signature of

```
bigDog::trick()
```

matches the signature of

```
Rex->trick()
```

just as the signature of

```
littleDog::trick()
```

matches the signature of

```
Fifi->trick()
```

This is why it is so easy in C++ to change `Rex` to a `littleDog`:

```
littleDog *Fifi = new littleDog;
littleDog *Rex = new littleDog;/* Rex is now a littleDog. */
Fifi->trick();
Rex->trick();                  /* Rex now does littleDog tricks. */
```

Although the invocation of **Rex**'s **trick()** has not changed, the signature of **Rex**'s **trick()** *has* changed. When this code is compiled, C++ now believes that **Rex**'s **trick()**'s signature includes a target object of type **littleDog** instead of type **bigDog**, and resolves this against the only method with the correct signature, **littleDog::trick()**.

The "type" of the target object is the same, regardless of whether the object is a pointer or an actual class instantiation. Thus in

```
littleDog *Fifi = new littleDog;
littleDog Toto;
Fifi->trick();
Toto.trick();
```

the signature of the **trick()** method invoked by **Fifi** and **Toto** is identical.

This resolution works the same for functions as for class methods. Therefore, we can overload a function name just as we can a class method. For example, we can create a file with two different versions of **bark()** as long as the signatures are different.

```
#include <stdio.h>
void bark()
{
  printf("How many times should I bark?\n");
}
void bark(int nTimes)
{
  int n;
  for (n=0; n<nTimes; n++) printf("Woof!\n");
}
```

The determination as to which of these will be invoked depends on the signature on the caller side. So, if a program looks like this

```
int main()
{
  bark(2);
}
```

we get this output

```
Woof!
Woof!
```

while a program that looks like

```
int main()
{
  bark();
}
```

gets an entirely different output

How many times should I bark?

Notice that the return value of the method (or function) is not part of the signature. Two methods which differ only in return value are considered to illegally share a signature. The following, for example, will not compile:

```
#include <stdio.h>
void show(int n)
{
  printf("Void version of show\n");
}
int show(int n2)
{
  printf("Int version of show\n");
  return n2;
}
```

When multiple versions of a method name exist, that method is said to be *overloaded*. This term is misleading, because it seems to imply that overloaded functions are resolved differently than nonoverloaded functions, which is not true. C++ does not distinguish between overloaded and nonoverloaded functions. Both are resolved strictly by signature.

The ability of C++ to allow the same method name to participate in more than one signature is often described as *polymorphism*. Overloaded methods are said to be *polymorphic*. This word adds little to our understanding of object-oriented programming, and is included here solely because it is encountered frequently in the literature.

Name overloading is frequently used even within a class. In this version of dog, both describe() and bark() are overloaded. Notice both method versions are described in the class header file

```
class dog {
public:
  void describe(char *newName, int newN, char *newBark);
  void describe(char *newName);
  void bark();
  void bark(int nTimes);
```

```
private:
  char myName[100];
  char myBark[100];
  int nBarks;
};
```

and both versions of the method are coded in the method code file

```
#include <stdio.h>
#include <string.h>
#include "dog.hpp"

/*
This <describe> resets all private data.
---------------------------------------- */
void dog::describe(char *newName, int newN, char *newBark)
{
  nBarks = newN;
  strcpy(myBark, newBark);
  strcpy(myName, newName);
}
/*
This <describe> uses defaults.
----------------------------- */
void dog::describe(char *newName)
{
  nBarks = 2;                    // Default
  strcpy(myBark, "bow wow");     // Default
  strcpy(myName, newName);
}
/*
This <bark> uses private data for iteration.
-------------------------------------------- */
void dog::bark()
{
  int n;
  printf("%s goes\n", myName);
  for (n=0; n<nBarks; n++) printf("  %s\n", myBark);
}
```

```
/*
This <bark> uses a parameter for iteration.
------------------------------------------ */
void dog::bark(int nTimes)
{
  int n;
  printf("%s goes\n", myName);
  for (n=0; n<nTimes; n++) printf("  %s\n", myBark);
}
```

As before, resolution is by signature. Although the two signatures match on target object, they differ on parameters.

```
#include <stdio.h>
#include "dog.hpp"

int main()
{
  dog *Fifi = new dog;
  dog *Rex = new dog;

  Fifi->describe("Little dog");            // Invoke 2nd
  Rex->describe("Big dog", 3, "BOW WOW");  // Invoke 1st

  Fifi->bark(1);     // Invoke 2nd
  Rex->bark();       // Invoke 1st
  return 0;
}
```

The result of overloading **bark()** is seen in the output.

```
Fifi goes
  bow wow
Rex goes
  BOW WOW
  BOW WOW
  BOW WOW
```

Some programmers use overloading to create implicit get and set methods for private data. Most classes have private data, and often this data is accessed through methods. Typically one method is used to set some data and another used to read the data. The same method name can be overloaded to perform both of these functions. The method name *with* parameters sets the item, and the method name *without* parameters gets the item. For example, this definition of dog:

```
class dog {
public:
  void name(char *newName);    // Set name
  char *name();                // Read name
private:
  char myName[100];
};
```

and this code file:

```
#include <string.h>
#include "dog.hpp"

void dog::name(char *newName)    // Set version
{
  strcpy(myName, newName);
}
char *dog::name()                // Overloaded get version
{
  return myName;
}
```

is used by this client:

```
#include <stdio.h>
#include "dog.hpp"

int main()
{
  dog *myDog = new dog;
  myDog->name("Toto");
  printf("My name is %s\n", myDog->name());
}
```

which gives this output:

```
My name is Toto
```

8.3 Virtual Methods

Overloading sometimes gives unexpected results. Let's consider another example, a further modification of the **dog** classes. We will use this class lattice, similar to

some we have already seen

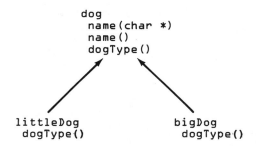

dog now looks like it did in the previous example, with another method, dogType(), which we plan on overloading in the derived classes.

Our dog definition file is

```
class dog {
public:
  void name(char *newName);
  char *name();
  void dogType();
private:
  char myName[100];
};
```

The dog implementation file has the new method dogType() added. It is set up to be a default, on the assumption that it will be redefined by derived classes littleDog and bigDog

```
#include <string.h>
#include <stdio.h>
#include "dog.hpp"

void dog::name(char *newName)
{
  strcpy(myName, newName);
}
char *dog::name()
{
  return myName;
}
```

```
void dog::dogType()
{
  printf("My type is unknown\n\n");
}
```

The `littleDog` definition files inherits everything from `dog`, including `dogType()` which it redefines

```
#include "dog.hpp"

class littleDog : public dog {
public:
  void dogType();
};
```

and the `littleDog` implementation file defines this method for `littleDogs`:

```
#include <stdio.h>
#include "ldog.hpp"

void littleDog::dogType()
{
  printf("My type is littleDog\n\n");
}
```

We define `bigDog` similarly

```
#include "dog.hpp"

class bigDog : public dog {
public:
  void dogType();
};
```

and again redefine `dogType()`

```
#include <stdio.h>
#include "bdog.hpp"

void bigDog::dogType()
{
  printf("My type is bigDog\n\n");
}
```

The following test program creates instances of `dog`, `littleDog`, and `bigDog`:

```
    #include <stdio.h>
    #include "bdog.hpp"
    #include "ldog.hpp"
    #include "dog.hpp"

    int main()
    {
      dog *Lassie = new dog;
      bigDog *RinTinTin = new bigDog;
      littleDog *Toto = new littleDog;

      Lassie->name("Lassie");
      RinTinTin->name("RinTinTin");
      Toto->name("Toto");

      printf("My name is: %s\n", Lassie->name());
      Lassie->dogType();

      printf("My name is %s\n", RinTinTin->name());
      RinTinTin->dogType();

      printf("My name is: %s\n", Toto->name());
      Toto->dogType();
      return 0;
    }
```

and the output looks exactly as we would expect

```
    My name is: Lassie
    My type is unknown

    My name is RinTinTin
    My type is bigDog

    My name is: Toto
    My type is littleDog
```

Notice that three different versions of **dogType()** are being called, controlled by the signatures of **dogType()** on the client side. This is all working just as we would expect.

Now let's make a slight change in the client program. We decide to eliminate some code repetition by creating a new function, **printDog()**, which takes a **dog** pointer and prints the dog's name and type. The new version of the client program looks like this

```
#include <stdio.h>
#include "bdog.hpp"
#include "ldog.hpp"
#include "dog.hpp"

printDog(dog *thisDog);        // Prototype for printDog

int main()
{
  dog *Lassie = new dog;
  bigDog *RinTinTin = new bigDog;
  littleDog *Toto = new littleDog;

  Lassie->name("Lassie");
  RinTinTin->name("RinTinTin");
  Toto->name("Toto");

  printDog(Lassie);
  printDog(Toto);
  printDog(RinTinTin);
  return 0;
}

printDog(dog *theDog)
{
  printf("My name is: %s\n", theDog->name());
  theDog->dogType();
}
```

But when we run this version, we no longer get

```
My name is: Lassie
My type is unknown

My name is RinTinTin
My type is bigDog

My name is Toto
My type is littleDog
```

Now our result is

```
My name is: Lassie
My type is unknown

My name is: Toto
My type is unknown

My name is: RinTinTin
My type is unknown
```

Suddenly the same `dogType()` is being invoked for all three objects. The problem is that the signature of `dogType()` on the client side is now the same regardless of whether the target object is `Toto`, `RinTinTin`, or `Lassie`.

We need a different kind of signature resolution, one which allows the type of the target object to be determined at run time, not compile time. This distinction is subtle, but very important. With standard method overloading, the method is resolved based on the declared type of the target object or pointer. We are looking for a way to resolve based on the actual run time type of the target object or pointer.

Remember, a pointer to a base type (say `dog`) can point to an object of either the base type or a derived type. We discussed this earlier in the `dogHouse` example. So a pointer to `dog` can point to a `dog`, a `littleDog`, or a `bigDog` object. We need a method resolution that checks the actual type of the object at run time, instead of assuming that because we are invoking through a `dog` pointer, the target object is necessarily of base type `dog`.

Virtual method resolution gives us the resolution we are looking for. When a base class defines one of its methods as *virtual*, the compiler uses a different method resolution, one which takes into account the run time type of the target object.

The virtual keyword is needed only in the base class definition. Any class derived from the base class which redefines the virtual method inherits the virtual characteristics.

We can see how this works by making one slight change in the `dog` header file

```
#ifndef DOG_CLASS
#define DOG_CLASS 1

class dog {
public:
  void name(char *newName);
  char *name();
  virtual void dogType();      // dogType is now virtual
```

```
private:
  char myName[100];
};
#endif
```

This is the only change needed to make **dogType** virtual. The **dog** method code file, the client file, and all of **littleDog** and **bigDog** are unchanged. Now our output looks like this

```
My name is: Lassie
My type is unknown

My name is: Toto
My type is littleDog

My name is: RinTinTin
My type is bigDog
```

Let's look once more at the mechanisms at play here, because the difference between virtual methods and overloaded methods, though not obvious, is very important. First, look carefully at **printDog()**:

```
printDog(dog *theDog)
{
  printf("My name is: %s\n", theDog->name());
  theDog->dogType();
}
```

Consider the resolution of **dogType()** when **printDog()** is invoked with **Toto**. When **dogType()** is nonvirtual, the resolution is done by simple signature. The signature of **dogType()** is

```
   method name: dogType
 target object: dog
     arguments: none
```

With **dogType()** now virtual, the class of the target object, **Toto**, is now checked at run time, and is allowed to be any class derived directly or indirectly from dog. The *run time* signature of **dogType** is

```
   method name: dogType
 target object: littleDog (derived from dog)
     arguments: none
```

The virtual method resolution then looks for a method named `dogType()` defined in the class `littleDog()`, and finds `littleDog::dogType()`.

When a base class defines a virtual method, and a derived class defines its own version of the virtual method, the derived class method is said to *override* the base class method.

The first important difference between virtual resolution and overload resolution is the time at which the resolution occurs. Virtual resolution occurs at run time, because only at run time can we know what object the pointer is actually pointing at. Overload resolution occurs at compile time, because the signature of the method can be fully determined at compile time. Therefore, we can expect virtual resolution to be slower at run time than overload resolution.

The second important different difference is the signature. When a method overrides a virtual method, the signatures must be the *same* with the exception of the type of the target object, which must be related through *is a* relationships. When a method name is overloaded, the method signatures must be *different*.

Derived classes are not required to redefine virtual methods. If they choose not to, they pick up the method as defined in the base class. So if we rewrite the `littleDog` class, removing the redefinition of `dogType()` as

```
#include "dog.hpp"
class littleDog : public dog {
public:
};
```

Then remove the method code from the implementation file, and recompile and rerun the last test program, we get a new result

```
My name is: Lassie
My type is unknown

My name is: Toto
My type is unknown

My name is: RinTinTin
My type is bigDog
```

`Toto`, who before had overridden `dog::dogType()` now uses `dog::dogType()` directly. Since the `bigDog` class still has a virtual `dogType()` to override the base class method, `RinTinTin` uses `bigDog` version.

Earlier we noted that a given method name can exist in multiple overloaded forms. The question now arises, if we have a virtual method in a base class, and several overloaded versions in the derived class, which one overrides?

The following simplified versions of **dog** and **littleDog** show how this could arise. First, look at the **dog** class, which defines two versions of **dogType()**, one of which is virtual. The class definition file for **dog**:

```
#ifndef DOG_CLASS
#define DOG_CLASS 1

class dog {
public:
  virtual void dogType();
  void dogType(char *mySpecies);
};
#endif
```

and the method code file

```
#include <stdio.h>
#include "dog.hpp"

void dog::dogType()
{
  printf("My type is Unknown\n");
}
void dog::dogType(char *mySpecies)
{
  printf("My type is Unknown... My species is %s\n", mySpecies);
}
```

Now for **littleDog**. The class definition file

```
#include "dog.hpp"

class littleDog : public dog {
public:
  void dogType();
  void dogType(char *mySpecies);
};
```

and the method code file

```
#include <stdio.h>
#include "ldog.hpp"
```

```
void littleDog::dogType()
{
  printf("My type is littleDog\n");
}
void littleDog::dogType(char *mySpecies)
{
  printf("Type is littleDog, species is %s\n", mySpecies);
}
```

Our client looks like

```
#include <stdio.h>
#include "dog.hpp"
#include "ldog.hpp"

printDog(dog *thisDog);      // Prototype for printDog
int main()
{
  littleDog *Toto = new littleDog;
  printDog(Toto);
  return 0;
}
printDog(dog *theDog)
{
  theDog->dogType();
  theDog->dogType("Unknown");
}
```

The function printDog() now invokes two different versions of dogType(). Both versions are defined in dog and littleDog. One of the dog versions is declared virtual. From looking at the littleDog definition, we can't tell which, if either, of littleDog::dogType() will take on the virtual characteristics.

When we run this program, we get the following output:

```
My type is littleDog
My type is Unknown... My species is Unknown
```

From this output we can see that the first invocation of dogType() invoked the littleDog version of the first form of dogType() (the one with no parameters). The second invocation of dogType() invoked the dog version of dogType(char *).

The first invocation clearly used the virtual mechanism. The second clearly used standard overloading, since it based its choice of dogType() on the type of the pointer, not the type of the target object.

As we can guess from this example, a virtual method in a base class is matched against a method with a similar signature in the derived class (with allowances made for the target object type). The signature of the virtual function in `dog` was

```
          method name: dogType
        target object: dog (which includes littleDogs)
   number of arguments: 0
```

There is only one form of `dogType()` in `littleDog` which has a matching signature, and it becomes the virtual method. The other form has no matching virtual declaration in the base class, and therefore, becomes a nonvirtual method. If no method in the derived class matched the signature of the virtual `dog::dogType()`, then we would have no overriding, similar to what we saw earlier with `littleDog`.

The use of virtual methods can lead to confusing situations. Remember, there is no way a derived class can tell which of its methods are virtual. Even worse, you can take a method which had been virtual, make a slight signature change, and suddenly end up with a nonvirtual method.

Changing the signature of a method is quite easy, in fact, much too easy. A signature change occurs when a parameter is added or deleted, or even when one of the parameters simply changes its type. There is not much you can do to protect yourself against losing the virtual characteristic of a method outside of always checking the signatures of methods you expect to be virtual, and being especially wary of making any changes which alter a method signature.

8.4 Using Virtual Methods

Virtual methods are frequently used to provide for class customization. When building a class, the class designer should be trying to think of which characteristics of a class might be changed in derived classes. These characteristics can then be embedded inside virtual methods, and can be overridden as appropriate in latter class derivations.

As an example of this technique, let's look again at the book ordering program of the last two chapters. This program used two classes, `Order` and `LineItem`. The `Order` class contained one method for entering the order and another for printing the order. We discussed the changes a store might make to track salespeople and include a trailing advertisement on the order printout.

We accomplished these changes by deriving a new class from `Order` called `Order2` which added two new methods and one new data member to those derived from `Order`. The data member was the string `SalesPerson`. The methods were `SetSalesPerson()` and `DisplayFooter()`. The bookstore C++ programmer then modified the main program in two ways. First, the class used was changed to the newly derived class. Second, invocations of the newly defined methods were inserted at the appropriate places.

Deriving the new class was easy enough. The new class definition looked like

```
#include "order.hpp"
class Order2 : public Order {
public:
  void SetSalesPerson();
  void DisplayFooter();
private:
  char salesPerson[100];
};
```

Modifying the program was not difficult either. The new version looked like

```
#include <stdio.h>
#include "order2.hpp"

int main()
{
  Order2 *op = new Order2();    // Changed from Order
  op->InitOrder();
  op->SetSalesPerson();         // Added
  op->EnterOrder();
  op->DisplayOrder();
  op->DisplayFooter();          // Added
  return 0;
}
```

A good class designer could have foreseen these changes, not in their exact final form, but as typical adaptations a store might want to make in the program. The designer could have assumed that a store might want to include some store specific information in the order, and that the store might want special information included on the printout.

The virtual mechanism allows the class designer to invoke a concept rather than a specific method. In this case, the class designer can invoke the concept of initializing store specific information and the concept of including store specific printings even without knowing what form these concepts will eventually take.

Let's see how the class designer can define the Order class, taking into account these possible changes. The original version looked like this

```
#ifndef OrderClass
#define OrderClass 1
#include "1_item.hpp"
```

```
class Order {
public:
  void InitOrder();
  void EnterOrder();
  void DisplayOrder();
  int CostOfOrder();
  float TaxRate();
private:
  /* ... */
};
#endif
```

Now two new virtual methods are added

```
#ifndef OrderClass
#define OrderClass 1
#include "l_item.hpp"

class Order {
public:
  void InitOrder();
  void EnterOrder();
  void DisplayOrder();
  int CostOfOrder();
  float TaxRate();
  virtual void InitStoreInfo();      // Store will overload
  virtual void DisplayFooter();      // Store will overload
private:
  /* ... */
};
#endif
```

The class designer then implements default versions of these methods. In this case, these default versions might be quite trivial

```
void Order::InitStoreInfo()
{
}
void Order::DisplayFooter()
{
}
```

Appropriate invocations to these virtual methods are added wherever appropriate. We might, for example, decide that initializing store information is part of initializing the store order, in which case we modify `InitOrder()`:

```
void Order::InitOrder()
{
  nItems = 0;
  subtotal = 0;
  tax = 0;
  total = 0;
  InitStoreInfo();      // Initialize store specific information,
                        // if any.

}
```

Printing store specific information seems to belong logically within `DisplayOrder()`, so it gets one new line added at the end

```
void Order::DisplayOrder()
{
/* Local Declarations.
   ------------------ */
    int n;
    LineItem *lip;    // Line Item Pointer.
    int change;

/* Print name and address.
   ---------------------- */
    printf("\n*******************************\n");
    printf("%s\n", name);
    printf("%s\n", address);

/* Print Line Items.
   ---------------- */
    DisplayLineItemHeading();
    for (n=0; n<nItems; n++) {
      lip = Item[n];
      lip->DisplayLineItem();
    }
/* Display Payment Information.
   -------------------------- */
    printf("\n********************************************\n");
    printf("  Subtotal: %10s\n", CentsToDollars(subtotal));
    printf("       Tax: %10s\n", CentsToDollars(tax));
```

```
      printf("     Total: %10s\n", CentsToDollars(total));
      printf("*********************************************\n");
      printf("   Payment: %10s\n", CentsToDollars(payment));
      change = -(total-payment);
      printf("Change Due: %10s\n", CentsToDollars(change));

  /* Display store specific information, if any.
     ------------------------------------------- */
      DisplayFooter();
  }
```

The client can then derive from this class much as they did before. Now, however, the client must use agreed on conventions for the concept of initializing store information and printing store specific footers. So where as before the derived class looked like this

```
  #ifndef ORDER2_CLASS
  #define ORDER2_CLASS 1
  #include "order.hpp"

  class Order2 : public Order {
  public:
    void SetSalesPerson();
    void DisplayFooter();
  private:
    char salesPerson[100];
  };
  #endif
```

now it looks like this

```
  #ifndef ORDER2_CLASS
  #define ORDER2_CLASS 1
  #include "order.hpp"

  class Order2 : public Order {
  public:
    void InitStoreInfo();    // Conform to virtual definition
    void DisplayFooter();    // Already conformed.
  private:
    char salesPerson[100];
  };
  #endif
```

Other than changing the method name `SetSalesPerson()` to `InitStoreInfo()`, the code for the new class is unchanged

```
#include <stdio.h>
#include "order2.hpp"
#include "helper.hpp"

void Order2::InitStoreInfo()
{
  PromptForString("What is your name? ", salesPerson);
}
void Order2::DisplayFooter()
{
  printf("\n\n");
  printf("Your sales person was %s, ", salesPerson);
  printf("and we appreciate your business\n");
  printf("***********************************************\n");
  printf("Have you seen the latest work, Romeo and Juliet\n");
  printf("by that new playwrite William Shakespeare?\n\n");
  printf("The New York Times has praised this play as\n");
  printf(
      "\"...an interesting concept ... engaging dialogue\"\n\n");
  printf(
      "Please stop by our drama section and examine this work.\n");
}
```

So far the virtual mechanism has not made much of a difference. The store modifications have required the same work both with and without virtual methods. Now, however, is when the payoff occurs. Without virtual methods, the store programmer had to locate each section of code where `InitStoreInfo()` and `DisplayFooter()` needed to be invoked. With virtual methods, the provider of the `Order` class has already done this work. The store programmer makes only one change to the main program: changing the class of the order pointer (`op`) from `Order` to `Order2`.

```
#include <stdio.h>
#include "order2.hpp"
```

```
int main()
{
  Order2 *op = new Order2();
  op->InitOrder();
  op->EnterOrder();
  op->DisplayOrder();
  return 0;
}
```

Admittedly, this has saved the store programmer only two lines of code, and the location of those lines was fairly obvious. But suppose the **main** program had been coded slightly differently, say

```
#include <stdio.h>
#include "order.hpp"

processOrder(Order *nextOrder);
int main()
{
  Order *op = new Order();
  processOrder(op);
  return 0;
}
```

with `processOrder()` in a separate file, whose source may or may not be distributed:

```
#include "order.hpp"
processOrder(Order *nextOrder)
{
  nextOrder->InitOrder();
  nextOrder->EnterOrder();
  nextOrder->DisplayOrder();
}
```

This is a more likely scenario. If **Order** did not use virtual methods, the store programmer will now have much more difficulty locating the areas needing changing, and if the source for `processOrder()` is not included in the package, the changes will not even be possible.

If **Order** was coding using the virtual methods, only the main program needs changing

```
#include <stdio.h>
#include "order2.hpp"              // Used to include order.hpp
```

```
processOrder(Order *nextOrder);
int main()
{
    Order2 *op = new Order2();      // op used to point to an Order
    processOrder(op);
    return 0;
}
```

Just to make sure the virtual mechanism is clear, let's walk through the programming flow as `processOrder()` is invoked. `processOrder()` is a regular function, not a member method of any class. Its parameter is a pointer to an `Order` object. A pointer to an `Order` can legally point not only to an `Order` object, but to an object of any class derived, directly or indirectly, from the `Order` class. We say that an object of a class derived from `Order` is also an `Order`, just as a `littleDog` is also a `dog`.

Knowing that the parameter is an `Order` gives us only incomplete information about the class of the object. The true nature of the object can only be determined at run time.

Regardless of what the class of the parameter eventually turns out to be, we know it supports the `InitOrder()`, because we know the parameter is an object of some class derived from `Order`, and therefore, inherits the method. So `processOrder()` invokes the `InitOrder()` method which initializes some data items, and then invokes `InitStoreInfo()`, a virtual method. Because `InitStoreInfo()` is virtual, we expect many possible versions of the method, each corresponding to one of the classes which might be derived, directly or indirectly from `Order`.

As the software was distributed, the target object is an `Order` and `InitStoreInfo()` resolves to `Order::InitStoreInfo()`, which does nothing. If the store programmer has modified the main program as we discussed, then the target object will be an `Order2`, in which case `InitStoreInfo()` resolves to `Order2::InitStoreInfo()`. The `Order2` version sets another data member, the `salesPerson` string. This data member isn't even part of the `Order` class. It is part of the definition of `Order2`.

The same process results in the appropriate `DisplayFooter()` being invoked, either a do nothing version, for an `Order`, or a store defined version, for an `Order2`. The program flow is left as an exercise.

8.5   Abstract Classes

It is often useful in C++ to design a class that has nothing but virtual methods. Frequently this class is never instantiated, but used only as a base for further class derivation. Such a class is called an *abstract class*. An abstract class is usually used to define a framework on which further class development proceeds.

As usual, virtual methods in an abstract class are overridden in any derived classes. The virtual methods typically define application specific code, allowing generic code to be written which can manipulate any object of a class derived from the abstract class.

Let's consider the problem of rewriting in C++ the C version of the linked list class shown in Chapter 4. The linked list allowed programmers to manipulate any type of object. The linked list imposed one requirement on the manipulated class. The class had to define a `match()` method. And not just any `match()` method, but a very specific `match()` function. Let's look at where this requirement originated.

The `match()` method is used by the linked list method `ll_find()`, whose purpose is to scan a linked list and find a specific target. The method `ll_find()` is general, and part of a body of code that works for a variety of classes. `ll_find()` has no way of knowing if its target is a `physician`, `patient`, or `dog`. Therefore, it has no way to know if the target should be checked against a `physician->emp_id`, a `patient->name`, or a `dog->breed`, and therefore, defers this judgment to a client identified `match()` function. The code for `ll_find()` looks like

```
int ll_find(linked_list * pll, void *lookfor)
{
    ll_head(pll);
    for (;;) {
      if ((*pll->match)(pll->pcl->pcontents, lookfor)) return 1;
      if (ll_istail(pll)) return 0;
      ll_next(pll);
    }
}
```

The address of the client identified `match()` function is contained in `pll->match`. The data member `match` is part of the linked list structure defined as

```
struct linked_list_type {
  link *pcl;
  link *phead;
  link *ptail;
  int listlength;
  int (*match)();    /* Pointer to match function */
};
typedef struct linked_list_type linked_list;
```

and is initialized by the client when this method is invoked

```
void *ll_new(int (*newmatch)())
{
  linked_list *this;
  this = malloc(sizeof(linked_list));
  this->pcl = this->phead= this->ptail = 0;
  this->listlength = 0;
  this->match = newmatch;
  return (void *) this;
}
```

Although `ll_new()` looks complex, from a client perspective, it is not difficult to use. It takes only one parameter, the name of the match method defined in the manipulated class. If the manipulated class is **patient**, the invocation might look like this

```
#include "ll.h"
#include "patient.h"
int main()
{
    pat_list =
      (linked_list *) ll_new(patient_match);
```

The match definition requirements stem from this line in `ll_find()`

```
if ((*pll->match)(pll->pcl->pcontents, lookfor))
return 1;
```

`ll_find()` makes several assumptions about the **match()** method. The method will take two parameters. The first parameter will be a pointer to the object being checked. The second parameter will be a pointer to some undefined memory block defining the target. The **match()** method will return 1 if the target matches the object. The **match()** method will return 0 otherwise. If all of these requirements are met, the **match()** method is compatible. If any of these requirements are not, the offending **match()** will cause `ll_find()` to fail.

We can abstractly define the type of class our C linked list can contain. We expect the manipulated class to provide a **match()** method which follows a strict protocol. We could similarly require a **print()** method and a **copy()** method.

Whatever methods are eventually used, we end up with a set of methods, each with a defined protocol, which must be provided by any class which might someday find itself placed in our linked list. We can call this set of methods an abstract definition of any linked list manipulatable class.

In C++, we can carry this concept further. We have discussed class hierarchy discovery through seeking class intersections. The intersection of two classes is removed from both classes, and placed in a base class from which the two original classes become derived. Since every linked list manipulatable class must support the set of methods the linked list class expects, we see that this set of methods is a class intersection of all manipulatable classes. Logic dictates this intersection can be removed and formed into a base class. Since this base class is the abstract definition of a manipulatable class, we call this an *abstract base class*.

An abstract base class has one peculiar characteristic: it is never directly instantiated. Only classes derived from it are instantiated. This makes sense when we consider the base class necessarily defines only protocols. It does not define how those protocols are to be implemented. In fact, it cannot define any implementations. If it did, it would no longer represent the class intersection of all manipulatable classes.

Let's consider an abstract base class definition. The class `baseType` defines methods which are expected from all classes, but whose implementation will vary. The `match()` method is one example of such a class specific method. The definition of `baseType` looks like

```
#ifndef BASETYPE_CLASS
#define BASETYPE_CLASS 1
#include <stdio.h>

class baseType {
public:
  virtual int match(void *target) = 0;
  virtual void print(FILE *output) = 0;
  virtual void replace(baseType *dest) = 0;
  virtual baseType *newCopy() = 0;
};
#endif
```

Notice we are using a slightly different syntax in defining the methods. Until now we have been using the syntax

```
class baseType {
public:
  virtual int match(void *target);
  /* ... */
};
```

whereas the syntax here is

```
class baseType {
public:
  virtual int match(void *target) = 0;
  /* ... */
};
```

Setting a virtual method equal to 0 tells C++ that the method is not going to be implemented in this class, but will instead be coded in derived classes. If we had not set `match()` to 0, then C++ would expect code for `match()` to exist in the `baseType` class. A virtual method which is prototyped but not coded is called a *pure virtual method.*

The existence of a pure virtual method in a class tells us something about the characteristics of the class. First, we cannot instantiate objects of such a class. If we could, we would have an object with a valid method prototyped, but no corresponding executable code. Second, any derived classes which will have instantiated objects *must* override all pure virtual methods declared in the base class. If they do not override the pure virtual methods, they will be unable to instantiate for the same reason the base class cannot instantiate.

Thus, the use of pure virtual methods ensures that first, we will not attempt to instantiate such a class, and second, we will define the necessary methods in any derived classes. Formally an *abstract class* can be defined as a class containing at least one pure virtual method.

The abstract class serves an important function in C++. It allows highly generic code to be written which deals with a variety of classes, knowing nothing about those classes except that they are derived, directly or indirectly, from some specific abstract class. For example, we can rewrite the linked list class in C++ so that it can be used to manipulate any class, as long as that class is derived from the `baseType` class.

The linked list definition looks like this

```
#ifndef LINKED_LIST_CLASS
#define LINKED_LIST_CLASS 1
#include <stdio.h>
#include "link.hpp"
#include "bt.hpp"

class linkedList {
public:
  void init();
  void head();
  void tail();
  int isTail();
  int isHead();
  void next();
  void previous();
  baseType *retrieve();
  void addHead(baseType *newElement);
  void promote();
```

```
      void replace(baseType *newElement);
      int find(void *findme);
      void addTail(baseType *newElement);
      int length();
      void remove();
      void print(FILE *output);
  private:
      link *pcl;         // Pointer to current link.
      link *phead;       // Pointer to head of list.
      link *ptail;       // Pointer to tail of list.
      int listLength;    // Number of links in list.
  };
  #endif
```

The definition of a link is also changed. Instead of being a structure, we make it a class. More substantively, instead of containing a pointer to **void**, it now contains a pointer to a **baseType**.

```
  #ifndef LINK_CLASS
  #define LINK_CLASS 1
  #include "bt.hpp"

  class link {
  public:
    link *pnext;
    link *pprevious;
    baseType *pcontents;
  };
  #endif
```

The overall functionality of the various linked list members should be clear from reviewing the C version of the linked list described in Chapter 4. The translation of most of the methods from C to C++ should also be fairly obvious. The only translations that are conceptually different are those impacted by the assumption that the stored class is one derived from **baseType**. These methods are

```
      baseType *retrieve();
      void addHead(baseType *newElement);
      void replace(baseType *newElement);
      int find(void *findme);
      void addTail(baseType *newElement);
      void print(FILE *output);
```

All but two of these methods are impacted only in that they now use **baseType *** instead of **void ***. The other two are **find()** and **print()**, both of which need to invoke class specific methods for classes they know nothing about except that the classes are derived from **baseType**.

Let's first consider **find()**, whose purpose is to find the link containing a particular item. Its code looks like

```
int linkedList::find(void *lookfor)
{
/* Initialize.
   ----------- */
   baseType *nextElement;
   head();

/* Loop through the list.
   ---------------------- */
   for (;;) {
     nextElement = pcl->pcontents;

/*   See if this link contains the desired item.
     ------------------------------------------- */
     if (nextElement->match(lookfor)) return 1;

/*   If we are at the end, the item must not be here.
     ------------------------------------------------ */
     if (isTail()) return 0;

/*   Prepare to check next link.
     --------------------------- */
     next();
   }
}
```

The most interesting lines are these

```
baseType *nextElement;
nextElement = pcl->pcontents;
if (nextElement->match(lookfor)) return 1;
```

which, between them, demonstrate the power of the abstract base class. Let's look at these lines one by one.

The first is

```
baseType *nextElement;
```

which just declares a local variable, a pointer to a **baseType**.

The second is

```
nextElement = pcl->pcontents;
```

which assigns to this local variable the address of the item contained in the current link. We don't know anything about this item other than it is some class derived from `baseType`. Because a pointer to a class can point to either an object of that class, or to an object of some derived class, this assignment is legal.

The third is

```
if (nextElement->match(lookfor)) return 1;
```

which invokes `baseType::match()` on the object pointed to by `nextElement`. However the class `baseType` defined `match()` to be virtual (also, incidentally, pure virtual) therefore, virtual method resolution is used. The actual class of the object pointed to by `nextElement` is checked. An overriding `match()` method is looked for in that class, and that becomes the `match()` method invoked. The fact that such a method is really defined is guaranteed by the definition of `match()` as a pure virtual method in `baseType`.

This same mechanism is used in the linked list method `print()`, which walks through the linked list printing out each item stored in each link. It knows only that these items are of some class derived from `baseType`. By necessity, any such class must override `baseType::print()` with a method which presumably prints out an object of that class in some intelligible format.

```
void linkedList::print(FILE *output)
{
  int n;
  int nend;
  baseType *nextElement;
  nend = length();
  head();
  for (n=1; n<=nend; n++) {
    nextElement = retrieve();
    nextElement->print(output);
    next();
  }
}
```

Having written the linked list to accept objects of classes derived from `baseType`, let's look at a few such objects. Going back to the HMO program of Chapter 4, we will recreate the `physician` and `patient` classes, making them derived from `baseType`, and thus manipulatable by our linked list. First, the `physician` class definition.

```
#ifndef PHYSICIAN_CLASS
#define PHYSICIAN_CLASS 1
#include <stdio.h>
#include "bt.hpp"               // Base Type Definition

class physician : public baseType {
public:

/* Virtual overrides of baseType.
   --------------------------- */
   int match (void *target);       // Match by id.
   void replace(baseType *source);
   void print(FILE *output);
   baseType *newCopy();

/* New methods specific for physician.
   --------------------------------- */
   void getInfo();
   int matchSpeciality (void *target);

private:
   char empID[10];
   char name[80];
   char specialty[2];
};
#endif
```

Notice a few details about this class definition. First, the class is derived from **baseType**, so it is compatible with our linked list. Second, all of the pure virtual methods of **baseType** are overridden in this class so this class can be instantiated. Third, there is no way to tell from this definition (except from comments) that the first four methods are virtual. The virtual characteristic is discernible only by examining the base class definition.

The code file for physician contains nothing unexpected. It looks like

```
#include <stdio.h>
#include <string.h>
#include "phys.hpp"
#include "helper.h"
```

```
int physician::match(void *target)
{
  return (!strcmp(empID, target));
}


void physician::replace(baseType *source)
{
  physician *physSrc = (physician *) source;
  strcpy(empID, physSrc->empID);
  strcpy(name, physSrc->name);
  strcpy(specialty, physSrc->specialty);
}


void physician::print(FILE *output)
{
  fprintf
  (output,"-----------------------------------------------\n");
  fprintf(output, "      Physician ID: %s\n", empID);
  fprintf(output, "    Physician Name: %s\n", name);
  fprintf(output, "Assigned Specialty: %s\n", specialty);
}


baseType *physician::newCopy()
{
  physician *newPhysician = new physician();
  newPhysician->replace(this);
  return newPhysician;
}


void physician::getInfo()
{
  printf("  Physician ID: "); get_line(empID);
  printf("Physician Name: "); get_line(name);
  printf("      Specialty: "); get_line(specialty);
}


int physician::matchSpeciality(void *target)
{
  return (!strcmp(specialty, target));
}
```

We can now test our **physician** and **linkedList** class with programs such as this

```
#include <stdio.h>
#include "phys.hpp"
#include "ll.hpp"
#include "helper.h"
int main()
{
  linkedList *plist = new linkedList;
  physician *pp;

  plist->init();
  pp = new physician;
  pp->getInfo();
  plist->addHead(pp);

  pp = new physician;
  pp->getInfo();
  plist->addHead(pp);
  plist->print(stdout);

  if (plist->find("2")) {
     printf("found\n");
  }
  else printf ("not found\n");
  return 0;
}
```

The **patient** class follows the same pattern. The definition looks like

```
#ifndef PATIENT_CLASS
#define PATIENT_CLASS 1
#include <stdio.h>
#include "bt.hpp"                // Base Type Definition

class patient : public baseType {
public:
  int match(void *target);
  void replace(baseType *source);
  void print(FILE *output);
  baseType *newCopy();
  void getInfo();
```

```
    private:
      char name[80];
      char ssn[15];
      char symptoms[100];
      char specialty[2];
    };
    #endif
```

and the code looks like

```
    #include <stdio.h>
    #include <string.h>
    #include "patient.hpp"
    #include "helper.h"

    int patient::match(void *target)
    {
      return (!strcmp(ssn, target));
    }


    void patient::replace(baseType *source)
    {
      patient *patSrc = (patient *) source;
      strcpy(name, patSrc->name);
      strcpy(ssn, patSrc->ssn);
      strcpy(symptoms, patSrc->symptoms);
      strcpy(specialty, patSrc->specialty);
    }


    void patient::print(FILE *output)
    {
      fprintf
      (output, "---------------------------------------------\n");
      fprintf(output, "      Patient Name: %s\n", name);
      fprintf(output, "       Patient SSN: %s\n", ssn);
      fprintf(output, "  Patient Symptoms: %s\n", symptoms);
      fprintf(output, "Assigned Specialty: %s\n", specialty);
    }
```

```
baseType *patient::newCopy()
{
  patient *newPatient = new patient();
  newPatient->replace(this);
  return newPatient;
}


void patient::getInfo()
{
  printf("        Patient Name: "); get_line(name);
  printf("         Patient SSN: "); get_line(ssn);
  printf("    Patient Symptoms: "); get_line(symptoms);
  printf("Assigned Specialty: "); get_line(specialty);
}
```

We can even put both **physician** and **patient** objects in the same linked list. For example, this program

```
#include <stdio.h>
#include "phys.hpp"
#include "patient.hpp"
#include "ll.hpp"
#include "helper.h"
int main()
{
  linkedList *plist = new linkedList;
  physician *pp;
  patient *patientp;

  plist->init();

  pp = new physician;
  pp->getInfo();
  plist->addHead(pp);

  pp = new physician;
  pp->getInfo();
  plist->addHead(pp);

  patientp = new patient;
  patientp->getInfo();
  plist->addHead(patientp);
```

```
    patientp = new patient;
    patientp->getInfo();
    plist->addHead(patientp);

    plist->print(stdout);
    return 0;
}
```

If we run this program and insert the physicians Pierce and Casey, and the patients Hamlet and Socrates, we get the following printed:

```
      Patient Name: Socrates
       Patient SSN: 2222
  Patient Symptoms: Seems to have drunk too much of something.
Assigned Specialty: G
------------------------------------------
      Patient Name: Hamlet
       Patient SSN: 1234
  Patient Symptoms: Stab Wound
Assigned Specialty: G
------------------------------------------
      Physician ID: 2222
    Physician Name: Casey
Assigned Specialty: I
------------------------------------------
      Physician ID: 1111
    Physician Name: Pierce
Assigned Specialty: G
```

We can see the virtual mechanism at work here. The method linkedList::print() is running through the list invoking the virtual baseType::print() on each element. When the element is a pointer to a physician, physician::print() is invoked. When the element is a patient, patient::print() is invoked.

Although we can legally place both patients and physicians in the same list, our linked list method find() does not handle such a case well. For example, an invocation to locate physician cases in the above list would look like

```
    plist->find("2222")
```

However, this would unexpectedly locate the patient Socrates, since its match() also returns true with the string "2222."

8.6   C++ Version of Linked List

For completeness, we will show the remaining C++ linked list method implementation here. They should all be readily interpretable by comparison with their C analogs in Chapter 4.

```
#include <stdio.h>
#include "ll.hpp"

void linkedList::init()
{
   pcl = phead = ptail = 0;
   listLength = 0;
}


void linkedList::head()
{
   pcl = phead;
}


void linkedList::tail()
{
   pcl = ptail;
}


int linkedList::isTail()
{
   return (pcl == ptail);
}


int linkedList::isHead()
{
  return (pcl == phead);
}


void linkedList::next()
{
   if (!isTail()) pcl = pcl->pnext;
}
```

```
void linkedList::previous()
{
   if (!isHead()) pcl = pcl->pprevious;
}


baseType *linkedList::retrieve()
{
   return pcl->pcontents;
}


void linkedList::addHead(baseType* newElement)
{
/* Set up new link.
   --------------- */
   link *newLink = new link;
   newLink->pcontents = newElement;
   listLength++;

/* Check for special case of first time call.
   ---------------------------------------- */
   if (listLength == 1) {
       phead = ptail = pcl = newLink;
       newLink->pnext = newLink->pprevious = 0;
       return;
   }

/* Handle general case.
   ------------------- */
   phead->pprevious = newLink;
   newLink->pnext = phead;
   newLink->pprevious = 0;
   phead = pcl = newLink;
   return;
}
```

```
void linkedList::promote()
{
/* Special case: current link is head, then nothing to do.
   ------------------------------------------------------- */
   if (isHead()) return;

/* If this is the tail, back up the tail to previous link.
   ------------------------------------------------------- */
   if (isTail()) ptail = ptail->pprevious;

/* Promote current to head.
   ----------------------- */
   pcl->pprevious->pnext = pcl->pnext;
   pcl->pnext->pprevious = pcl->pprevious;
   pcl->pnext = phead;
   pcl->pprevious = 0;
   phead->pprevious = pcl;
   phead = pcl;
   return;
}


void linkedList::replace(baseType *newElement)
{
   pcl->pcontents = newElement;
}


void linkedList::addTail(baseType *newElement)
{
/* Set up new link.
   ---------------- */
   link *newLink = new link;
   newLink->pcontents = newElement;
   listLength++;
```

```
/* Check for special case of first time call.
   ----------------------------------------- */
   if (listLength == 1) {
      phead = ptail = pcl = newLink;
      newLink->pnext = newLink->pprevious = 0;
      return;
   }
/* Handle general case.
   -------------------- */
   ptail->pnext = newLink;
   newLink->pprevious = ptail;
   newLink->pnext = 0;
   ptail = pcl = newLink;
   return;
}


int linkedList::length()
{
   return listLength;
}


void linkedList::remove()
{
/* General activity.
   ----------------- */
   link *plink = pcl;            /* Link to remove. */
   if (length() < 1) return;     /* Error check. */
   listLength--;                 /* Decrement link count. */

/* Special case: only one link.
   --------------------------- */
   if (length() == 0) {
      pcl = phead = ptail = 0;
   }
/* If this is the tail, back up the tail to previous link.
   ----------------------------------------------------- */
   if (isTail()) ptail = ptail->pprevious;

/* If this is the head, move head up to next link.
   --------------------------------------------- */
   if (isHead()) phead = phead->pnext;
```

```
/* Excise current link.
   ------------------- */
   if (pcl->pprevious)
       pcl->pprevious->pnext = pcl->pnext;
   if (pcl->pnext)
       pcl->pnext->pprevious = pcl->pprevious;

/* Reset current link and delete.
   ---------------------------- */
   if (pcl->pnext) pcl = pcl->pnext;
   else pcl = pcl->pprevious;
   delete plink;
   return;
}
```

8.7   Exercises

Exercise 8.1 Given this definition of dog

```
class dog{
public:
  /* ... */
private:
  char myName[100];
  char myBark[100];
};
```

add two init() methods. The first takes one parameter, a new name, and uses a default bark. The second takes two parameters, a new name and a new bark. Add code and create a test program.

Exercise 8.2 To the dog definition in Exercise 1, add a third init(). This takes a new bark and initializes using a default name. Modify your test program to make use of the new init(). Observe what happens to your dog class and explain your observations.

Exercise 8.3 Define, code, and test the following class lattice:

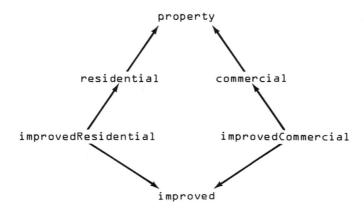

All properties have a base tax which will change in time. A residential property is taxed at the base rate. A commercial property is taxed at 1.2 times the base rate. An improved property is taxed at 1.2 times the rate of the same property unimproved. Write a function (not method) which takes a pointer to any property and calculates a property tax. Write another function (not method) which can be called by any property to find out the current base tax.

Exercise 8.4 In the newly modified version of the book store program, discuss the program flow which allows the proper version of `DisplayFooter()` to be invoked.

Exercise 8.5 Earlier we rewrote `patient` and `physician` to be derived classes from `baseType`. We then looked at a test program which included these lines

```
pp->getInfo();
plist->print(stdout);
patientp->getInfo();
```

Explain which of these invocations uses virtual resolution, and which overload resolution. Justify your answer.

For we brought nothing into this world, and it is
certain we can carry nothing out.

- 1 Timothy 6:7

Chapter 9

Managing Memory

In the C versions of our classes, we typically wrote allocation and construction methods for each class. A C **dog** class, for example, might look like

```
/* Data Portion.
   ------------- */
struct dogType {
  char myNoise[100];
};
typedef struct dogType dog;

/* Method portion.
   --------------- */
dog *dogNew();   /* dog allocator */
void dogConstr(dog *thisDog, char *newNoise);
                /* dog constructor */
void dogSpeak(dog *thisDog);
                /* Ask dog object to speak. */
```

As we discussed earlier, a method whose purpose is to initialize memory is called a *constructor*. A method whose purpose is final cleanup before memory release is called a *destructor*. Because constructors are so intimately associated with memory allocation, and because of a somewhat misleading name, many programmers assume that constructors allocate memory. This is incorrect. Constructors deal only with allocated memory.

The C version of the **dog** allocator, constructor, and deallocator might look like

```
dog *dogNew()                          /* Allocator   */
{
  return malloc(sizeof(dog));
}
                                       /* Constructor */
void dogConstr(dog *thisDog, char *newNoise)
{
  strcpy(thisDog->myNoise, newNoise);
}
void dogFree(dog *thisDog)             /* Deallocator */
{
  free (thisDog);
}
```

Since this class has no need for cleanup, it defines no destructor.

9.1 Default Memory Management in C++

In C++, it is unnecessary to write such simple common methods. The language automatically provides default allocator, constructor, destructor, and deallocators for each class. Writing this same dog class definition in C++ is as simple as

```
class dog {
public:
  void init(char *newNoise);
  void speak();
private:
  char myNoise[100];
};
```

With the exception of the class and object identification syntax, the C++ implementations look similar to what you would expect of their C counterparts

```
#include <stdio.h>
#include <string.h>
#include "dog.hpp"

void dog::init(char *newNoise)
{
    strcpy(myNoise, newNoise);
}
```

```
void dog::speak()
{
    printf("%s\n", myNoise);
}
```

But we can easily get into trouble using such a simple class definition. The following program, for example, unexpectedly prints a string of garbage characters:

```
#include "dog.hpp"
int main()
{
    dog *myDog = new dog;
    myDog->speak();
}
```

This program has erred in forgetting to invoke `dog::init()`. Our class definition, however, is also at fault in being so unforgiving of this easily made error. The problem occurs because the default constructor initializes none of the allocated memory, one reason the default constructor is rarely useful in practice. Most classes will need to overwrite the constructor, which is done by defining a method named with the name of the class. The simplest version of this method takes no parameters. All constructors return pointers to objects of their class. The return value is implicit and not declared. For the **dog** class, the parameter is **dog()**. We declare a **dog** constructor like this

```
class dog {
public:
    dog();                              // Constructor declaration
    void init(char *newNoise);
    void speak();
private:
    char myNoise[100];
};
```

The code file looks the same, with this addition

```
dog::dog()        // Constructor
{
    strcpy(myNoise, "Generic Dog Noise");
}
```

Our test program,

```
#include "dog.hpp"
int main()
{
    dog *myDog = new dog;
    myDog->speak();
}
```

may still not perform as we expect, but at least we now get an interpretable message:

```
Generic Dog Noise
```

We can also define constructors which do take parameters. In fact, we can define any number of constructors through the standard mechanism of overloading. As we have already discussed, we can overload any C++ method, as long as each overloaded version has a unique signature. This is also true for constructors. A constructor is identified as such by having a name which matches the name of the class. As a constructor, it must have no return type defined (not even **void**). Within these constraints, you may use any parameters you wish.

An obvious change to our **dog** class is to remove the **init()** method and replace it by a second constructor. With this change, our **dog** header file becomes

```
class dog {
public:
  dog();                    // Default constructor
  dog(char *newNoise);  // Constructor given a noise
  void speak();
private:
  char myNoise[100];
};
```

The **dog** code file now contains two constructors

```
dog::dog()
{
  printf("Constructing new dog with generic noise\n");
  strcpy(myNoise, "Generic Dog Noise");
}
dog::dog(char *newNoise)
{
    printf("Constructing new dog with noise: %s\n", newNoise);
    strcpy(myNoise, newNoise);
}
```

Print statements in the constructors allow us to observe program flow. This program uses both constructors

```
#include "dog.hpp"
int main()
{
                        // Construct generic dog
    dog *littleDog = new dog;
                        // Construct dog with noise
    dog *bigDog = new dog("Woof");

    littleDog->speak();
    bigDog->speak();
}
```

The first two lines of program output show the two different constructors in use.

```
Constructing new dog with generic noise
Constructing new dog with noise: Woof
```

The second two lines show the results of the different style of **dog** initialization.

```
Generic Dog Noise
Woof
```

As discussed earlier, a programmer can obtain memory for an object in one of two ways. The programmer can either define an object or can define a pointer to an object. In the former, the compiler statically allocates the necessary memory. In the latter, the programmer dynamically allocates the needed memory, with **malloc()**, for C classes, or **new**, for C++ classes.

A C program might look like

```
/* ... */
dog realDog;                    /* Object */
dog *pointerToDog = dogNew();   /* Pointer to object */
/* ... */
```

While the equivalent C++ program looks like

```
// ...
dog realDog;                    // Object
dog *pointerToDog = new dog;    // Pointer to object
// ...
```

An object, like any variable, has an associated scope. An object's scope is the time period during which the object can be thought of as existing. A given object, or variable, is said to *come into scope* when that time period begins, and to *go out of scope* when that time period ends. When the object memory is under the control of the C++ compiler, such as **realDog**, the compiler will automatically invoke the constructor as the object comes into scope, as shown by this program

```
#include "dog.hpp"
int main()
{
    dog littleDog;
    dog bigDog("Woof");

    littleDog.speak();
    bigDog.speak();
}
```

which gives this output

```
Constructing new dog with generic noise
Constructing new dog with noise: Woof
Generic Dog Noise
Woof
```

9.2   Constructors as Type Convertor

When constructing objects, initializing information can also be passed into the constructor using this syntax

```
#include "dog.hpp"
int main()
{
    dog littleDog = "Woof";
    littleDog.speak();
}
```

giving this output

```
Constructing new dog with noise: Woof
Woof
```

Notice how much this looks like a type conversion, going from **char *** to **dog**. In fact, classic type casting syntax is also acceptable here

```
#include "dog.hpp"
int main()
{
    dog littleDog = (dog) "Woof";
    littleDog.speak();
}
```

with the same output as before

```
Constructing new dog with noise: Woof
Woof
```

We can conclude that there is little difference between *construction* and *type conversion*. Let's examine this issue further by looking at two classes, cat and dog, and the use of constructors as type convertors between the two classes. Our cat will have a similar header file to dog

```
#ifndef CAT_CLASS
#define CAT_CLASS 1

class cat {
public:
  cat();                  // Default constructor.
  cat(char *newNoise);    // Constructor from noise.
  char *noise();          // Readonly gate to private data.
  void speak();           // Similar to dog method.
private:
  char myNoise[100];
};

#endif
```

and a similar code file

```
#include <stdio.h>
#include <string.h>
#include "cat.hpp"

cat::cat()
{
  printf("Constructing new cat with generic noise\n");
  strcpy(myNoise, "Generic Cat Noise");
}
cat::cat(char *newNoise)
{
  printf("Constructing new cat with noise: %s\n", newNoise);
  strcpy(myNoise, newNoise);
}
```

```
char *cat::noise()
{
    return myNoise;
}
void cat::speak()
{
    printf("%s\n", myNoise);
}
```

The `dog` class now defines a new constructor which takes a `cat` argument.

```
#include "cat.hpp"
class dog {
public:
    dog();                    // Construct given nothing.
    dog(char *newNoise);      // Construct given a noise string.
    dog(cat);                 // Construct given a cat.
    void speak();
private:
    char myNoise[100];
};
```

The code file now contains the same constructors as before, with one addition

```
#include <stdio.h>
#include <string.h>
#include "dog.hpp"
#include "cat.hpp"

dog::dog()
{
    printf("Constructing new dog with generic noise\n");
    strcpy(myNoise, "Generic Dog Noise");
}

dog::dog(char *newNoise)
{
    printf("Constructing new dog with noise: %s\n", newNoise);
    strcpy(myNoise, newNoise);
}
```

```
dog::dog(cat usedToBeCat)   // Newly added to handle cats.
{
    printf("Constructing a dog from a cat\n");
    strcpy(myNoise, usedToBeCat.noise());
    strcat(myNoise, "... I mean, Woof!");
}

void dog::speak()
{
    printf("%s\n", myNoise);
}
```

The following program demonstrates the use of "typical" **cat** and **dog** constructors, as well as the **dog** constructor which converts from cats to dogs

```
#include "dog.hpp"
#include "cat.hpp"
int main()
{
    dog myDog("Woof");
    cat myCat("Meow");
    dog usedToBeCat = (dog) myCat;

    myDog.speak();
    myCat.speak();
    usedToBeCat.speak();
}
```

with this output

```
Constructing new dog with noise: Woof
Constructing new cat with noise: Meow
Constructing a dog from a cat
Woof
Meow
Meow... I mean, Woof!
```

9.3   Reference Variables

In the previous definition of **dog**, we had a constructor taking a cat object as a parameter. What happens when we pass an object as a parameter? We can use this stripped down version of **dog** to explore this issue. First, the header file

```
class dog {
public:
  dog(char *newNoise);
  void speak();
  char myNoise[100];    // Changed from private to public
};
```

and the code file

```
#include <string.h>
#include <stdio.h>
#include "dog.hpp"

dog::dog(char *newNoise)
{
    strcpy(myNoise, newNoise);
}
void dog::speak()
{
    printf("%s\n", myNoise);
}
```

Now let's consider a function (*not* method) which accepts a dog object. Notice myNoise, the data member, is now public, and available to the public for update. Our test function looks like this:

```
#include "dog.hpp"
#include <string.h>
#include <stdio.h>

void silence(dog thisDog)
{
    thisDog.speak();
    strcpy(thisDog.myNoise, "I don't bark anymore");
    thisDog.speak();
}
```

Our test program

```
#include "dog.hpp"
#include <stdio.h>
```

```
void silence(dog thisDog);
int main()
{
    dog myDog("Woof");

    myDog.speak();
    silence(myDog);
    myDog.speak();
}
```

and our test output

```
Woof
Woof
I don't bark anymore
Woof
```

The first and fourth lines of output come from the main program. The second and third lines come from **silence()**, before and after **myNoise** is updated. Lines two and three show that **myNoise** has indeed been updated. But lines one and four show that the update is never seen by the main program's **myDog**.

In C++, when an object is passed as a parameter to a method or function, it is passed by value. Passing by value means that the entire object is copied, byte by byte, to another object seen only within the method or function. This is consistent with how C defines parameters.

One of the C++ embellishments to C is the concept of passing by reference. When a function is defined as accepting a reference variable, C++ does not make a private copy, and any changes made to the parameter are reflected in the parameter on the caller's side.

The syntax for describing a reference variable is reminiscent of that which describes a pointer, and indeed there is a relationship between these concepts. If we wanted to define **silence()** to take a *pointer* to a **dog**, we would define it as

```
void silence (dog *thisDog)
```

and then use pointer syntax to refer to members.

To define **silence()** as taking a *reference* to a **dog** object, we define it as

```
void silence (dog &thisDog)
```

Now, instead of using pointer syntax to refer to members, we use object syntax to refer to members. Thus, the **silence()** code looks like

```
#include "dog.hpp"
#include <string.h>
#include <stdio.h>

void silence(dog &thisDog)
{
   thisDog.speak();
   strcpy(thisDog.myNoise, "I don't bark anymore");
   thisDog.speak();
}
```

Our program behaves very differently when run with this version of silence()

```
Woof
Woof
I don't bark anymore
I don't bark anymore
```

Just as a variable can be declared as a *pointer* to an object, a variable can also be declared as a *reference* to an object. If myDog is declared as a reference to a dog and then set to yourDog, any updates to yourDog will be reflected in myDog. The following code makes use of a function loudest(), which takes references to two dogs, and returns a reference to a dog. First, the dog definition, which is unchanged from the previous example

```
class dog {
public:
   dog(char *newNoise);
   void speak();
   char myNoise[100];
};
```

and the implementation of loudest()

```
#include "dog.hpp"
#include <string.h>

dog &loudest(dog &dog1, dog &dog2)
{
   if (strlen(dog1.myNoise) >= strlen(dog2.myNoise))
     return dog1;
   else return dog2;
}
```

Notice the definition of `loudest()`, which effectively acts as an arithmetic comparison for dogs. The following program uses this function to find the loudest of four dogs

```
#include "dog.hpp"
#include <stdio.h>

void silence(dog &thisDog);
dog &loudest(dog &dog1, dog &dog2);
int main()
{
    dog quietDog("Woof");
    dog normalDog("Woof Woof");
    dog loudDog("Woof Woof Woof");
    dog veryLoudDog("Woof Woof Woof Woof");
    dog &loudestDog = loudest(loudest(quietDog, normalDog),
                             loudest(loudDog, veryLoudDog));
    loudestDog.speak();
    silence(veryLoudDog);
    loudestDog.speak();
    return 0;
}
```

This program defines `loudestDog` as a reference to an object returned by `loudest()`, and `loudest` gets set to `veryLoudDog`. Since `loudestDog` is now really a reference to `veryLoudDog`, `silence()`ing `veryLoudDog` also `silence()`s `loudestDog`. This is all apparent in the following output:

```
Woof Woof Woof Woof
Woof Woof Woof Woof
I don't bark anymore
I don't bark anymore
```

If we change `loudestDog` to be a `dog`, rather than a reference to a `dog`, we find that `silence()`ing `veryLoudDog` has no effect on `loudestDog`. This new version,

```
#include "dog.hpp"
#include <stdio.h>
void silence(dog &thisDog);
dog &loudest(dog &dog1, dog &dog2);
```

```
int main()
{
    dog quietDog("Woof");
    dog normalDog("Woof Woof");
    dog loudDog("Woof Woof Woof");
    dog veryLoudDog("Woof Woof Woof Woof");
    dog loudestDog = loudest(loudest(quietDog, normalDog),
                             loudest(loudDog, veryLoudDog));

    loudestDog.speak();
    silence(veryLoudDog);
    loudestDog.speak();
    return 0;
}
```

gives this output:

```
Woof Woof Woof Woof
Woof Woof Woof Woof
I don't bark anymore
Woof Woof Woof Woof
```

9.4   const Qualifier — Protecting Reference Variables

There are two reasons for using reference variables as parameters. The first is to allow the function to directly update the object without going through pointers. The second, and much more common reason, is to avoid the potentially expensive copying of possibly large object parameters

It is true that copy avoidance can also be achieved with object pointers. However, object pointers have one significant drawback: Parameters can't be protected from update. Reference variables can be protected.

The C++ mechanism for protecting reference objects is the **const** qualifier. A reference variable that is also declared **const** is passed without copying, giving the efficiency of pointer parameters, but cannot be updated, giving the safety of nonpointing parameters. Thus, **const** reference parameters give the best of both worlds, and incidentally reduce the need for pointer parameters.

Constructors with object parameters are among the prime candidates for **const** reference types. Notice the definitions of the third and fourth constructors in this version of **dog**

```
#include "cat.hpp"
class dog {
public:
  dog();
  dog(char *newNoise);
  dog(const cat&);        // Constructor from cat object
  dog(const dog&);        // Constructor from dog object
  void speak();
private:
  char myNoise[100];
};
```

The four dog constructors are defined as

```
#include <stdio.h>
#include <string.h>
#include "dog.hpp"
#include "cat.hpp"

dog::dog()
{
   printf("Constructing new dog with generic noise\n");
   strcpy(myNoise, "Generic Dog Noise");
}
dog::dog(char *newNoise)
{
   printf("Constructing new dog with noise: %s\n", newNoise);
   strcpy(myNoise, newNoise);
}
dog::dog(const cat &usedToBeCat)
{
   printf("Constructing new dog from a cat\n");
   strcpy(myNoise, usedToBeCat.noise());
   strcat(myNoise, "... I mean, Woof!");
}
dog::dog(const dog &otherDog)
{
   printf("Constructing new dog from another dog\n");
   strcpy(myNoise, otherDog.myNoise);
}
```

This program makes use of all four constructors. Notice that the client program has little interest in whether the object parameter is constant and/or reference. This is a detail of the class implementation.

```
#include "dog.hpp"
#include "cat.hpp"
int main()
{
    dog myDog("Woof");
    cat myCat("Meow");
    dog usedToBeCat = myCat;
    dog likeMyDog = myDog;

    myDog.speak();
    myCat.speak();
    usedToBeCat.speak();
    likeMyDog.speak();
    return 0;
}
```

The first four lines of output show the different constructor invocations

```
Constructing new dog with noise: Woof
Constructing new cat with noise: Meow
Constructing new dog from a cat
Constructing new dog from another dog
```

The next two lines show typical **dog** and **cat** constructor results

```
Woof
Meow
```

The next line shows what happens when a **dog** is constructed from a **cat**

```
Meow... I mean, Woof!
```

Finally, a **dog** constructed using a default constructor, and then reset to a normal dog.

```
Woof
```

9.5 Destructors

None of these versions of **dog** are particularly memory efficient. They allocate space for 99 character barks, even though most barks are relatively small, and when a dog does comes around with a *very* long bark these class definitions fail. This version provides a better solution

```
class dog {
public:
  dog(char *newNoise);
  void speak();
private:
  char *myNoise;       // Now a character pointer.
};
```

Each of the constructors now needs changing. In addition to their old responsibilities, they now must allocate enough space for the bark string.

```
#include <stdio.h>
#include <string.h>
#include <stdlib.h>
#include "dog.hpp"

dog::dog(char *newNoise)
{
    printf("Constructing new dog with noise: %s\n", newNoise);
    myNoise = new char[strlen(newNoise)+1];
    strcpy(myNoise, newNoise);
}
void dog::speak()
{
    printf("%s\n", myNoise);
}
```

But we now have a problem. When the program deletes a dog object, it does not deallocate the memory pointed to by **myNoise**, behavior which is considered socially incorrect. This program, for example, does everything it can to properly delete created objects, but the **delete** invocation frees only that memory pointed to by **littleDog**:

```
#include "dog.hpp"
int main()
{
    dog *littleDog = new dog("Woof");
    littleDog->speak();
    delete littleDog;
}
```

We can solve this problem by creating an explicit destructor for the **dog** class. A destructor is the opposite of a constructor. It prepares an object to release memory. It is declared with the ~ symbol followed by the class name. A **dog** class which declares a destructor looks like

```
class dog {
public:
  dog(char *newNoise);
  ~dog();                        // Destructor for dog class
  void speak();
private:
  char *myNoise;
};
```

The code for this class looks like

```
#include <stdio.h>
#include <string.h>
#include <stdlib.h>
#include "dog.hpp"

dog::dog(char *newNoise)
{
    printf("Constructing new dog with noise: %s\n", newNoise);
    myNoise = new char[strlen(newNoise)+1];
    strcpy(myNoise, newNoise);
}
dog::~dog()
{
    printf("Destroying dog\n");
    delete myNoise;
}

void dog::speak()
{
    printf("%s\n", myNoise);
}
```

The `delete` operation now invokes the newly defined destructor, which properly frees our dynamically allocated memory. This is demonstrated in this program

```
#include "dog.hpp"
int main()
{
    dog *littleDog = new dog("Woof");
    littleDog->speak();
    delete littleDog;
}
```

with this output

```
Constructing new dog with noise: Woof
Woof
Destroying dog
```

new and delete come as a matched set, much like malloc() and free(). One may not delete objects which were not acquired via new. The following gives compile errors when the program attempts to delete littleDog.

```
#include "dog.hpp"
int main()
{
    dog littleDog("Woof");
    littleDog.speak();
    delete littleDog;    // Gives compile error
}
```

Just as a constructor is automatically invoked when an object comes into scope, the destructor is automatically invoked as the object leaves scope. We can see this in the following program:

```
#include "dog.hpp"
int main()
{
    void dogDemo();
    int n;
    for (n=0; n<3; n++) dogDemo();
}
void dogDemo()
{
    dog littleDog("Woof");
    littleDog.speak();
}
```

Since littleDog is in scope only within dogDemo(), it enters and leaves scope three times, each time invoking the constructor and the destructor.

```
Constructing new dog with noise: Woof
Woof
Destroying dog
Constructing new dog with noise: Woof
Woof
Destroying dog
```

```
Constructing new dog with noise: Woof
Woof
Destroying dog
```

9.6   Overloading the Assignment Operator

Next we will investigate assignments using this definition of dog

```
class dog {
public:
  dog(char *newNoise);
  dog(const dog &);
  ~dog();
  void speak();
  void newBark(char *newNoise);
private:
  char *myNoise;
};
```

Most of the methods are unchanged, but just to be sure we are all looking at
the same code

```
#include <stdio.h>
#include <string.h>
#include <stdlib.h>
#include "dog.hpp"

dog::dog(char *newNoise)
{
    printf("Constructing new dog with noise: %s\n", newNoise);
    myNoise = new char[strlen(newNoise)+1];
    strcpy(myNoise, newNoise);
}

dog::dog(const dog &otherDog)
{
    printf("Constructing new dog from other dog\n");
    myNoise = new char[strlen(otherDog.myNoise)+1];
    strcpy(myNoise, otherDog.myNoise);
}
```

```
dog::~dog()
{
   printf("Destroying dog\n");
   delete myNoise;
}

void dog::speak()
{
   printf("%s\n", myNoise);
}

void dog::newBark(char *newNoise)
{
   delete myNoise;
   myNoise = new char[strlen(newNoise)+1];
   strcpy(myNoise, newNoise);
}
```

Assignment statements are not necessarily easy to recognize. Consider this program

```
#include "dog.hpp"
int main()
{
   dog littleDog = "Woof";
   dog bigDog = littleDog;

   littleDog.speak();
   bigDog.speak();
}
```

The line

```
   dog bigDog = littleDog;
```

looks like an arithmetic assignment, but actually invokes the dog::dog(const dog&) constructor as can be seen from the second line of output

```
Constructing new dog with noise: Woof
Constructing new dog from other dog
Woof
Woof
Destroying dog
Destroying dog
```

This next program uses the same **dog** class, and looks very similar.

```
#include "dog.hpp"
int main()
{
    dog littleDog = "Woof";
    dog bigDog = "Woof Woof";

    bigDog = littleDog;
    littleDog.speak();
    bigDog.speak();
}
```

The only difference is that what had been

```
    dog bigDog = littleDog;
```

is now replaced by

```
    dog bigDog = "Woof Woof";
    bigDog = littleDog;
```

You might expect identical results from these two programs. However the output now looks quite different:

```
Constructing new dog with noise: Woof
Constructing new dog with noise: Woof Woof
Woof
Woof
Destroying dog
Destroying dog
Heap is corrupted
```

The significant difference between these two programs lies in assignment. The former program never does a true assignment. It uses a constructor with a syntax that appears to be assignment. The latter program takes one existing object and assigns it to another existing object. This is a true use of an assignment operator.

Before we can understand why our program crashed, we need to look at how the default assignment operator works. The default assignment operator does a strict member by member copy between two objects. If the member data item is an address, then this results in the overwriting of one address by another. This is rarely what we want. Consider the use of littleDog and bigDog in our test program. When we finish

```
    dog littleDog = "Woof";
    dog bigDog = "Woof Woof";
```

we may end up, for example, with "Woof" stored in memory locations 1000–1004, and `littleDog.myNoise,` therefore, equal to 1000. `Woof Woof`" may be stored in memory locations 2010–2019, and `bigDog.myNoise` is, therefore, set to 2010.

The default assignment,

```
bigDog = littleDog;
```

then overwrites the 2010 that was stored in `bigDog.myNoise` by the new value 1000, the value of `littleDog.myNoise.` The output lines

```
Woof
Woof
```

generated by

```
littleDog.speak();
bigDog.speak();
```

are a little misleading. It appears as if two different memory locations both containing the same values are being printed. In fact, the exact same memory location is printed twice.

When `littleDog` and `bigDog` go out of scope, the destructor is invoked twice. Both invocations are going to attempt to free memory location 1000. The first time this works fine. The second time, we are freeing memory which has already been freed, a sure way to corrupt the memory allocation scheme.

The solution is to overwrite the assignment operator. Instead of an address copy, we want a `strcpy()`. This definition of `dog` shows the syntax for overloading an assignment operator. Other than the newly defined operator, our `dog` class is unchanged.

```
class dog {
public:
  dog(char *newNoise);
  dog(const dog &);
  ~dog();
  void speak();
  void newBark(char *newNoise);
  void operator=(const dog& otherDog);   // Redefinition of "="
private:
  char *myNoise;
};
```

The code for the assignment operator looks like this

```
void dog::operator=(const dog &otherDog)
{
   printf("Assigning one dog to another\n");
   delete myNoise;
   myNoise = new char[strlen(otherDog.myNoise)+1];
   strcpy(myNoise, otherDog.myNoise);
}
```

and now this program,

```
#include "dog.hpp"
int main()
{
   dog littleDog = "Woof";
   dog bigDog = "Woof Woof";

   bigDog = littleDog;
   littleDog.speak();
   bigDog.speak();
}
```

which moments before resulted in corrupted memory allocation, works as expected

```
Constructing new dog with noise: Woof
Constructing new dog with noise: Woof Woof
Assigning one dog to another
Woof
Woof
Destroying dog
Destroying dog
```

We are still not totally in the clear. Consider this program, using the same dog definition

```
#include "dog.hpp"
int main()
{
   dog littleDog = "Woof";
   littleDog.speak();
   littleDog = littleDog;
   littleDog.speak();
}
```

This gives an unexpected result:

```
Constructing new dog with noise: Woof
Woof
Assigning one dog to another
(garbage character string)
Destroying dog
```

Everything seems to be working fine until we process the second `speak()`. Instead of the expected `Woof`, we get a stream of garbage characters. What is going on here?

Notice the special use of assignment in this program. Unlike the last program, which assigned one object to another, this program assigns an object to itself. Assigning an object to itself should result in no change to the object. Obviously our assignment operator does not work in this special case.

Let's take a close look at the assignment operator

```
void dog::operator=(const dog &otherDog)
{
    printf("Assigning one dog to another\n");
    delete myNoise;
    myNoise = new char[strlen(otherDog.myNoise)+1];
    strcpy(myNoise, otherDog.myNoise);
}
```

The first line prints a trace statement. The second line frees `littleDog.myNoise`, making `littleDog.myNoise` point to undefined memory. The next two lines assume that `littleDog.myNoise` points to a string, an assumption invalidated by the second line. Thus, this assignment fails when assigning an object to itself.

The proper way to deal with this special case is as a special case, by checking the address of both objects. If the addresses of the objects are the same, then the objects must be the same. Not merely identical, but literally the same object. This new version fixes the problem

```
void dog::operator=(const dog &otherDog)
{
    printf("Assigning one dog to another\n");
    if (this == (dog *) &otherDog) return;
    delete myNoise;
    myNoise = new char[strlen(otherDog.myNoise)+1];
    strcpy(myNoise, otherDog.myNoise);
}
```

Although we earlier discussed the variable `this`, the implicit pointer to the target object, this is the first time we have seen it used in practice. When the

address of the target object (contained in **this**) is the same as the address of the
parameter object (contained in **otherDog**), we know the two objects are identical.
The casting of **&otherDog** is required because of a slight difference in address types.
this is the address of a **dog**, while **&otherDog** is the address of a reference to a
dog, a seemingly subtle distinction, but apparently enough to make some compilers
complain.

Now our test program,

```
#include "dog.hpp"
int main()
{
    dog littleDog = "Woof";
    littleDog.speak();
    littleDog = littleDog;
    littleDog.speak();
}
```

behaves as expected.

```
Constructing new dog with noise: Woof
Woof
Assigning one dog to another
Woof
Destroying dog
```

There is one more refinement we might consider for our **dog** assignment operator.
Arithmetic assignment operators can logically be used in constructions like

```
#include <stdio.h>
int main()
{
  int n3 = 1;
  int n1, n2;
  n1 = n2 = n3;        // Note special usage here.
  printf("n1: %d n2: %d n3: %d\n", n1, n2, n3);
  return 0;
}
```

giving

```
n1: 1 n2: 1 n3: 1
```

If we were to try this with our dog assignment operator, as in

```
int main()
{
  dog d1 = "woof";
  dog d2 = "woof";
  dog d3 = "woof woof";
  d1 = d2 = d3;        // Usage here similar to above.
  d1.speak();
  d2.speak();
  d3.speak();
  return 0;
}
```

we get a compile error. The problem is with the statement

```
d1 = d2 = d3;
```

which says, in effect,

```
assign(d1, assign(d2, d2));
```

Our assignment operator returns nothing, so its return value cannot be used as a method parameter. We can fix this by changing the return type of the assignment operator. The most logical type for it to return is the same type as it expects as a parameter. This new version shows the change.

```
const dog &dog::operator=(const dog &otherDog)
{
  printf("Assigning one dog to another\n");
  delete myNoise;
  myNoise = new char[strlen(otherDog.myNoise)+1];
  strcpy(myNoise, otherDog.myNoise);
  return *this;        // Note addition of return value.
}
```

Now the program behaves as expected

```
Constructing new dog with noise: woof
Constructing new dog with noise: woof
Constructing new dog with noise: woof woof
Assigning one dog to another
Assigning one dog to another
woof woof
woof woof
woof woof
```

```
Destroying dog
Destroying dog
Destroying dog
```

9.7   Constructors and Assignment Operators

Assignment and constructors are often associated, because constructors are often needed to help resolve assignments. Consider the following program

```
#include "dog.hpp"
int main()
{
    dog littleDog = "Woof";
    littleDog = "Woof Woof";
    littleDog.speak();
}
```

We are not surprised to find the `dog::dog(char*)` constructor invoked as a result of

```
dog littleDog = "Woof";
```

since clearly a `littleDog` is coming into scope. But it may be surprising to see that same constructor invoked again as a result of this line

```
littleDog = "Woof Woof";
```

However we see exactly this happening in the output

```
Constructing new dog with noise: Woof
Constructing new dog with noise: Woof Woof
Assigning one dog to another
Woof Woof
Destroying dog
Destroying dog
```

The constructor is needed to deal with the assignment. Our `dog` class defines only one assignment operator, and this works only when both sides of the assignment are `dog` objects.

As C++ looks over the situation, it realizes it cannot deal with the assignment directly, because the types are wrong. However there is an available path for correcting the types. The program has requested an assignment of a string to a `dog`. It has only defined the meaning of assigning a `dog` to a `dog`. However it has also defined a constructor for `dog`, which takes a string. As we have already seen, this constructor can also be interpreted as a type convertor from string to `dog`.

So C++ resolves the assignment the only way it can. It creates a new temporary dog from a string. It then assigns this temporary dog to littleDog, and finally, it frees both our littleDog and its own temporary dog as both objects leave scope.

We can avoid creating this extra temporary object by just defining an assignment operator which assigns a string to a dog. If we do this, C++ can accomplish the assignment directly. This new version of dog defines such an assignment.

```
class dog {
public:
  dog(char *newNoise);
  dog(const dog &);
  ~dog();
  void speak();
  void newBark(char *newNoise);
  const dog &operator=(const dog& otherDog);
  const dog &operator=(char *newNoise);
private:
  char *myNoise;
};
```

This second assignment operator looks like this

```
const dog &dog::operator=(char *newNoise)
{
    printf("Assigning string to a dog\n");
    delete myNoise;
    myNoise = new char[strlen(newNoise)+1];
    strcpy(myNoise, newNoise);
    return *this;
}
```

and now this same program,

```
#include "dog.hpp"
int main()
{
    dog littleDog = "Woof";
    littleDog = "Woof Woof";
    littleDog.speak();
}
```

completes the assignment without creating temporary objects

```
Constructing new dog with noise: Woof
Assigning string to a dog
Woof Woof
Destroying dog
```

9.8   Managing Memory Allocation

As we have said, the constructor, `dog::dog()`, does not allocate object memory.
The only memory it allocates is orthogonal memory, memory needed by but not
for the object. In this case, this memory is needed to contain the **bark** string.

The operators that control memory allocation are **new** and **delete**, both of which
are considered operators even though they have method like names. When we need
to take control of memory allocation, we do so by overloading these operators.

Let's consider a simple example of memory allocation for our **dog** class. This **dog**
definition shows **new** and **delete** overloaded. Notice **new** takes a single parameter
of type **size_t**, which is defined in **stddef.h**, one of the standard C++ header
files.

```
class dog {
public:
   dog();
   ~dog();
   void speak();
   void *operator new(size_t);
   void operator delete(void *);
private:
   char *myNoise;
};
```

Our memory allocation makes use of a static block of memory large enough to
contain three **dog** objects. This memory is named **dogArray**, and will be allocated
once, when the first call to **new** is made. From then on, we will recycle through
this memory pool. We will use another static array, this one of integers, named
inUse. The nth element of **inUse** will tell us if the nth element of the static memory
block has been assigned. If **inUse[n]** is true, then the nth element in **dogArray** is
currently allocated. If it is false, then the nth element is available.

The new **dog** method code file looks like this

```
#include <stdio.h>
#include <string.h>
#include <stddef.h>    // Required
#include <stdlib.h>
#include "dog.hpp"

#define NDOGS 3                     // Maximum number of dogs.
static dog *dogArray = 0;           // Initialize to 0.
static int inUse[NDOGS] = {0,0,0}; // Set slots to available.

/* ... */

void *dog::operator new(size_t size)
{
    int n;

/* Allocate memory block if necessary.
   -------------------------------- */
    if (!dogArray)
        dogArray = malloc(sizeof(dog) * NDOGS);

/* Find first available slot.
   ------------------------ */
    for (n=0; n<NDOGS; n++) {
        if (!inUse[n]) {
            inUse[n] = 1;
            printf("Assigning dog %d\n", n);
            return dogArray+n;
        }
/* If none are available, print error.
   ---------------------------------- */
    }
    printf("Sorry... no more dogs available\n");
    return 0;
}
```

When **new** is invoked, the single parameter is set to the number of bytes needed, which should be the number of bytes needed by an object of this class. In many cases, this parameter can be ignored.

The **delete** operator receives one parameter, a pointer set to the address of the object to be deleted. Since this pointer is defined to be **void ***, it will need casting before being checked. The **delete** operator looks like this

```
void dog::operator delete(void *thisDog)
{
    int n;

    /* Find slot whose address we had assigned, and mark as free.
       ------------------------------------------------------------- */
    for (n=0; n<NDOGS; n++) {
        if (dogArray+n == (dog *) thisDog) {
            inUse[n] = 0;
            printf("Freeing dog %d\n", n);
            return;
        }
    }
    printf("Error... couldn't find your dog\n");
}
```

Our testing program,

```
#include <stddef.h>
#include <stdio.h>

#include "dog.hpp"
int main()
{
    dog myDog;
    dog *myDogPtr = new dog;

    myDog.speak();
    myDogPtr->speak();

    delete myDogPtr;
}
```

gives this output

```
Constructing new dog with generic noise
Assigning dog 0
Constructing new dog with generic noise
Generic Dog Noise
Generic Dog Noise
Destroying a dog
Freeing dog 0
Destroying a dog
```

Notice we get two invocations of the constructor and only one of **new**. Similarly, we get two invocations of the destructor and only one of **delete**. Constructors are invoked when either a variable comes into scope such as **myDog** *or* when an object is instantiated such as the object pointed to by **myDogPtr**. However, the overloaded **new** is invoked *only* when the object is instantiated. The destructor and **delete** operator follow a similar pattern.

9.9 Hierarchical Constructors

Now that we understand how constructors and destructors work within a simple, non derived class, let's extend this discussion to derived classes. The behavior we expect from constructors and destructors in derived classes is not entirely obvious. Consider this class lattice.

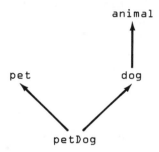

Remember, we read

$$\text{dog} \quad \longrightarrow \quad \text{animal}$$

as "dog derived from animal."

If each class in the lattice has both private data and various flavors of constructors, what happens when a **petDog** comes into scope? We certainly don't expect **petDog** constructors to initialize data which is private to **dog**, not to mention **animal**. On the other hand, a constructor of **petDog** can't leave base class data uninitialized.

Let's construct some simple examples of these classes, and investigate the constructor behavior. We will start with overwritten default constructors, so we can temporarily ignore the issue of parameters.

We will define each of these four classes with one private data element, one default constructor which will set that element, and one **display()** method to display an object of its class.

Displaying an object of a derived class requires a little sophistication. A display method can only display data members of that class. Each of our display methods will therefore follow this rule. First they display their own data. Then they invoke the `display()` method of their immediate base classes.

This might look like a violation of encapsulation, since it requires a method to know about its derivation. However `petDog::display()` is written by the class designer of `petDog`, who has defined the base classes of `petDog` to start with. This scheme only requires knowledge of the *immediate* base classes of `petDog`. It will then be the responsibility of the **dog** designer to know about the **dog** base class(es).

One further note: `display()` is logically defined as virtual, to ensure correct run time behavior.

Our four classes look like this

```
class animal {
public:
  animal();        // animal constructor
  virtual void display();
private:
  char *myFood;
};


class dog: public animal {
public:
  dog();           // dog constructor
  void display();
private:
  char *myNoise;
};


class pet {
public:
  pet();           // pet constructor
  virtual void display();
private:
  char *myOwner;
};


class petDog : public pet, dog {
public:
  petDog();        // pet constructor
  void display();
```

```
private:
  char *myName;
};
```

The four default constructors are shown next. They are shown together even though they live in four different files.

```
#define defaultFood "Generic Animal Food"
animal::animal()
{
   printf("Generic animal constructor\n");
   myFood = new char[strlen(defaultFood)+1];
   strcpy(myFood, defaultFood);
}


#define defaultNoise "Generic Dog Noise"
dog::dog()
{
   printf("Generic dog constructor\n");
   myNoise = new char[strlen(defaultNoise)+1];
   strcpy(myNoise, defaultNoise);
}


#define defaultPetOwner "Generic Pet Owner"
pet::pet()
{
   printf("Generic pet constructor\n");
   myOwner = new char[strlen(defaultPetOwner)+1];
   strcpy(myOwner, defaultPetOwner);
}


#define defaultName "Generic Pet Dog Name"
petDog::petDog()
{
   printf("Generic petdog constructor\n");
   myName = new char[strlen(defaultName)+1];
   strcpy(myName, defaultName);
}
```

and next, the four display() methods.

```
void animal::display()
{
   printf(" My Food: %s\n", myFood);
}

void dog::display()
{
   printf("My Noise: %s\n", myNoise);
   animal::display();
}

void pet::display()
{
   printf("My Owner: %s\n", myOwner);
}

void petDog::display()
{
   printf(" My Name: %s\n", myName);
   pet::display();
   dog::display();
}
```

Now let's observe the behavior of a test program, paying particular attention to the constructor invocations as a **petDog** is instantiated. Our program

```
#include <stdio.h>
#include "petdog.hpp"
int main()
{
   void displayAnimal(const animal&);
   petDog *myDog = new petDog;
   displayAnimal(*myDog);
}

void displayAnimal(const animal &thisAnimal)
{
   printf("\n");
   printf("This is an animal\n");
   printf("----------------\n");
   thisAnimal.display();
}
```

and the output:

```
Generic pet constructor
Generic animal constructor
Generic dog constructor
Generic petdog constructor

This is an animal
-----------------
 My Name: Generic Pet Dog Name
My Owner: Generic Pet Owner
My Noise: Generic Dog Noise
 My Food: Generic Animal Food
```

From this output we can learn something about the behavior of these constructors. First, we see that all base class constructors (both direct and indirect) are invoked. Second, we see a correlation between the order of invocation and the derivation graph. Compare these lines of output

```
Generic pet constructor
Generic animal constructor
Generic dog constructor
Generic petdog constructor
```

to the original derivation graph:

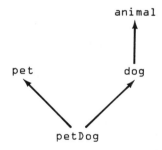

From the output we see that each class invokes the constructors of its base classes before it invokes its own constructor. It does this in the same order as the classes are defined as base classes. Since each class is following the same algorithm, we end up with the "leaf" constructors being the first invoked.

Now that we have a basic understanding of constructor flow in derived classes, let's see how parameter information is passed up the constructor hierarchy. As far as the class definitions themselves go, there is nothing particularly special about constructor hierarchies, except that each level needs to define the information

used at its own and more basic levels (including indirect base classes). Thus, the
prototype for the **animal** constructor looks like

```
animal(char *food);
```

and the prototype for the **dog** constructor (derived from **animal**) looks like

```
dog(char *noise, char *food);
```

and so on. Our new class definition then looks like this

```
class animal {
public:
  animal();
  animal(char *food);
  virtual void display();
private:
  char *myFood;
};


class dog: public animal {
public:
  dog();
  dog(char *noise, char *food);
  void display();
private:
  char *myNoise;
};


class pet {
public:
  pet();
  pet(char *owner);
  virtual void display();
private:
  char *myOwner;
};
```

```
class petDog : public pet, dog {
public:
  petDog();
  petDog(char *name, char *owner, char *noise, char *food);
  void display();
private:
  char *myName;
};
```

It is in the method code that we specify how these parameters are to be parceled out. This specification is done through a mechanism known as an *initialization list*. This is a list of constructors for all classes from which this class is immediately derived. The initialization list comes immediately after the method prototype and before the body of the method. The initialization list is separated from the prototype by a : character. Each constructor is given its share of the parameters.

The syntax for a constructor with initialization list is this

```
className::className(parameters):initializationList
{
  /* body of method */
}
```

Our **animal** and **pet** classes are not derived, and therefore do not have initialization lists.

```
animal::animal(char *food)
{
  printf("Constructing animal with food: %s\n", food);
  myFood = new char[strlen(food)+1];
  strcpy(myFood, food);
}

pet::pet(char *owner)
{
  printf("Constructing pet with owner: %s\n", owner);
  myOwner = new char[strlen(owner)+1];
  strcpy(myOwner, owner);
}
```

The **dog** class is derived from only one class, **animal**, so its constructor contains a one element initialization list containing the constructor for **animal**.

```
dog::dog(char *noise, char *food) : animal(food)
{
    printf("Constructing dog with noise: %s\n", noise);
    myNoise = new char[strlen(noise)+1];
    strcpy(myNoise, noise);
}
```

The line

```
dog::dog(char *noise, char *food) : animal(food)
```

can be read as saying, "This dog constructor takes two parameters, but the second parameter is just passed off to the next level constructor for animal."

The petDog class is derived from two classes, dog and animal, so both of these classes are represented in the initialization lists.

```
petDog::petDog(char *name, char *owner, char *noise,
               char *food) : dog(noise, food), pet(owner)
{
    printf("Constructing petdog with name: %s\n", name);
    myName = new char[strlen(name)+1];
    strcpy(myName, name);
}
```

The line

```
petDog::petDog(char *name, char *owner, char *noise,
       char *food) : dog(noise, food), pet(owner)
```

can be read as saying, "This petDog constructor takes four parameters, but the second is just passed off to the next level constructor for pet, and the third and fourth are just passed off to the next level constructor for dog."

Other than shunting off arguments through the initialization lists, a constructor does not deal with arguments destined for more basic level constructors. Each constructor deals only with constructors of its immediate base class(es), consistent with the ideal that a class implementation should depend only on the *definition* of its immediate base class, but independent of the *implementation* of its base classes. It should be *completely* independent of any base classes further removed.

The relationship between constructors does not concern the class client. A petDog user does not care about the disposition of parameters, in fact, never sees the initialization lists. The petDog users want to know only what information is expected by the constructor, and in what order. Our test program modified to use these new constructors looks like this

```
#include <stdio.h>
#include "petdog.hpp"

int main()
{
    void displayAnimal(const animal&);
    petDog *myDog = new petDog
      ("Abigail", "Emily", "Woof Woof Woof",
        "Anything I can get");
    displayAnimal(*myDog);
}
```

and the output shows the new constructors replacing the old defaults

```
Constructing pet with owner: Emily
Constructing animal with food: Anything I can get
Constructing dog with noise: Woof Woof Woof
Constructing petdog with name: Abigail

This is an animal
-----------------
  My Name: Abigail
 My Owner: Emily
 My Noise: Woof Woof Woof
  My Food: Anything I can get
```

9.10 Hierarchical Destructors

Destructors work much like default constructors. They are prototyped as if the class is nonderived. Our class definitions with destructors added look like

```
class animal {
public:
  animal();
  animal(char *food);
  ~animal();
  virtual void display();
private:
  char *myFood;
};
```

```
class pet {
public:
  pet();
  pet(char *owner);
  ~pet();
  virtual void display();
private:
  char *myOwner;
};


class dog: public animal {
public:
  dog();
  dog(char *noise, char *food);
  ~dog();
  void display();
private:
  char *myNoise;
};


class petDog : public pet, dog {
public:
  petDog();
  petDog(char *name, char *owner, char *noise, char *food);
  ~petDog();
  void display();
private:
  char *myName;
};
```

Each destructor is responsible only for preparing its own class members for release. So we have

```
animal::~animal()
{
  printf("Destroying animal\n");
  delete myFood;
}
```

```
dog::~dog()
{
    printf("Destroying dog\n");
    delete myNoise;
}


pet::~pet()
{
    printf("Destroying pet\n");
    delete myOwner;
}


petDog::~petDog()
{
    printf("Destroying petDog\n");
    delete myName;
}
```

Our program needs no changes.

```
#include <stdio.h>
#include "petdog.hpp"

int main()
{
    void displayAnimal(const animal&);
    petDog *myDog = new petDog
      ("Abigail", "Emily", "Woof Woof Woof",
        "Anything I can get");
    displayAnimal(*myDog);
    delete myDog;
}
```

and gives this new output:

```
Constructing pet with owner: Emily
Constructing animal with food: Anything I can get
Constructing dog with noise: Woof Woof Woof
Constructing petdog with name: Abigail
```

```
This is an animal
------------------
 My Name: Abigail
My Owner: Emily
My Noise: Woof Woof Woof
 My Food: Anything I can get

Destroying petDog
Destroying dog
Destroying animal
Destroying pet
```

As this output shows, the destructors are invoked pretty much as we expect, except possibly for the order of invocation. The order of invocation for destructors is the mirror image of the order of invocation of constructors. This is perhaps easier to see if we edit out some of the output lines and add indentation.

```
Constructing pet with owner: Emily
| Constructing animal with food: Anything I can get
| | Constructing dog with noise: Woof Woof Woof
| | | Constructing petdog with name: Abigail
| | | Destroying petDog
| | Destroying dog
| Destroying animal
Destroying pet
```

The constructors are invoked in left to right, bottom to top order, and the destructors are invoked right to left, top to bottom order. Both of these are strictly defined by the ANSI standard [Ellis and Stroustrup].

There is one last problem with the destructors as shown here. Consider this program, which looks similar to the last.

```cpp
#include <stdio.h>
#include "petdog.hpp"

int main()
{
    void deleteAnimal(animal *animalToDelete);
    petDog *myDog = new petDog
      ("Abigail", "Emily", "Woof Woof Woof",
        "Anything I can get");
    deleteAnimal(myDog);
}
```

```
void deleteAnimal(animal *animalToDelete)
{
   delete animalToDelete;
}
```

The output from this program shows only one destructor being called, the **animal** destructor:

```
Constructing pet with owner: Emily
Constructing animal with food: Anything I can get
Constructing dog with noise: Woof Woof Woof
Constructing petdog with name: Abigail
Destroying animal
```

This is in marked contrast to the four destructor outputs we saw in the last program

```
Destroying petDog
Destroying dog
Destroying animal
Destroying pet
```

The problem is that we did not declare the destructors to be virtual. Thus the resolution of the destructor within **deleteAnimal()** is based on the type of the pointer, not the type of the object the pointer references. We fix this by declaring the destructor to be virtual in **animal** and **pet**. Since **dog** and **petDog** are derived from **animal** and **pet**, the prior declaration of the destructor as virtual automatically makes it virtual for these classes. The only two necessary changes are in the **animal** and **pet** definitions

```
class animal {
public:
   animal();
   animal(char *food);
   virtual ~animal();        // Now virtual
   virtual void display();
private:
   char *myFood;
};

class pet {
public:
   pet();
   pet(char *owner);
```

```
  virtual ~pet();            // Now virtual
  virtual void display();
private:
  char *myOwner;
};
```

With just these two changes, we see the expected output

```
Constructing pet with owner: Emily
Constructing animal with food: Anything I can get
Constructing dog with noise: Woof Woof Woof
Constructing petdog with name: Abigail
Destroying petDog
Destroying dog
Destroying animal
Destroying pet
```

The lesson is that you should be very wary of nonvirtual destructors. If there is any chance of a destructor being invoked when the type of the target object cannot be known at compile time, the destructor should be virtual. In fact, there is little reason to ever declare a destructor nonvirtual, with the highly questionable exception of performance.

9.11   Allocating and Deallocating Memory in Hierarchies

Last on the memory agenda are **new** and **delete** within a class derivation context. Let's redefine these classes once more, now adding **new** and **delete** operators. The syntax here is no different that **new** and **delete** with non derived classes. So we have

```
class animal {
public:
  animal();
  animal(char *food);
  ~animal();
  void *operator new(size_t);
  void operator delete(void *);
  virtual void display();
private:
  char *myFood;
};
```

```
class pet {
public:
  pet();
  pet(char *owner);
  ~pet();
  void *operator new(size_t);
  void operator delete(void *);
  virtual void display();
private:
  char *myOwner;
};


class dog: public animal {
public:
  dog();
  dog(char *noise, char *food);
  ~dog();
  void *operator new(size_t);
  void operator delete(void *);
  void display();
private:
  char *myNoise;
};


class petDog : public pet, dog {
public:
  petDog();
  petDog(char *name, char *owner, char *noise, char *food);
  ~petDog();
  void *operator new(size_t);
  void operator delete(void *);
  void display();
private:
  char *myName;
};
```

We will implement a trivial, even useless memory allocation scheme, allowing us to focus on the mechanisms of allocation rather than on allocation algorithms. The new **new** operator for each class contains a static pointer to an object of its type. This pointer is initialized to zero. The first time **new** is invoked, the allocator resets the pointer to a dynamically allocated block of memory, sufficient in size to

hold one object. From then on **new** just returns that pointer. The **delete** operator
will do nothing except announce its invocation.

The **animal** set:

```
void *animal::operator new(size_t size)
{
    static animal *storage = 0;
    printf("New animal called\n");
    if (!storage) storage = new animal;
    return storage;
}

void animal::operator delete (void *thisAnimal)
{
    printf("Delete animal called\n");
}
```

The **pet** set:

```
void *pet::operator new(size_t size)
{
    static pet *storage = 0;
    printf("New pet called\n");
    if (!storage) storage = new pet;
    return storage;
}

void pet::operator delete (void *thisPet)
{
    printf("Delete pets called\n");
}
```

The **dog** set:

```
void *dog::operator new(size_t size)
{
    static dog *storage = 0;
    printf("New dog called\n");
    if (!storage) storage = new dog;
    return storage;
}

void dog::operator delete (void *thisDog)
{
    printf("Delete dog called\n");
}
```

and the petDog set:

```
void *petDog::operator new(size_t size)
{
    static petDog *storage = 0;
    printf("New petDog called\n");
    if (!storage) storage = new petDog;
    return storage;
}

void petDog::operator delete (void *thisPetDog)
{
    printf("Delete petDog called\n");
}
```

Once again, our program.

```
#include <stdio.h>
#include "petdog.hpp"

int main()
{
    void displayAnimal(const animal&);
    petDog *myDog = new petDog
      ("Abigail", "Emily", "Woof Woof Woof",
        "Anything I can get");
    displayAnimal(*myDog);
    delete myDog;
}
```

Before we look at the new output, let's reexamine the output from our last version of these classes, before overloading **new** and **delete**. That output looked like this

```
Constructing pet with owner: Emily
Constructing animal with food: Anything I can get
Constructing dog with noise: Woof Woof Woof
Constructing petdog with name: Abigail

This is an animal
----------------
 My Name: Abigail
My Owner: Emily
My Noise: Woof Woof Woof
 My Food: Anything I can get
```

```
Destroying petDog
Destroying dog
Destroying animal
Destroying pet
```

Try to guess where the output from these various allocator/deallocators is going to appear. Will the **new** operators kick in before or after the constructors? Will their invocation order follow the order of constructors or of the destructors?

The actual output may seem surprising

```
New petDog called
Constructing pet with owner: Emily
Constructing animal with food: Anything I can get
Constructing dog with noise: Woof Woof Woof
Constructing petdog with name: Abigail

This is an animal
------------------
 My Name: Abigail
My Owner: Emily
My Noise: Woof Woof Woof
 My Food: Anything I can get

Destroying petDog
Destroying dog
Destroying animal
Destroying pet
Delete petDog called
```

Only one of our four allocators is invoked, the one explicitly invoked in this line

```
petDog *myDog = new petDog
  ("Abigail", "Emily", "Woof Woof Woof",
    "Anything I can get");
```

Similarly, only one of our deallocators is ever invoked, the one explicitly invoked by this line

```
delete myDog;
```

We can draw several interesting conclusions from this output. For one, the memory is allocated before any of the constructors are invoked, certainly reasonable enough. Two, the memory is deallocated after all of the destructors have finished their work, also quite reasonable. The third conclusion is perhaps more of a surprise.

Even though the memory is *managed* as a series of separate, independent regions, each region under the control of the constructors and destructors for a particular class, the memory is *allocated* in one, single chunk. We will better understand the reasons for this when we go to Chapter 10, How C++ Works.

9.12 Exercises

Exercise 9.1 Given this class definition

```
class houseCat{
public:
  void display();
private:
  char *name;
  char *coloring;
  char *owner;
  houseCat *mother;
  houseCat *father;
};
```

write a constructor which takes initializing values for all five private data members. Write a `display()` method which displays a `houseCat`. Write a main program which exercises the class.

Exercise 9.2 Given these definitions

```
class dog {
public:
  dog(char *);       /* Constructor */
  void display();
private:
  char name[50];
};

class dogHouse {
public:
  dogHouse(char *);  /* Constructor */
  void display();
```

```
private:
  dog *dogArray[50];
  int ndogs;
};
```

Fill in the code for these classes and write an exercising program. Create the
`dogHouse()` constructor so that it takes a single string of the form

```
"Lassie Rover RinTinTin"
```

that is, a string of blank separated dog names and initializes the `dogHouse` so that
each name is an element in `dogArray`. In your main program demonstrate this
constructor used as a type convertor.

Exercise 9.3 Given this definition

```
class animal {
public:
  animal (char *noise);
  char *says();
private:
  char *myNoise;
};
```

Fill in the code. Then write a function (not method) called `converse()`, which
takes two animals and has them converse with each other. By *converse*, we mean
alternate their sounds for three cycles. Then, if our exercising program instantiates
`Silvester`, who says "Meow," and `TweetiePie`, who says "I thought I saw a Pussy
Cat," and passes these two objects to `converse()`, the output will look like

```
I thought I saw a Pussy Cat
Meow
I thought I saw a Pussy Cat
Meow
I thought I saw a Pussy Cat
Meow
```

Exercise 9.4 Given the `dogHouse` definition in exercise 2, add a `dogHouse`
destructor. Decide what the destructor should do and prove it works.

Exercise 9.5 Given the classes in exercise 4, change the private data member
`name` to be a character pointer. Add a destructor to the `dog` class. Demonstrate
the relationship between the `dogHouse` and the `dog` destructors.

Exercise 9.6 Given the classes after exercise 5, add an assignment operator which allows one `dogHouse` to be assigned to another.

Exercise 9.7 Given the classes after exercise 6, add trivial memory allocators and deallocators to both classes. Show that *both* are called in response to a line like

```
dogHouse *myDogHouse = "RinTinTin Lassie Snoopie";
```

Explain this in light of the earlier discussion of this chapter, in which we showed that when a derived class is instantiated, only *one* allocator is called.

Exercise 9.8 Earlier we saw this code

```
#include <stdio.h>
#include "petdog.hpp"

int main()
{
    void displayAnimal(const animal&);
    petDog *myDog = new petDog
      ("Abigail", "Emily", "Woof Woof Woof",
        "Anything I can get");
    displayAnimal(*myDog);
    delete myDog;
}
```

Given this prototype

```
void displayAnimal(const animal&);
```

explain why we have this

```
displayAnimal(*myDog);
```

instead of this

```
displayAnimal(myDog);
```

The gods love the obscure and hate the obvious.

-Brihadaranyaka Upanishad 4.2.2
(The Upanishads)
Translated by R.C. Zaehner

Chapter 10

How C++ Works

We have now been introduced to C++. We have discussed the concepts of classes, method overloading, inheritance, and memory utilization among others. This chapter discusses how C++ is implemented.

10.1 Introduction

There are many implementations of C++, and the standards for the language have little to say about implementation. However, the most commonly used C++ is implemented as a C preprocessor. This is the AT&T C++ preprocessor. The discussions in this chapter are about AT&T C++ version 2.1, but the principles apply to most C++ implementations.

Let's consider the following class definition of **animal**, and follow its transformation from C++ source to an executable program. Our **animal** class defines two data members, two methods for setting these data members, and two display methods. Our class definition looks like

```
class animal {
public:

    void setFood(char *newFood);        // Reset Food
    void setHabitat(char *newHabitat);  // Reset Habitat
    void shortDisplay();                // Brief Display of Data
    void longDisplay();                 // Long Display of Data
```

317

```
private:
  char food[100];
  char habitat[100];
};
```

The code for this class is

```
#include "animal.hpp"
#include <stdio.h>
#include <string.h>
#include <stdlib.h>

void animal::setFood(char *newFood)
{
    strcpy(food, newFood);
}

void animal::setHabitat(char *newHabitat)
{
    strcpy(habitat, newHabitat);
}

void animal::shortDisplay()
{
    printf("%s\n%s\n", food, habitat);
}

void animal::longDisplay()
{
    printf("     My food: %s\n", food);
    printf("   My habitat: %s\n", habitat);
}
```

Our test program is

```
#include "animal.hpp"

int main()
{
    animal *pooh = new animal();

    pooh->setFood("Honey");
    pooh->setHabitat("Hundred Acre Woods");
```

```
    pooh->shortDisplay();
    pooh->longDisplay();

    delete pooh;
    return 0;
}
```

which gives this output, the first two lines from **shortDisplay()** and the second two lines from **longDisplay()**.

```
Honey
Hundred Acre Woods
        My food: Honey
    My habitat: Hundred Acre Woods
```

This code consists of three separate files. The header file, **animal.hpp**, defines the class. This header file is **#include**d in any source file which needs to know the definition of an **animal**. This definition needs to be known by the animal implementation file and by clients who instantiate objects of that class. Both must, therefore, **#include** this file.

The processing of a C++ program occurs in three steps.

Step one is under control of the C++ preprocessor. The preprocessor reads through the C++ source, say **animal.c**. When an **#include** directive is encountered, the appropriate file is read in, and treated as if its text was part of the source at that point. From the preprocessor's perspective, there is no difference between a block of text being inserted into a source file through the **#include** directive and that same block of text physically residing in the source file. The sole purpose of the **#include** directive is eliminating the duplicate and redundant information that would otherwise exist in multiple files.

The end result of this first step is a new C source file. This C source file is the C equivalent to the original C++ source file. Every C++ source file has a corresponding C file. We will call the C source file the *emitted code*, because it is the code emitted by the C++ preprocessor.

In stages two and three, this C file is processed as if it were a valid C source file, and in fact, it is exactly that, a fully valid C source file. In step two this C file is compiled into an object file. In step three this object file is linked together with other object files to form an executable program.

From this discussion, we can see that our animal code will require two runs of the C++ preprocessor — one to create **animal** C code from our **animal** C++ code and one to create **test** C code from our **test** C++ code. These C programs must fully implement the functionality we specified in C++. Let's first consider the emitted code for the animal implementation file. The emitted code, with unrelated headers expansions removed, looks like this

```
/* <<AT&T C++ Translator 2.1.0 03/31/90>> */
/* < animal.c > */

char *__vec_new ();

char __vec_delete ();
typedef int (*__vptp)();
struct __mptr {short d; short i; __vptp f; };


struct animal {      /* sizeof animal == 200 */

char food__6animal [100];
char habitat__6animal [100];
};

extern struct __mptr* __ptbl_vec__animal_c_setFood_[];

char setFood__6animalFPc (__0this , __0newFood )
struct animal *__0this ;

char *__0newFood ;
{
( __strcpy ( ((char *)__0this -> food__6animal ), ((char
*)__0newFood )) ) ;
}


char setHabitat__6animalFPc (__0this , __0newHabitat )
struct animal *__0this ;

char *__0newHabitat ;
{
( __strcpy ( ((char *)__0this -> habitat__6animal ), ((char
*)__0newHabitat )) ) ;
}

extern int printf ();

char shortDisplay__6animalFv (__0this )
struct animal *__0this ;
```

```
{
printf ( (char *)"%s\n%s\n", __0this -> food__6animal,
__0this -> habitat__6animal ) ;
}


char longDisplay__6animalFv (__0this )
struct animal *__0this ;

{
printf ( (char *)"     My food: %s\n",
__0this -> food__6animal
) ;
printf ( (char *)"  My habitat: %s\n", __0this ->
habitat__6animal ) ;
}
/* the end */
```

This file looks difficult to read, and indeed, is not designed for human readability. Other than wanting to understand the process, there is little reason to read this file. However, this emitted code is not quite as bad as it seems at first. Let's clean it up slightly by removing extraneous information and applying some visual reformatting. This file now looks like

```
struct animal
{
  char food__6animal [100];
  char habitat__6animal [100];
};


char setFood__6animalFPc (__0this, __0newFood)
struct animal *__0this;
char *__0newFood;
{
    __strcpy (__0this->food__6animal, __0newFood);
}


char setHabitat__6animalFPc (__0this, __0newHabitat)
struct animal *__0this;
char *__0newHabitat;
{
    __strcpy (__0this->habitat__6animal, __0newHabitat);
}
```

```
char shortDisplay__6animalFv (__0this)
struct animal *__0this;
{
   printf ("%s\n%s\n",
     __0this->food__6animal, __0this->habitat__6animal);
}

char longDisplay__6animalFv (__0this)
struct animal *__0this;
{
   printf ("     My food: %s\n",
           __0this->food__6animal);
   printf ("  My habitat: %s\n",
           __0this->habitat__6animal);
}
```

The emitted code is starting to look better, but still has a peculiar feel to it. Let's further edit the file by changing valid, but ugly identifiers by equally valid, but nice looking identifiers. Making these substitutions:

original	*new*
food__6animal	food
habitat__6animal	habitat
__0this	this
__0newHabitat	newHabitat
__0newFood	newFood
longDisplay__6animalFv	longDisplay
shortDisplay__6animalFv	shortDisplay
setHabitat__6animalFPc	setHabitat
setFood__6animalFPc	setFood

we get this new file

```
struct animal
{
  char food [100];
  char habitat [100];
};
```

```
char setFood (this, newFood)
struct animal *this;
char *newFood;
{
    __strcpy (this->food, newFood);
}

char setHabitat (this, newHabitat)
struct animal *this;
char *newHabitat;
{
  __strcpy (this->habitat, newHabitat);
}

char shortDisplay (this)
struct animal *this;
{
    printf ("%s\n%s\n", this->food, this->habitat);
}

char longDisplay (this)
struct animal *this;
{
    printf ("    My food: %s\n", this->food);
    printf ("  My habitat: %s\n", this->habitat);
}
```

Now this C code is looking not only interpretable, but even recognizable. In fact, it's starting to look very much like our own C classes. Let's continue with the test program file, the file that started out life as this C++ program

```
#include "animal.hpp"
int main()
{
    animal *pooh = new animal();
    pooh->setFood("Honey");
    pooh->setHabitat("Hundred Acre Woods");
    pooh->shortDisplay();
    pooh->longDisplay();
    delete pooh;
    return 0;
}
```

The preprocessor emitted version looks like

```
/* <<AT&T C++ Translator 2.1.0 03/31/90>> */
/* < test.c > */

char *__vec_new ();

char __vec_delete ();
typedef int (*__vptp)();

struct __mptr {short d; short i; __vptp f; };


struct animal {      /* sizeof animal == 200 */

char food__6animal [100];
char habitat__6animal [100];
};

char setFood__6animalFPc ();
char setHabitat__6animalFPc ();

char shortDisplay__6animalFv ();
char longDisplay__6animalFv ();
extern struct __mptr* __ptbl_vec__test_c_main_[];

extern char __dl__FPv ();

extern char *__nw__FUl ();

int main (){ _main(); {
struct animal *__1pooh ;

__1pooh = (((struct animal *)__nw__FUl
( sizeof (struct animal ))));

setFood__6animalFPc ( __1pooh , (char *)"Honey") ;
setHabitat__6animalFPc ( __1pooh ,
(char *)"Hundred Acre Woods") ;
```

```
    shortDisplay__6animalFv ( __1pooh ) ;
    longDisplay__6animalFv ( __1pooh ) ;

    __dl__FPv ( (char *)__1pooh ) ;
  }
}

/* the end */
```

After the same name substitution, reformatting, and extraneous information reduction, we get

```
struct animal {
  char food [100];
  char habitat [100];
};

char setFood ();
char setHabitat ();
char shortDisplay ();
char longDisplay ();

extern char __dl__FPv ();
extern char *__nw__FUl ();

int main ()
{
  _main();
  {
    struct animal *__1pooh ;
    __1pooh = (((struct animal *)
              __nw__FUl (sizeof(struct animal)) ));
    setFood ( __1pooh, "Honey");
    setHabitat ( __1pooh, "Hundred Acre Woods");

    shortDisplay ( __1pooh ) ;
    longDisplay ( __1pooh ) ;

    __dl__FPv ( (char *)__1pooh ) ;
  }
}
```

Although this file is not quite as easy to relate to as our **animal** emitted file, it is still possible to make some sense out of what is happening.

The file starts by defining an **animal** structure and a set of functions. Assuming the functions are all methods of the **animal** class, and the first four certainly are, then this emitted class definition

```
struct animal {
  char food__6animal [100];
  char habitat__6animal [100];
};

char setFood__6animalFPc ();
char setHabitat__6animalFPc ();
char shortDisplay__6animalFv ();
char longDisplay__6animalFv ();
```

which is equivalent to this name substituted version

```
struct animal {
  char food [100];
  char habitat [100];
};

char setFood ();
char setHabitat ();
char shortdisplay ();
char longDisplay ();
```

is very similar to our own concept of C classes. We can start to see how the class concept is implemented in C++. The "class" becomes a data structure and a set of associated functions. The C++ class we defined as

```
class animal {
public:

  void setFood(char *newFood);
  void setHabitat(char *newHabitat);
  void shortDisplay();
  void longDisplay();
```

```
private:

  char food[100];
  char habitat[100];
};
```

becomes

```
struct animal {
  char food__6animal [100];
  char habitat__6animal [100];
};

char setFood__6animalFPc ();
char setHabitat__6animalFPc ();

char shortDisplay__6animalFv ();
char longDisplay__6animalFv ();
```

Except for the odd looking identifiers, the C++ concept of C classes is very similar to our own. A class definition becomes a structure definition. An object becomes either a structure, or, as in this test program, a pointer to a structure. Our C++ line

```
animal *pooh = new animal();
```

becomes

```
struct animal *__1pooh ;
__1pooh = (((struct animal *)
        __nw__FU1 ( sizeof (struct animal )) ));
```

whereas, had we been writing in C, our test program would have been

```
animal *pooh;
pooh = newAnimal ();
```

The parallels here are clear. There are only two significant differences between C++ generated C code and our C code. First, the name of the variables are odd, though recognizable. Second, instead of allocating memory with a class allocator, C++ uses some intermediate memory allocator.

C++ also uses a method invocation scheme which is similar to ours. The C++ line

```
pooh->setFood("Honey");
```

becomes

```
setFood__6animalFPc(__1pooh,(char*)"Honey");
```

which is similar to what we would have written

```
setFood(pooh, "Honey");
```

Finally, there is a strong similarity in the method code itself. Our C++ version,

```
void animal::setFood(char *newFood)
{
    strcpy(food, newFood);
}
```

becomes

```
char setFood__6animalFPc (__0this , __0newFood )
struct animal *__0this ;
char *__0newFood ;
{
  ( __strcpy ( ((char *)__0this -> food__6animal ),
               ((char *)__0newFood ))
  );
}
```

which we would have written with this equivalent, simpler version

```
setFood(this, newFood)
animal *this;
char *newFood;
{
    strcpy(this->food, newFood);
}
```

Like our own C code, C++ uses the first method parameter to identify the target object. Notice the parallel construction between the C++ version of a method declaration

```
char setFood__6animalFPc (__othis , __0newFood )
```

and our own:

```
setFood(this, newFood)
```

10.2 Default Memory Management

We can also learn something about default memory management from our current version of **animal**. Our C++ class redefined neither constructors, destructors, allocators, nor deallocators. In the absence of such redefinitions, our

```
animal *pooh = new animal();
```

becomes

```
    struct animal *__1pooh ;
    __1pooh = (((struct animal *)
            __nw__FU1 ( sizeof (struct animal )) ));
```

We can't tell what the function `__nw__FU1()` does exactly, but based on its parameter, which says how much memory is required for an **animal**, the fact that it returns a pointer, and the context in which it is used, we can safely assume that at least one of its purposes is allocating memory.

Similarly, our C++ line,

```
    delete pooh;
```

becomes

```
    __dl__FPv((char *)__1pooh);
```

which has all the appearance of a function whose purpose is freeing the memory allocated by `__nw__FU1()`.

Overall, a few points seem clear. Default memory allocation is fairly simple. It consists of simple allocation, possibly with initialization. Since the only memory allocator parameter is the object size, any initialization can consist only of zeroing.

We can start to see why classes with either orthogonal memory requirements or more sophisticated initialization expectations are going to have to override this scheme.

10.3 Overloaded Method Resolution

Methods in C++ can be overloaded. In the last section, we saw that methods in C++ map into C functions. Functions in C cannot be overloaded. How is this resolved?

We saw some clues if we noticed the name changes as C++ methods became C functions. The C++ method **setFood()**, for example, turned into the C function **setFood__6animalFPc()**. To better understand what is happening, let's redefine the C++ class, adding some seriously overloaded method names. Our new class definition looks like

```
class animal {
public:

  void setFood(char *newFood);
  void setHabitat(char *newHabitat);

  void testMethod(int n);         // Dummy method name.
  void testMethod(int n, int m); // Overloaded dummy method.
  void testMethod(char *n);       // Even more overloaded.
  void testMethod(char *n, int m); // Really overloaded.

  void shortDisplay();
  void longDisplay();

private:

  char food[100];
  char habitat[100];
};
```

We will add the most trivial possible implementations of these four overloaded **testMethods()**, since we aren't interested in these methods *per se*, only in how the method resolution works. This code, trivial by any standards, is added to the implementation file:

```
void animal::testMethod(int n)
{
}

void animal::testMethod(int n, int m)
{
}

void animal::testMethod(char *n)
{
}

void animal::testMethod(char *n, int m)
{
}
```

We modify the test program to "invoke" these new **animal** methods

```
#include "animal.hpp"

int main()
{
    animal *pooh = new animal();

    pooh->setFood("Honey");
    pooh->setHabitat("Hundred Acre Woods");

    pooh->shortDisplay();
    pooh->longDisplay();

    pooh->testMethod(1);        // Invoke first definition
    pooh->testMethod(1, 2);     // Invoke second definition
    pooh->testMethod("1");      // Invoke third definition
    pooh->testMethod("1", 2);   // Invoke fourth definition

    delete pooh;
    return 0;
}
```

As we look at our emitted code, we notice a change in our **animal** class. The old version was

```
struct animal {
  char food__6animal [100];
  char habitat__6animal [100];
};

char setFood__6animalFPc ();
char setHabitat__6animalFPc ();

char shortDisplay__6animalFv ();
char longDisplay__6animalFv ();
```

The new version is

```
struct animal {
  char food__6animal [100];
  char habitat__6animal [100];
};

char setFood__6animalFPc ();
char setHabitat__6animalFPc ();
```

```
char shortDisplay__6animalFv ();
char longDisplay__6animalFv ();

char testMethod__6animalFi ();
char testMethod__6animalFiT1 ();
char testMethod__6animalFPc ();
char testMethod__6animalFPci ();
```

We can hypothesize that C++ has mapped these four methods

```
void testMethod(int n);
void testMethod(int n, int m);
void testMethod(char *n);
void testMethod(char *n, int m);
```

to these four C functions, respectively

```
char testMethod__6animalFi ();
char testMethod__6animalFiT1 ();
char testMethod__6animalFPc ();
char testMethod__6animalFPci ();
```

This hypothesis is further supported by an examination of the preprocessor produced version of the method code file, which includes these new definitions

```
char testMethod__6animalFi (__Othis , __On )
struct animal *__Othis ;
int __On ;
{
}

char testMethod__6animalFiT1 (__Othis , __On , __Om )
struct animal *__Othis ;
int __On ;
int __Om ;
{
}

char testMethod__6animalFPc (__Othis , __On )
struct animal *__Othis ;
char *__On ;
{
}
```

```
char testMethod__6animalFPci (__0this , __0n , __0m )
struct animal *__0this ;
char *__0n ;
int __0m ;
{
}
```

Finally, we have the direct evidence of the emitted test program, which started out life, back in C++ as

```
pooh->testMethod(1);
pooh->testMethod(1, 2);
pooh->testMethod("1");
pooh->testMethod("1", 2);
```

and becomes

```
testMethod__6animalFi ( __1pooh , 1 ) ;
testMethod__6animalFiT1 ( __1pooh , 1 , 2 ) ;
testMethod__6animalFPc ( __1pooh , (char *)"1") ;
testMethod__6animalFPci ( __1pooh , (char *)"1", 2 ) ;
```

From this analysis, we can see that method overloading is based on a scheme of method renaming, or what is frequently referred to as name mangling. Earlier we encountered a limitation on overloading, that every overload for a given method must have a unique signature. This limitation now makes sense. The signature of every method is actually embedded in the name of the resulting function. We can even see the various signature elements represented in the name: the target class, the method name, and some encoding of the parameters.

10.4 Constructor and Destructor Overriding

The next issue we will examine is redefinitions of the constructor and destructor. We start by changing our definition of **animal**. The two private data members, **food** and **habitat** will change from character arrays to character pointers. This immediately suggests the need for explicitly defining class constructors and destructors. We will use **malloc()** and **free()** for setting up these pointers to simplify the analysis of the emitted file. Our new C++ class definition

```
class animal {
public:

  animal();
  ~animal();

  void setFood(char *newFood);
  void setHabitat(char *newHabitat);

  void shortDisplay();
  void longDisplay();

private:

  char *food;      // Now a pointer, not an array.
  char *habitat;   // Ditto.
};
```

Our new constructor and destructor

```
animal::animal()
{
    food = (char *) malloc(strlen(defaultFood)+1);
    habitat = (char *) malloc(strlen(defaultHabitat)+1);

    strcpy(food, defaultFood);
    strcpy(habitat, defaultHabitat);
}

animal::~animal()
{
    free(food);
    free(habitat);
}
```

Our unchanged C++ test program now has some changes in the emitted code. The line

```
animal *pooh = new animal();
```

which until now transformed into this invocation of the default memory allocator

```
__1pooh = (((struct animal *)
         __nw__FUl ( sizeof (struct animal )) ));
```

now transforms into something quite different:

```
__1pooh = __ct__6animalFv ( (struct animal *)0 ) ;
```

Similarly, the line which in our test program deallocated memory,

```
delete pooh;
```

and used to transform to

```
__dl__FPv((char *)__1pooh);
```

now transforms to

```
__dt__6animalFv ( __1pooh , 3) ;
```

Two questions arise. First, what are these new functions, `__ct__6animalFV()` and `__dt__6animalFv()`? Second, what happened to the memory allocators?

The answer to these questions lies in the emitted version of the method code file. There we find these two new functions:

```
struct animal *__ct__6animalFv (__0this )
register struct animal *__0this ;

{ if (__0this || (__0this = (struct animal *)__nw__FUl (
(unsigned long )(sizeof (struct animal))) )){
__0this -> food__6animal = (((char
*)malloc ( strlen ( (char *)"Food has not been set")
+ 1 ) ));
__0this -> habitat__6animal = (((char *)malloc
( strlen ( (char
*)"Habitat has not been set") + 1 ) ));

( __strcpy ( __0this -> food__6animal , ((char *)
"Food has not been set")) ) ;
( __strcpy ( __0this -> habitat__6animal ,
((char *)"Habitat has not been set")) ) ;
} return __0this ;

}

extern char free ();

extern char __dl__FPv ();
```

```
char __dt__6animalFv (__Othis , __O__free )
struct animal *__Othis ;

int __O__free ;

{ if (__Othis ){
free ( (char *)__Othis -> food__6animal ) ;
free ( (char *)__Othis -> habitat__6animal ) ;
if (__Othis )if (__O__free & 1)__dl__FPv ( (char *)__Othis ) ;
}
}
```

Let's look at the first of these, cleaned up a bit

```
struct animal *__ct__6animalFv (__Othis )
register struct animal *__Othis ;
{
  if (__Othis ||
      (__Othis = (struct animal *)__nw__FU1
                 (sizeof(struct  animal)) )){

    __Othis -> food__6animal =
       (((char *)malloc(strlen((char *)
       "Food has not been set")+1)));

    __Othis -> habitat__6animal =
       (((char *)malloc(strlen((char *)
       "Habitat has not been set")+1)));

    __strcpy(__Othis->food__6animal,
    "Food has not been set");

    __strcpy(__Othis->habitat__6animal,
            "Habitat has not been set");
  }
  return __Othis ;
}
```

This function, or at least part of it, represents our newly defined constructor. The beginning **if** statement, however, seems quite unrelated to anything we wrote and within it we see the reappearance of the default memory allocator, __nw__FU1().

Therefore, we find that memory allocation is handled quite differently, depending on whether or not a class defines a constructor. If the class does define a constructor, allocation is done inside the constructor. If the class does not define a constructor, allocation is done directly at the client side.

When memory allocation moves inside a constructor, it becomes a more complicated affair. Before, allocation consisted only of

```
__1pooh = (((struct animal *)
          __nw__FUl ( sizeof (struct animal )) ));
```

Now it has become

```
if (__Othis ||
(__Othis = (struct animal *)__nw__FUl
            (sizeof(struct  animal)) )){
```

When memory is allocated inside the constructor, it must be allocated conditionally. Remember, a constructor gets invoked when either an object comes into scope *or* becomes instantiated. Both of these statements invoke the constructor

```
animal *pooh = new animal();
animal rabbit();
```

even though only the first dynamically allocates an object. Thus, the conditional is necessary to determine if object memory really needs to be allocated.

If we look once again at the constructor invocation from our test program:

```
__1pooh = __ct__6animalFv ( (struct animal *)0 ) ;
```

we see that the signal to allocate memory is a null pointer. We can assume that the signal to construct without allocating would have been a pointer to an existing structure. The interpretation of this signal occurs in the **if** statement, inside the constructor, which takes the form of

```
if (A || B) /* ... */
```

or, in English, "If A is true (nonzero) or B is true (nonzero)..."

The semantics of C *guarantee* that the evaluation of a logical expression ceases as soon as the result of the expression can be determined. Thus, here, if __Othis is true (nonzero), the evaluation stops. There is no need to continue because if A is true, then (A or B) is always true regardless of the value of B. The pseudocode for this constructor could be written as

```
if((memory was already allocated) or
   (we are successful in allocating memory now)) {
        proceed with constructor;
}
```

The destructor has similar concerns. Again, it is called when either memory has been freed or an object is leaving scope. Only in the first case do we want to free any memory. The C version of the destructor, when made presentable, looks like

```
char __dt__6animalFv(__0this,__0__free )
struct animal *__0this;
int __0__free;
{
   if(__0this ){
     free(__0this->food__6animal ) ;
     free(__0this->habitat__6animal ) ;
     if(__0this)
          if (__0__free & 1)__dl__FPv ( (char *)__0this ) ;
   }
}
```

and is invoked by this C code:

```
__dt__6animalFv ( __1pooh , 3) ;
```

There is one important difference between the constructor allocation and the destructor deallocation. The constructor can use a null pointer as a special flag. The destructor cannot. The destructor is always passed a valid pointer, because it is always passed an object to destroy. The issue is not whether the object exists or not. The object always exists. The issue is whether the object should be freed or not. If the object is merely going out of scope, then "destruction" means freeing only orthogonal memory. If the object is to be deleted, then destruction means freeing the object as well as the orthogonal memory.

Since the pointer parameter cannot be used as a flag, a different mechanism must be used. C++ chose to add another parameter, a flag used to indicate which mode of destruction is being called for. The pseudocode for the destructor looks like

```
if (this is valid) {
   execute C++ destructor code;
   if (this is still valid) and if (this should be freed)
      free this;
}
```

10.5 Overriding Memory Allocation and Deallocation

Once constructors and destructors are understood, and their relationship to default allocators and deallocators is clear, then overriding allocators and deallocators is an extension of these principles.

Consider this version of the `animal` class

```
class animal {
public:

    animal();
    ~animal();

    void *operator new(size_t);     // Overwritten Allocator
    void operator delete(void *);   // Overwritten Deallocator

    void setFood(char *newFood);
    void setHabitat(char *newHabitat);

    void shortDisplay();
    void longDisplay();

private:

    char *food;
    char *habitat;
};
```

We will again use a trivial memory allocator and deallocator, since we are interested only in the mechanism of overloading here.

```
void *animal::operator new(size_t size)
{
    return (animal *) malloc(sizeof(animal));
}

void animal::operator delete(void *thisAnimal)
{
    free(thisAnimal);
}
```

This is our test program

```
#include "animal.hpp"

int main()
{
    animal *pooh = new animal();

    pooh->setFood("Honey");
    pooh->setHabitat("Hundred Acre Woods");

    pooh->shortDisplay();
    pooh->longDisplay();

    delete pooh;
    return 0;
}
```

The emitted code for this looks the same, with or without overwriting of **new** and **delete**. The change after overwriting occurs in the emitted methods file, where we find these new functions defined, shown here in their beautified form:

```
char *__nw__6animalSFUl(__0size)
size_t __0size;
{
    return (char *) malloc(sizeof(struct animal));
}

char __dl__6animalSFPv(__0thisAnimal)
char *__0thisAnimal;
{
  free(__0thisAnimal);
}
```

Clearly, these are the mangled forms of our own **new** and **delete**. The other change occurs in the constructor and destructor, where the code that had called the default allocator and deallocator,

```
struct animal *__ct__6animalFv (__0this )
register struct animal *__0this ;
{
  if (__0this ||
      (__0this = (struct animal *)__nw__FUl
                  (sizeof(struct  animal)))){
  /* ... */
```

```
char __dt__6animalFv(__0this,__0__free )
struct animal *__0this;
int __0__free;
{
   if(__0this){
     free(__0this->food__6animal);
     free(__0this->habitat__6animal);
     if(__0this)
         if (__0__free & 1)__dl__FPv ((char *)__0this ) ;
   }
}
```

now calls our own versions

```
struct animal *__ct__6animalFv (__0this )
register struct animal *__0this ;
{
   if (__0this ||
      (__0this = (struct animal *)__nw__6animalSFU1
                 (sizeof (struct animal)))){
   /* ... */

char __dt__6animalFv(__0this,__0__free)
struct animal *__0this;
int __0__free;
{
  if (__0this){
     free (__0this->food__6animal);
     free (__0this->habitat__6animal);
     if (__0this)
         if (__0__free & 1)__dl__6animalSFPv((char *)__0this);
  }
}
```

We are starting to see a logic to this system. What had first appeared to be a mass of tangled C code is starting to coalesce into an understandable system very much like our own.

10.6 Assignment Operator

We have discussed overloading the assignment operator. Actually, any operator can be overloaded in C++, but this book has focused on three such overloads: assignment, **new**, and **delete**.

Before we see how the overloaded assignment is implemented, let's look at the default assignment operator. We will start with this version of **animal**, which does not redefine assignment

```
class animal {
public:

  animal();
  ~animal();

  void setFood(char *newFood);
  void setHabitat(char *newHabitat);
  void shortDisplay();
  void longDisplay();

private:

  char *food;
  char *habitat;
};
```

This program uses the default assignment operator to assign one object to another

```
#include "animal.hpp"

int main()
{
   animal pooh;
   animal rabbit;

   pooh.setFood("Honey");
   pooh.setHabitat("Hundred Acre Woods");

   rabbit = pooh;

   pooh.shortDisplay();
   rabbit.shortDisplay();
   return 0;
}
```

Although this program gives us the output we expect, our previous examination of assignments should remind us that what we see is not necessarily what we get

```
Honey
Hundred Acre Woods
Honey
Hundred Acre Woods
```

Upon examining the emitted C code, we find that this C++ line

```
rabbit = pooh;
```

turns into this emitted C line

```
__1rabbit = __1pooh ;
```

telling us that the default C++ assignment is the standard C assignment.

The standard ANSI C assignment is a block memory copy. Since objects of class `animal` contain pointers to orthogonal memory, we need to come up with something better. The following version of `animal` redefines assignment

```
class animal {
public:

  animal();
  ~animal();

  void *operator new(size_t);
  void operator delete(void *);

  void setFood(char *newFood);
  void setHabitat(char *newHabitat);

  void operator=(const animal &otherAnimal);  // Overwritten

  void shortDisplay();
  void longDisplay();

private:

  char *food;
  char *habitat;
};
```

The code for this new assignment looks like

```
void animal::operator=(const animal &otherAnimal)
{
    if (this == (animal *) &otherAnimal) return;
    setHabitat(otherAnimal.habitat);
    setFood(otherAnimal.food);
}
```

Now our C++ line

```
rabbit = pooh;
```

emits something quite different

```
__as__6animalFRC6animal(&__1rabbit,
        (struct animal *)(&__1pooh ));
```

After seeing this it comes as no surprise to find that our definition of assignment transforms into the function `__as__6animalFRC6animal()`, and we see in the C version of the methods code file (beautified, of course)

```
char __as__6animalFRC6animal (__0this , __0otherAnimal )
register struct animal *__0this ;
struct animal *__0otherAnimal ;
{
    if (__0this ==__0otherAnimal) return ;

    setHabitat__6animalFPc(__0this,
        ((*__0otherAnimal)).habitat__6animal);

    setFood__6animalFPc(__0this,
        ((*__0otherAnimal)).food__6animal) ;
}
```

Besides showing how operators are transformed into functions, this transformation also shows how reference types are dealt with. C, of course, does not have reference types.

As we see in this method transformation, reference types are turned back into addresses, with dereferencing managed automatically by the C++ preprocessor. The dereferencing use the less familiar form

```
((*__0otherAnimal)).food__6animal
```

instead of this equivalent, more familiar syntax

```
__0otherAnimal->food__6animal
```

but the concept is the same.

As we see, the **const** declaration of the parameter is not reflected in the C file, indicating that the prohibition against changing **const** types is enforced only at the preprocessor level.

10.7 Virtual Methods

Virtual methods are an important C++ programming tool. They provide the standard mechanism for run time resolution of application specific code. They greatly reduce the need for function pointers, the standard C mechanism for run time function resolution. Since virtual methods have no obvious C counterpart, how are they handled by the preprocessor?

Let's start by modifying **animal**. The methods **shortDisplay()** and **longDisplay()** are good candidates for being made virtual.

```
class animal {
public:

    animal();
    ~animal();

    void setFood(char *newFood);
    void setHabitat(char *newHabitat);

    virtual void shortDisplay();    // Now declared virtual
    virtual void longDisplay();     // Ditto

private:

    char *food;
    char *habitat;
};
```

The code for these methods is unaffected

```
void animal::shortDisplay()
{
    printf("%s\n%s\n", food, habitat);
}
```

```
void animal::longDisplay()
{
    printf("     My food: %s\n", food);
    printf("   My habitat: %s\n", habitat);
}
```

Our test program is also unaffected. The only necessary change is the method prototype in the class header file.

```
#include "animal.hpp"

int main()
{
    animal *pooh = new animal();

    pooh->setFood("Honey");
    pooh->setHabitat("Hundred Acre Woods");

    pooh->shortDisplay();
    pooh->longDisplay();

    delete pooh;
    return 0;
}
```

The test program output is also unchanged

```
Honey
Hundred Acre Woods
      My food: Honey
    My habitat: Hundred Acre Woods
```

So what is different? The difference, and it is considerable, lies in the emitted C code. Consider these lines

```
pooh->shortDisplay();
pooh->longDisplay();
```

Before these methods were declared virtual, the emitted code was

```
shortDisplay__6animalFv ( __1pooh ) ;
longDisplay__6animalFv ( __1pooh ) ;
```

Now the emitted code is:

```
((*(((char (*)())(__1pooh -> __vptr__6animal [1]).f))))(
((struct animal *)((((char *)__1pooh ))+ (__1pooh ->
__vptr__6animal [1]).d))) ;

((*(((char (*)())(__1pooh -> __vptr__6animal [2]).f))))
(((struct animal *)((((char *)__1pooh ))+
(__1pooh -> __vptr__6animal [2]).d))) ;
```

What is happening? Let's start with a little cleanup. It doesn't help much, but with the removal of some extraneous type casting and some reformatting, we get

```
(*((__1pooh->__vptr__6animal[1]).f))
(((__1pooh)+(__1pooh->__vptr__6animal[1]).d)));

(*((__1pooh->__vptr__6animal[2]).f))
(((__1pooh)+(__1pooh->__vptr__6animal[2]).d)));
```

Whatever else this is, this is certainly an indirect function call. This is easier to see if we substitute

```
pointerToFunction and parameter
```

for

```
(__1pooh->__vptr__6animal[1]).f
```

and

```
((__1pooh)+(__1pooh->__vptr__6animal[2]).d))
```

respectively. Then

```
(*((__1pooh->__vptr__6animal[1]).f))
(((__1pooh)+(__1pooh->__vptr__6animal[1]).d)));
```

becomes the more recognizable

```
(*(pointerToFunction)
(parameter);
```

Where is this function pointer located? The statement

```
(__1pooh->__vptr__6animal[1]).f
```

is read as follows: __1pooh is a pointer to a structure. That structure contains as one of its members ___vptr__6animal, which is itself an array of some other structure. That structure has a member named f. Or working backwards, the pointer is stored in member **f** of the first element of the array **__vptr__6animal**, itself a member of the structure pointed to by **___1pooh**.

If this is all true, then **__1pooh** must point to a structure containing an element named **__vptr__6animal**. But when we last looked, **_1pooh** pointed to a structure of type **animal**, and **animal** had no such member.

Finding the definition of **animal** in the newly emitted C code, we see an interesting metamorphosis. What had been emitted as

```
struct animal {
  char *food__6animal ;
  char *habitat__6animal ;
};
```

is now emitted as

```
struct animal {
  char *food__6animal ;
  char *habitat__6animal ;
  struct __mptr *__vptr__6animal ;
};
```

Let's follow the trail. If **__vptr__6animal** is a pointer to a **__mptr**, what is a **___mptr**? Looking through the emitted code, we find this definition

```
struct __mptr {
  short d;
  short i;
  __vptp f;
};
```

Surely we are close to the end now. We have located the structure containing the member **f**. **f** is a **__vptp**. What is a **__vptp**? The answer, as always, is in the emitted code, where we find

```
typedef int (*__vptp)();
```

We can start to see where we are going. As a result of the virtual declaration, **animal** now contains a new member, **__vptr__6animal**, which points to a structure of type **__mptr**, possibly the first of an array of such structures. **__mptr** contains a member named **f** which is of particular interest to us. **f** is a pointer to a function, a function we expect to be intimately associated with one of our virtual functions.

If this is true, then the next missing piece is the code which initializes all these structures. We need code which sets up an array of structures, the first of which contains a pointer to a function related to **shortDisplay()**. We need code which sets the pointer **__vptr__6animal** to the first element of that array.

To find this code, we turn our attention from the emitted test file to the emitted `animal` methods file, and start by examining our emitted `shortDisplay()` and `longDisplay()`:

```
char shortDisplay__6animalFv(__Othis )
struct animal *__Othis ;
{
   printf("%s\n%s\n",
      __Othis->food__6animal,
      __Othis->habitat__6animal ) ;
}

char longDisplay__6animalFv(__Othis )
struct animal *__Othis ;
{
   printf("      My food: %s\n", __Othis->food__6animal);
   printf("   My habitat: %s\n", __Othis->habitat__6animal);
}
```

Whatever the answer to the virtual method riddle, we won't find much help here. We next look for code which initializes an array of `__mptr`, and find this in the global declarations

```
struct __mptr __vtbl__6animal[] = {
  0,0,0,
  0,0,(__vptp)shortDisplay__6animalFv,
  0,0,(__vptp)longDisplay__6animalFv,
  0,0,0
};
```

This code is setting up an array of four `__mptr` structures. Starting from zero, the first array element `f` member is set to the address of `shortDisplay()` and the second array element `f` member is set to the address of `longDisplay()`.

We also find the address of this array stored in this structure:

```
struct __mptr* __ptbl_vec__animal_c___ct_[] = {
  __vtbl__6animal
};
```

This array declaration is in isolation from the animal structure. How does the `__vptr__6animal` member of the particular animal structure associated with `pooh` get set to the `__vptr__6animal` array? If we look in the emitted methods file for code which assigns some value to `__1pooh->__vptr__6animal`, we find only one such spot, in the constructor, which has changed since our last visit. It now looks like

```
struct animal *__ct__6animalFv (__0this )
register struct animal *__0this ;
{
  if (__0this ||
    (__0this=(struct animal *)
              __nw__FU1((sizeof(struct animal))) ))
  {
    __0this->__vptr__6animal=
      (struct __mptr *) __ptbl_vec__animal_c___ct_[0];

    __0this ->food__6animal =
          ((malloc(strlen("Food has not been set")+1)));

    __0this ->habitat__6animal =
          ((malloc(strlen("Habitat has not been set")+1)));

    __strcpy(__0this->food__6animal, "Food has not been set"));
    __strcpy (__0this->habitat__6animal,
                            "Habitat has not been set"));
  }
  return __0this ;
}
```

And this completes the story. Now the constructor, in addition to its previous duties, assigns the new animal member to the value of the first element of `__ptbl_vec__animal_c___ct_`, which, as we have seen, contains the address of the `__vtbl__6animal` array. The preprocessor knows that any invocation of `shortDisplay()` or `longDisplay()` should be indirect, via the first or second table element, respectively.

We can diagram the data structures as follows:

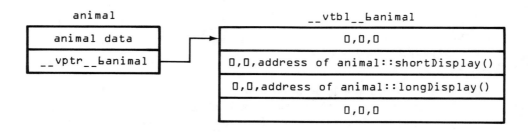

For our purposes, we can show this as

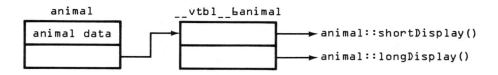

While the **animal** structure can be allocated either statically, at compile time, or dynamically, at runtime inside the constructor, the **__vtbl__6animal** structure is always allocated and initialized at compile time. The pointer **__vptr__6animal**, which connects these two structures, however, is set at run time, inside the constructor.

Notice one important point: These two structures are *not* in a 1:1 relationship. They are in a many:1 relationship. There may be many instances of **animal**, but there is exactly one **__vtbl__6animal structure**. While all **animals** have a pointer to a **__vtbl__6animal** structure, all pointers lead to the same structure. We can diagram this as

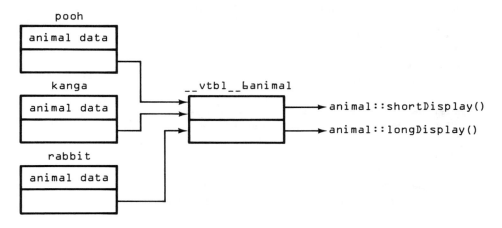

How do objects of derived classes end up with different virtual method tables? Let's consider a class derived from `animal`, say `pet`, which redefines these virtual methods. The definition of `pet` is

```
#include "animal.hpp"

class pet : public animal {
public:

  pet();
  ~pet();

  void setName(char *newName);
  void setOwner(char *newOwner);

  void shortDisplay();   // Virtual resolution.
  void longDisplay();    // Ditto.

private:

  char *name;
  char *owner;
};
```

Our nonvirtual `pet` method implementations are

```
#include "pet.hpp"
#include <stdio.h>
#include <string.h>
#include <stdlib.h>

#define defaultName "Name has not been set"
#define defaultOwner "Owner has not been set"

pet::pet()
{
    name= (char *) malloc(strlen(defaultName)+1);
    owner = (char *) malloc(strlen(defaultOwner)+1);

    strcpy(name, defaultName);
    strcpy(owner, defaultOwner);
}
```

```
pet::~pet()
{
    free(name);
}

void pet::setName(char *newName)
{
    free(name);
    name= (char *) malloc(strlen(newName)+1);
    strcpy(name, newName);
}

void pet::setOwner(char *newOwner)
{
    free(owner);
    owner = (char *) malloc(strlen(newOwner)+1);
    strcpy(owner, newOwner);
}
```

and our virtual methods are

```
void pet::shortDisplay()
{
    printf("%s\n%s\n", name, owner);
    animal::shortDisplay();
}

void pet::longDisplay()
{
    printf("      My name: %s\n", name);
    printf("      My owner: %s\n", owner);
    animal::longDisplay();
}
```

Our test program defines pooh (an animal) and shadow (a pet, derived from animal):

```
#include "animal.hpp"
#include "pet.hpp"
int main()
{
    animal *pooh = new animal();
    pet *shadow = new pet();

    pooh->setFood("Honey");
    pooh->setHabitat("Hundred Acre Woods");

    shadow->setName("Shadow");
    shadow->setOwner("Michael");
    shadow->setFood("Seeds and Nuts");
    shadow->setHabitat("Gerbil House");

    pooh->longDisplay();
    shadow->longDisplay();

    delete pooh;
    delete shadow;
    return 0;
}
```

The first two lines of output come from **pooh**

```
        My food: Honey
    My habitat: Hundred Acre Woods
```

and the next four from **shadow**.   Clearly **pooh** and **shadow** are resolving
longDisplay() to different methods, according to the rules of virtual resolution.

```
        My name: Shadow
       My owner: Michael
        My food: Seeds and Nuts
     My habitat: Gerbil House
```

From our last discussions, we know virtual resolution is through the virtual
method table. Each class has a unique, unchanging virtual resolution scheme.
Whenever a **shortDisplay()** is invoked on an **animal** object, the method will
resolve to **animal::shortDisplay()**. When **shortDisplay()** is invoked on a **pet**
object, the method will resolve to **pet::shortDisplay()**. We can assume the
virtual method table for **pets** is different from the one for **animals**. Our animal
table looked like this

```
struct __mptr __vtbl__6animal[] = {
  0,0,0,
  0,0,(__vptp)shortDisplay__6animalFv,
  0,0,(__vptp)longDisplay__6animalFv,
  0,0,0
};
```

and indeed, our **pet** version, from the emitted implementation file, looks like

```
struct __mptr __vtbl__3pet[] = {
  0,0,0,
  0,0,(__vptp)shortDisplay__3petFv,
  0,0,(__vptp)longDisplay__3petFv,
  0,0,0
};
```

We also have a corresponding **pet** version of

```
struct __mptr* __ptbl_vec__animal_c___ct_[] = {
  __vtbl__6animal
};
```

which is, as one might expect,

```
struct __mptr* __ptbl_vec__pet_c___ct_[] = {
  __vtbl__3pet
};
```

The identifiers shortDisplay__3petFv and longDisplay__3petFv are the emitted names of pet::shortDisplay() and pet::longDisplay(), as can be verified from the emitted **pet** methods file.

The next change we expect is in the **pet** constructor. The animal constructor resets the virtual method table pointer to the **animal** class's virtual method table, __vtbl__6animal[]. It follows that the **pet** constructor should set the **pet** object's virtual method table pointer to the **pet** class's virtual method table, __vtbl__3pet[]. Indeed, the cleaned up **pet** constructor looks like

```
struct pet *__ct__3petFv (__0this )
register struct pet *__0this ;
{
  if (__0this ||
      (__0this = __nw__FUl((sizeof (struct pet)))))
  {
      ((__0this = (struct pet *)__ct__6animalFv
                  (((struct animal *)__0this ))),
       (__0this->__vptr__6animal = (struct __mptr *)
       __ptbl_vec__pet_c___ct_[0])) ;

      __0this->name__3pet =
        ((malloc(strlen("Name has not been set")+1)));

      __0this->owner__3pet =
        ((malloc(strlen("Owner has not been set")+1)));

      __strcpy(__0this->name__3pet,
        "Name has not been set");
      __strcpy(__0this->owner__3pet,
        "Owner has not been set");
  }
  return __0this ;
}
```

and we see that the line which, in the **animal** constructor was

```
__0this->__vptr__6animal=
  (struct __mptr *) __ptbl_vec__animal_c___ct_[0];
```

in the **pet** constructor is

```
__0this->__vptr__6animal =
  (struct __mptr *) __ptbl_vec__pet_c___ct_[0]);
```

Notice that the name of the pointer to the virtual method table is the same for both **animals** and **pets**.

One last question before we leave this example. The emitted **animal** structure contained two data members and a pointer to a virtual method table. The **pet** structure contains two more data items. Where will they be placed? The animal structure looks like

```
struct animal {
  char *food__6animal ;
  char *habitat__6animal ;
  struct __mptr *__vptr__6animal ;
};
```

Will the new **pet** elements go before or after the virtual method table pointer? There is no way to predict, so turning to the emitted code we see

```
struct pet {
  char *food__6animal ;
  char *habitat__6animal ;
  struct __mptr *__vptr__6animal ;
  char *name__3pet ;
  char *owner__3pet ;
};
```

The net result of this is that **animals** and **pets** have both similarities and differences. Diagrammatically, if **pooh** is an **animal** and **shadow** is a **pet**, we have

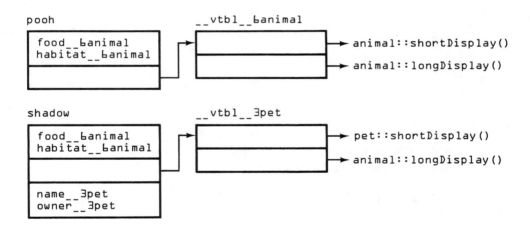

As we can see, the layout of an **animal** is a subset of the layout of a **pet**.

We have now seen how the virtual method table is set up when all virtual declarations come from a single class. In this example, the virtualness of **shortDisplay()** and **longDisplay()** originates in **animal**, and is inherited by **pet**.

Suppose some class derived from **animal** decides to declare some more methods as virtual. Does the second group go into the same or a new virtual method table?

Our existing C++ definitions are

```
class animal {
public:

  animal();
  ~animal();

  void setFood(char *newFood);
  void setHabitat(char *newHabitat);

  virtual void shortDisplay();
  virtual void longDisplay();

private:

  char *food;
  char *habitat;
};
```

and

```
class pet : public animal {
public:

  pet();
  ~pet();

  void setName(char *newName);
  void setOwner(char *newOwner);

  void shortDisplay(); // Virtual
  void longDisplay();  // Ditto.

private:

  char *name;
  char *owner;
};
```

Now we will add a pair of virtual methods to **pet**

```
class pet : public animal {
public:

  pet();
  ~pet();

  void setName(char *newName);
  void setOwner(char *newOwner);

  void shortDisplay(); // Virtual from animal
  void longDisplay();  // Ditto.

  virtual void testMethod1();  // New virtual method.
  virtual void testMethod2();  // Ditto.

private:

  char *name;
  char *owner;
};
```

and a new class derived from **pet**

```
#include "pet.hpp"
class housePet : public pet {
public:

  void testMethod1();   // Override pet virtual method.
  void testMethod2();   // Ditto.

private:

  char *characteristics;
  char *sleepingHours;
};
```

Now we can compare the three emitted class structures

```
struct animal {
  char *food__6animal ;
  char *habitat__6animal ;
  struct __mptr *__vptr__6animal ;
};
```

```
struct pet {
  char *food__6animal ;
  char *habitat__6animal ;
  struct __mptr *__vptr__6animal ;
  char *name__3pet ;
  char *owner__3pet ;
};
```

and

```
struct housePet {
  char *food__6animal ;
  char *habitat__6animal ;
  struct __mptr *__vptr__6animal ;
  char *name__3pet ;
  char *owner__3pet ;
  char *characteristics__8housePet ;
  char *sleepingHours__8housePet ;
};
```

Clearly the additional virtual methods have not created additional tables, or at least, if they have, they are not reflected in the class structures. The resulting virtual method tables are these

```
struct __mptr __vtbl__6animal[] = {
  0,0,0,
  0,0,(__vptp)shortDisplay__6animalFv ,
  0,0,(__vptp)longDisplay__6animalFv ,
  0,0,0
};
```

```
struct __mptr __vtbl__3pet[] = {
  0,0,0,
  0,0,(__vptp)shortDisplay__3petFv ,
  0,0,(__vptp)longDisplay__3petFv ,
  0,0,(__vptp)testMethod1__3petFv ,
  0,0,(__vptp)testMethod2__3petFv ,
  0,0,0
};
```

```
struct __mptr __vtbl__8housepet[] = {
  0,0,0,
  0,0,(__vptp)shortDisplay__3petFv ,
  0,0,(__vptp)longDisplay__3petFv ,
  0,0,(__vptp)testMethod1__8housepetFv ,
  0,0,(__vptp)testMethod2__8housepetFv ,
  0,0,0
};
```

Diagrammatically, we have

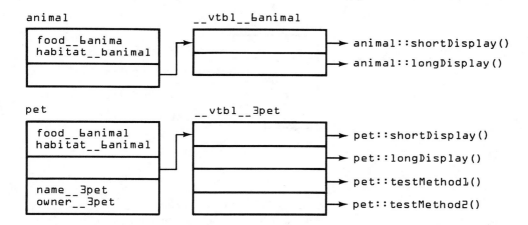

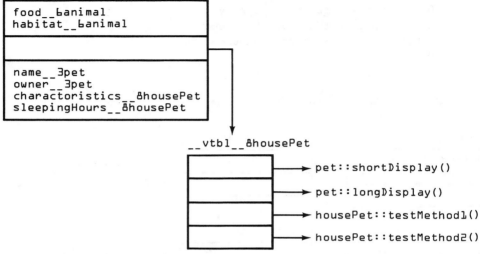

This shows that, at least in simple inheritance schemes, a given class has at most one virtual method table. Every object for a class which either defines virtual methods or is derived from such a class has similar overhead for those virtual methods: one pointer in the object structure.

We can also see how virtual but not overridden methods are managed. The **vtbl** for **housePet** includes pointers to the virtual but not overriden methods **shortDisplay()** and **longDisplay()**. Since **housePet()** does not override these methods, its **vtbl** uses the same slot values as the **vtbl** for **housePet**'s parent, **pet**.

This chapter is incomplete, and there are significant issues such as multiple inheritance that have not been discussed. However you should be getting a feel for how the language works and you should feel comfortable with using a new tool for helping you learn more. That tool is poking. You can learn a great deal through poking at the language. Design some test cases. Look at the emitted code. Rest assured that none of the emitted code you will be looking at will be any worse than what you have seen in here.

10.8 Exercises

Exercise 10.1 Given these class definitions

```
class dog {
public:
  void display();
  /* ... */
private:
  /* ... */
};

class cat {
public:
  void display();
  /* ... */
private:
  /* ... */
};
```

Fill in the method code and show how, in the emitted code, the `display()` associated with `dog` is distinguished from the `display()` associated with `cat`.

Exercise 10.2 Given the class definition

```
class dog {
public:
  void display();
  void display(int ndisplays);
  /* ... */
private:
  /* ... */
};
```

Fill in the method code and show how, in the emitted code, the two `display()` methods are distinguished.

Exercise 10.3 Given the class definition

```
class dog {
public:
  virtual void display();
  virtual void display(int ndisplays);
  /* ... */
private:
  /* ... */
};
```

Show how, on the client side, these two method calls are distinguished.

Exercise 10.4 Given the classes as they existed at the end of exercise 9-7, show in the emitted code how allocation, construction, destruction, and deallocation occur.

Also, show how the **dogHouse** assignment operator works.

Exercise 10.5 Comment on the following argument:

> C++ is very inefficient. Structures are largely replaced by objects. But whereas a structure only needs space for data, an object also needs space for a pointer for every virtual method. If a class needs 20 bytes for data storage, but has 20 virtual methods, most of the object space will be used for virtual method pointers. If we have 10000 objects of a given class, we can easily swamp our available memory just on method pointers.

Exercise 10.6 This chapter made a statement implying that changing data members from arrays to pointers immediately suggests the need to explicitly define class constructors and destructors. Do you agree? Explain your reasons.

Exercise 10.7 In an earlier test program, we showed that this line

```
animal *pooh = new animal();
```

turned into this constructor call

```
__1pooh = __ct__6animalFv ( (struct animal *)0 ) ;
```

What would this line

```
animal pooh;
```

have turned into?

Exercise 10.8 As we have seen in this chapter, when a client invokes a virtual method, the client code does an indirect invocation through pointers that are only set at run time. Explain this: If the client code doesn't know which method is really going to be invoked, how can the client code be so sure which parameter(s) should be passed in?

Thou art to me a delicious torment.

- On Friendship
Ralph Waldo Emerson

Chapter 11

C++ Problems

Now that we have looked in some depth at the many positive features of C++, it seems only fair to look at some of the failings of the language. Many of these can be worked around, but the work arounds are rarely trivial, obvious, or, in many cases, even completely satisfactory solutions.

These discussions should not be taken as a criticism of the language in the large. On the contrary, C++ is a wonderful language, and can provide an excellent introduction to object-oriented concepts. Without a doubt, C++ has been the primary force in popularizing object-oriented programming. However, every language makes tradeoffs, and the purpose of this chapter is to look at some of the tradeoffs made by C++.

11.1 Introduction

We will consider four issues here. Different programmers working on different projects will have different experiences with the languages, and different features they feel are lacking. This chapter represents one particular individual's experience with the language.

11.2 Poor Separation of Public and Private Information

C++ assumes that complete headers are distributed to clients. These complete headers include both public and private information. Private information is by definition not needed by clients, and may include proprietary information such as hints as to how classes are implemented. At the very least, the private information in the header files is distracting for the clients. Providing a standard facility for separating public and private information would be a significant improvement in the language.

11.3   Binary Version Incompatibility

C++ requires that all code modules using a common set of classes be compiled with the same set of class definitions. Say we have the class derivation graph

$$\text{dog} \quad \longrightarrow \quad \text{pet} \quad \longrightarrow \quad \text{animal}$$

and the code modules dog.c, pet.c, animal.c, and main.c. Even if main.c declares only pet objects, it must be compiled with the same versions of the class definitions for dog and animal as were dog.c and animal.c. We will look in more detail at why this is so, and the problems it can cause.

In Chapter 10 we considered these definitions

```
class animal {
public:

  animal();
  ~animal();

  void setFood(char *newFood);          // Non Virtual
  void setHabitat(char *newHabitat); // Ditto

  virtual void shortDisplay();          // Virtual
  virtual void longDisplay();           // Ditto

private:

  char *food;
  char *habitat;
};
```

```
class pet : public animal {
public:

  pet();
  ~pet();

  void setName(char *newName);     // Non Virtual
  void setOwner(char *newOwner);   // Ditto

  void shortDisplay();             // Virtual
  void longDisplay();              // Ditto

private:

  char *name;
  char *owner;
};
```

We found that the C++ preprocessor created **animal** and **pet** structures from the **animal** and **pet** class definitions. The structure declarations looked like

```
struct animal {
  char *food__6animal ;
  char *habitat__6animal ;
  struct __mptr *__vptr__6animal ;
};

struct pet {
   char *food__6animal ;
   char *habitat__6animal ;
   struct __mptr *__vptr__6animal ;
   char *name__3pet ;
   char *owner__3pet ;
};
```

We discovered that the element **__vptr__6animal** was used to point to an array of structures, each containing information about a method, including its address. The arrays were different for **animals** and **pets**. The **animal** method table was

```
struct __mptr __vtbl__6animal[] = {
  0,0,0,
  0,0,(__vptp)shortDisplay__6animalFv,
  0,0,(__vptp)longDisplay__6animalFv,
  0,0,0
};
```

while the pet method table was

```
struct __mptr __vtbl__3pet[] = {
    0,0,0,
    0,0,(__vptp)shortDisplay__3petFv,
    0,0,(__vptp)longDisplay__3petFv,
    0,0,0
};
```

Recall that the element shortDisplay__6animalFv is actually the mangled name of animal::shortDisplay(). Therefore, this element actually contains the address of the animal::shortdisplay() method.

We also looked at this main program

```
#include "animal.hpp"

int main()
{
    animal *pooh = new animal();

    pooh->setFood("Honey");
    pooh->setHabitat("Hundred Acre Woods");

    pooh->shortDisplay();
    pooh->longDisplay();

    delete pooh;
    return 0;
}
```

and found that the line

```
pooh->shortDisplay();
```

turned into emitted code of the form, after reformatting and simplification,

```
(*((__1pooh->__vptr__6animal[1]).f))
(((__1pooh)+(__1pooh->__vptr__6animal[1]).d)));
```

Had our program declared a pet, say kanga, the line

```
kanga->shortDisplay();
```

would have turned into the similar looking

```
(*((__1kanga->__vptr__6animal[1]).f))
(((__1kanga)+(__1kanga->__vptr__6animal[1]).d)));
```

but there would have been one important difference. pooh's `__vptr__6animal`
would be pointing at `__vtbl__6animal`, emitted as part of `animal.c`, which, as we
saw, looks like

```
struct __mptr __vtbl__6animal[] = {
  0,0,0,
  0,0,(__vptp)shortDisplay__6animalFv,
  0,0,(__vptp)longDisplay__6animalFv,
  0,0,0
};
```

kanga's `__vptr__6animal`, on the other hand, would be pointing at `__vtbl__3pet`,
emitted as part of `pet.c`, which, as we also saw, looks like

```
struct __mptr __vtbl__3pet[] = {
  0,0,0,
  0,0,(__vptp)shortDisplay__3petFv,
  0,0,(__vptp)longDisplay__3petFv,
  0,0,0
};
```

Diagrammatically, we have

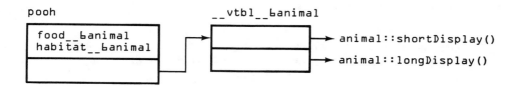

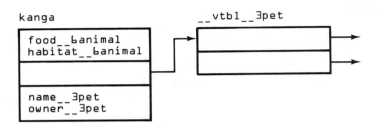

Now let's review the conceptual sequence of events that occurs when a section of code, say **main()**, wants to invoke a virtual method, say **shortDisplay()**, on an object of some class derived from **animal**.

1. **main()** assumes that it has the address of a block of memory representing an object, say **kanga**.

2. Although the exact class of **kanga** is unknown, it is assumed to be some class derived from **animal**. All objects of classes derived from **animal** start out with similar structures. Assuming that pointers require 4 bytes, the initial layout of **kanga** must look like

byte	variable	purpose
0-3	food__6animal	pointer to character array
4-7	habitat__6animal	pointer to character array
8-11	__vptr__6animal	pointer to virtual method table
12-...	different for different	derived classes

3. **main()**, therefore, looks to bytes 8 to 11 for an address of a block of memory which contains a table of virtual method. Once again, for all objects of classes derived from **animal**, this table starts out with similar structures. Assuming that integers also require 4 bytes, the initial layout of the structure pointed to by **__vptr__6animal** must look like

byte	contents	purpose
0–11	0	unknown
12–19	0	info about shortDisplay()
20–23	address	address of shortDisplay__3petFv
		or shortDisplay__6animalFv
24–35	0	info about longDisplay
36–39	address	address of longDisplay__3petFv
		or longDisplay__6animalFv
40–...		different for different derived classes

4. main(), therefore, looks to bytes 20 to 23 for the address of a shortDisplay() method. The address may be the address of animal::shortDisplay(), for pooh, the address of pet::shortDisplay(), for kanga, or the address of some other shortDisplay(), for an object of some other derived classes.

5. main() calls the method passing in the appropriate parameters.

Given this background, we can see some of the things that can go wrong if different code segments are compiled with different understandings of how a class is defined. Let's describe the current versions of animal and pet as A1 and P1 respectively.

Suppose animal gets redefined. Let's say this new version, A2, looks like this

```
class animal {
public:

    animal();
    ~animal();

    void setFood(char *newFood);        // Non Virtual
    void setHabitat(char *newHabitat);  // Ditto

    virtual void shortDisplay();        // Virtual
    virtual void longDisplay();         // Ditto

private:

    char *food;
    char *habitat;
    char *genus;        // Newly added information
    char *species;      // Ditto
};
```

Let's consider the scenario that `animal.c` and `pet.c` are compiled with A2 and main is compiled with A1. This can easily happen if the programmer changes the `animal` definition, and then recompiles the `animal` and `pet` implementation files, but forgets to recompile the main program.

Now we suddenly have a fundamental disagreement about the nature of an `animal` (or `pet`) object. `main()` still thinks the block of memory representing an `animal` looks as shown before, while the `animal` and `pet` implementation code thinks it looks like

byte	variable	purpose
0-3	`food__6animal`	pointer to character array
4-7	`habitat__6animal`	pointer to character array
8-11	`genus__6animal`	pointer to character array
12-15	`species__6animal`	pointer to character array
16-19	`__vptr__6animal`	pointer to virtual method table
12-...	different for different derived classes	

Diagrammatically, we have

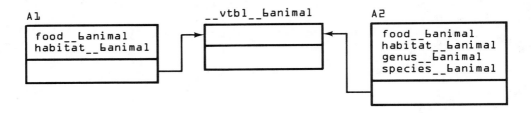

So `main()` follows bytes 8 to 11, thinking they point to a virtual method table, while in fact they point to a character array. `main()` then follows this address to another memory block. `main()` thinks that byte offsets 20 to 23 of this block contain the address of a method, which it then tries to call. In fact, bytes 20 to 23 are either undefined, or contain characters describing the genus of the animal. In either case, the program itself is about to become extinct.

Let consider one other example. Say the class designer wisely decides that `setFood()` and `setHabitat()` should become virtual methods. Now A2 looks like

```
class animal {
public:

    animal();
    ~animal();

    virtual void setFood(char *newFood);      // Now Virtual
    virtual void setHabitat(char *newHabitat); // Ditto

    virtual void shortDisplay();      // Always was virtual
    virtual void longDisplay();       // Ditto

private:

    char *food;
    char *habitat;
};
```

Now say the programmer recompiles `animal.c` and `main.c`, but forgets to recompile `pet.c`. `animal` and `main()` are now running with A2, and `pet` is running with A1.

We no longer have the same problem we had earlier. `main()`, `animal`, and `pet` all agree on the basic structure of an `animal`, and all agree on where the offset for the virtual method table is located. But now they disagree on what the virtual method table itself looks like. `pet` thinks it looks like it did before. `animal` and `main` think it looks like

byte	contents	purpose
0–11	0	unknown
12–19	0	info about `setFood()`
20–23	address	address of `setFood__3petFPc`
24–35	0	info about `setHabitat()`
36–39	address	address of `setHabitat__3petFPc`
40–51	0	info about `shortDisplay()`
52–55	address	address of `shortDisplay__3petFv` or `shortDisplay__6animalFv`
56–67	0	info about `longDisplay`
68–71	address	address of `longDisplay__3petFv` or `longDisplay__6animalFv`
72–...	different for different derived classes

Everything works fine as long as `main()` is invoking `pooh`'s virtual methods, but when `main()` tries to invoke one of `kanga`'s virtual method, say `shortDisplay()`, we have a problem. `main()` thinks that bytes 52 to 55 of the `pet` virtual method table contain the address of `shortDisplay()`. The `pet` code, still working with A1, is using bytes 20 to 23 to store the address of `pet::shortDisplay()`, and has no idea what, if anything, is stored in bytes 52 to 55. Clearly, `main()` is in for a big surprise when it tries to invoke `shortDisplay()` on `kanga`.

These kinds of problems mean that the C++ programmer has to be sure that all of the code is compiled using similar class definitions. Even minor changes to private areas of class definitions usually mean system wide recompiles.

For most large software systems this ripple effect is merely annoying. For others it is completely unmanageable.

Consider a vendor who wants to provide a popular C++ class library as a dynamically linked library. A dynamically linked library has the desirable characteristic of being loaded only once in memory regardless of how many programs on the system are making use it. So, if `animal` is distributed as a dynamically linked library, we can have any number of different programs all using `animal` objects and all sharing the same code, a very efficient use of memory.

Typically vendors, at least those with profit motives, distribute such libraries as object code and class definitions. Implementation code is not distributed.

However, suppose the `animal` library is supplied by one vendor, and the `pet` library is supplied by another. For efficiency, the `pet` library should make use of the dynamically linked version of the `animal` library. But there is no way to ensure that everything was compiled using the same class definitions. The user may have purchased `pet` library compiled using A2, but be using the A1 animal library. As the user purchases more and more class libraries, all based on the popular `animal` base class, this situation becomes hopelessly complex.

This scenario may seem far fetched, but this is exactly the scenario faced by distributors of system level class libraries, such as operating system interfaces. Using dynamic linking is highly desirable for such libraries. Yet there is no way to ensure that the different products being run on the system were all compiled using the same version of the library.

Problems like this will have to be solved before C++ can be considered an ideal tool for developing general purpose, system level class libraries.

11.4   Clashes Between Base and Derived Classes

Ideally, base class programmers and derived class programmers should be able to live in their respective happy worlds, and as long as each follows standard C++ rules, each should be oblivious to the work of the other. In reality, work done in one world often unexpectedly impacts work in the other.

Consider this simple `animal` definition

```
class animal {
private:
  char *food;
  char *habitat;
};
```

and this derived **pet** definition

```
class pet : public animal {
public:
  virtual void makeNoise();
private:
  char *name;
  char *owner;
};
```

with this implementation

```
#include "pet.hpp"
#include <stdio.h>

void pet::makeNoise()
{
  printf("a pet says: Please Pat Me\n");
}
```

This is all fine. A test program can declare and manipulate a pet. For example, this program

```
#include "pet.hpp"
#include <stdlib.h>

int main()
{
  pet *myPet = new pet;
  myPet->makeNoise();
  return 0;
}
```

gives this output

```
a pet says: Please Pat Me
```

Now suppose the **animal** programmer decides to add another method. The **animal** programmer has no idea that some other programmer has been using **animal** as a base class, and certainly doesn't expect the addition of a new method to break existing code. The new version of **animal** looks like

```
class animal {
public:
  virtual int makeNoise();
private:
  char *food;
  char *habitat;
};
```

and now has this implementation file

```
#include "animal.hpp"
#include <stdio.h>

int animal::makeNoise()
{
  printf("an animal says: Grrrrr\n");
}
```

The **animal** programmer's implementation file and test programs compile and work without incident. The **pet** programmer then makes some minor change to **pet** and recompiles. Suddenly **makeNoise()**, which had always compiled and worked, now has fatal compile errors. The unsuspecting **pet** programmer next spends an indeterminate amount of time trying to understand how this "minor" code change broke **makeNoise()**, eventually to discover it was the recompile that broke **pet**, not the code change.

Originally, **animal** did not have a **makeNoise()** method. When **pet** declared **makeNoise()** to be a nonvirtual method, there is no conflict, because there is only one **makeNoise()** defined in the **pet** class derivation graph.

When **animal** also declares **makeNoise()**, there is a conflict. **animal** says **makeNoise()** is virtual, so when **pet** is compiled, it is checked for a method declaration matching the signature of **makeNoise()**. Since the signature of **pet::makeNoise()** matches the signature of **animal::makeNoise()**, C++ assumes this is a virtual override of the base class virtual method. Unfortunately, although the signatures match, the return values do not. It is illegal for a virtual override not to have the same return value as the base method. Thus the compiler balks.

Of course, though the problem was caused by the base class programmer, it is the derived class programmer who is left to pick up the pieces.

Similar types of conflicts occur when multiple inheritance is used. Consider these class definitions

```
class animal {
public:
  void makeNoise(char *myNoise);
};
```

```
class performer {
public:
  void bargain(int bottomLine);
};

class animalPerformer : public animal, public performer {
};
```

This test code

```
int main()
{
  animalPerformer *Lassie = new animalPerformer;
  Lassie->makeNoise("woof woof");
}
```

works fine until **performer** is modified to this

```
class performer {
public:
  void bargain(int bottomLine);
  void makeNoise(char *myNoise);    // New method
};
```

Now the line

```
Lassie->makeNoise("woof woof");
```

gives a compile error, because the compiler doesn't know which **makeNoise()** is being used, **animal::makeNoise()** or **performer::makeNoise()**. Once again we have a seemingly innocuous change in a base class causing errors in code which is far removed from the source of the "problem."

Base classes and derived classes can also clash over virtual declarations. Consider this definition of **animal**

```
class animal {
public:

  animal();
  ~animal();

  void setFood(char *newFood);       // Non Virtual
  void setHabitat(char *newHabitat); // Ditto
  void shortDisplay();               // Ditto
  void longDisplay();                // Ditto
```

```
    private:

      char *food;
      char *habitat;
    };
```

If we decide to write **pet** derived from **animal** and use the virtual method resolution to override **shortDisplay()** and **longDisplay()**, we are stuck. Only the base class has the right to decide a method is virtual.

In most cases, it is probably the base class which is best able to judge whether it is reasonable for a particular method to be virtual. However, it also seems reasonable to allow the derived class to overrule the base class's decision. In C++, whatever the base class has decided, the derived class is forced to follow suit. For this reason this book recommends as many methods as possible be declared virtual, and that the internal class implementation be consistent with this choice.

Sometimes we may even have descriptive name clashes between base and derived classes. A method name that seemed appropriate for a base class may seem out of context in a derived class. Suppose, for example, we decide to implement a stack as a class derived privately from a linked list class, with the methods **addHead()** and **removeTail()** redeclared as public. This gives a perfectly reasonable stack, except for the names of the methods **addHead()** and **removeTail()**.

The names of these methods have two problems. First, they betray they origins as derived from a linked list, which is a violation of implementation hiding. Second, they are not the names we would expect in a stack context. The obvious names we expect to see are **push()** and **pop()**. This problem occurs because C++ offers no mechanism to rename an inherited method within the context of the derived class.

11.5   Class Is Not a Class

Many object-oriented programmers find that the concept of a class being a class in its own right can be helpful. Within this model, every object is associated with some object that defines its class. Every instantiation of a given class is associated with the same class object. So, if **Toto**, **Lassie**, and **RinTinTin** are all instantiations of **pet**, they are all associated with the same class object, say **petClassObject**, an object of type **classObject**.

We then expect all objects to support a **getClassObject()** method, which returns a pointer to the class object. The class object itself would support methods which deal with the class as a whole. For example, the **new** function, which C++ treats as a special case, would logically become one of the methods supported by the class object. The definition of a class object might start with some very basic class related methods.

```
class classObject{
  void *new(int nbytes);    // Create new object
  void delete(void *);      // Delete existing object
  char *className();        // Name of class, say "dog"
  char *size();             // Size of object, say "Lassie"
  char *base();             // Pointer to parent class object
};
```

We might also want methods to give us some run time information about the nature of objects. Such methods might look like

```
/* ... */
  int nDataItems();         // How many data items in an object?
  validTypes itemType(int n);
                            // What is the type of the nth item?
  int itemSize(int n);      // What is the size of the nth item?
/* ... */
```

We might want methods to give us more flexibility on choosing and applying methods such as

```
/* ... */
  methodPtr getMethod(char *methodName);
// Return a pointer to the method whose name is methodName.
```

which would allow us to write code like

```
/* ... */
  printf("What would you like to do to Lassie?\n");
  getString(response);
  doToLassie = petClassObject->getMethod(response);
  Lassie->*doToLassie();
/* ... */
```

We also might expect to be able to derive new classes from old, adding, for example, our own methods. We have seen examples in this book of class methods, that is, methods which were logically associated with a class rather than an object of that class. Because C++ does not directly support the concept of class classes, we implemented these class methods as dangling functions, that is, functions declared in the class definition file and implemented along in the class definition file, where they were placed only for lack of a better idea. One example of such dangling function was `DisplayLineItemHeading()` back in Chapter 6, which appeared as part of this class definition

```
class LineItem {
public:
  void InitLineItem();
  int  EnterLineItem();
  void DisplayLineItem();
  int  GetLineItemPrice();

private:
  char BookTitle[100];
  int BookQuantity;
  int BookPrice;
};
void DisplayLineItemHeading(); // Should be class method
```

The lack of a class, like all the problems in this chapter can be worked around. In most of these cases, C++ has made the choice to sacrifice breadth for performance, and assumes programmers will implement additional features on an as needed basis. The problem, of course, is that one person's options are another person's requirements.

11.6 Exercises

Exercise 11.1 Say P2 of **pet** adds a private data item. Then **animal** and **pet** are recompiled, but **main** is not. What problems, if any, does this cause?

Exercise 11.2 Say A2 of **animal** adds a new virtual method, and declares it after **longDisplay()**. Then **animal** is recompiled, but **main** and **pet** are not. What problems, if any, does this cause?

Exercise 11.3 Say A2 of **animal** adds a new virtual method, and declares it before **shortDisplay()**. Then **animal** is recompiled, but **main** and **pet** are not. What problems, if any, does this cause?

Exercise 11.4 Say A2 of **animal** adds a new virtual method, and declares it after **longDisplay()**. Say P2 of **pet** adds a new virtual method, and declares it after **longDisplay()**. Say **animal** is recompiled with A2, **pet** is recompiled with A1 and P2. What problems, if any, does this cause? Analyze the situation with **main** compiled with each of A1/P1, A1/P2, A2/P1, and A2/P2.

Exercise 11.5 We saw how the addition of

```
virtual int makeNoise();
```

to `animal` broke `pet`. Suppose `animal::makeNoise()` had been declared to return `void`. What difference would this have made?

Exercise 11.6 Suppose the next person to recompile after the addition of `animal::makeNoise()` was not the `pet` programmer, but the programmer of this

```
#include "pet.hpp"
#include <stdlib.h>

int main()
{
  pet *myPet = new pet;
  animal *myAnimal = new animal;

  myPet->makeNoise();
  myAnimal->makeNoise();

  return 0;
}
```

What would this programmer have experienced?

Exercise 11.7 Implement a class scheme of the type discussed in this chapter. Decide what methods it will support, how it will serve as a basis for further derivation, and how it will know about class definitions. Write sample code making use of your scheme.

*I beg your Grace... will show us some portrait of this
lady, even though it be no larger than a grain of
wheat, for by the thread one comes to the ball of yarn;
and with this we shall remain satisfied and assured.
The truth is, I believe that we have already so much of
your way of thinking that though it should show her to
be blind of one eye and distilling vermilion and
brimstone from the other, nevertheless, to please your
Grace, we would say in her behalf all that you desire.*

- Don Quixote de la Mancha
Miguel de Cervantes Saavedra
Translated by Samuel Putnam

Chapter 12

Final Example

Up until now we have been focusing on the C++ language syntax, and using simple
classes with little practical use. Even the most complex of our examples, the HMO
program managing patients and physicians, used less than a half dozen classes
and made minimal use of inheritance. These examples served their purpose in
illustrating language features. However, such small programs can not really prepare
one for what a large, complex, object-oriented system might look like.

12.1 Introduction

In this chapter, we will look at such a program. We will look at a highly object
oriented and relatively complex system. This system consists of 18 classes and over
1700 lines of code. The system makes extensive use of code reuse through both
inheritance and construction. This program illustrates different techniques class
designers use, and many of the tradeoffs class designer's face.

We will also introduce some of the parlance of Object-Oriented Design and

Analysis. This is a large topic, and is not part of the scope of this book, but at least this chapter offers an introduction to this closely related field. Our terminology generally follows the lead of Wirfs-Brock [Wirfs-Brock et al.].

12.2   Design Rules

We will start by considering a set of design rules which, with some exceptions, we will follow and recommend for the reader's own endeavors. This rules should be thought of as guidelines, not absolutes. Situations will come up when these guidelines cannot be followed exactly, but these situations should be few and far between. If you find yourself consistently "working around" these rules, then there is almost certainly something wrong with your approach.

Rule 1. Place each class definition in a separate file.

This makes it easy to locate the definitions of classes. The definition for the **dog** class lives in **dog.h**. The definition for **animal** lives in **animal.h**. The file names need not match the class names, and for portability reasons should always be kept to eight characters plus extension. The file name should be at least suggestive of the class name.

Rule 2. Enclose class definitions within #ifndef.

This guarantees that code will not be broken by indirect includes. If we don't follow this rule, then code using a base class will break if it later makes use of another class derived from the base class. So if we have, say, **animal.hpp**, which looks like

```
class animal {
  /* ... */
};
```

and **dog.hpp**, which looks like

```
#include "animal.hpp"
class dog : public animal {
  /* ... */
};
```

then our main program can either have

```
#include "animal.hpp"
```

or

```
#include "dog.hpp"
```

but not

```
#include "animal.hpp"
#include "dog.hpp"
```

because the animal call ends up being defined twice, once from the direct include of `animal.hpp`, and once through the indirect include through `dog.hpp`. Unlike `typedefs`, class definitions may not appear twice. Bracketing every class definition by `#ifndefs`, as in

```
#ifndef CLASS_ANIMAL
#define CLASS_ANIMAL
class animal {
/* ... */
};
#endif
```

and

```
#ifndef CLASS_DOG
#define CLASS_DOG
#include "animal.hpp"
class dog : public animal {
/* ... */
};
#endif
```

ensures the double definition never occurs.

Rule 3. Define all member data as private.

Member data should be treated as an implementation detail of the class. The distinction between member data and member methods may often seem blurred, and this rule may seem pedantic. For example, in

```
class dog : public animal {
public:
  virtual void setBark(char *newBark);
  virtual char *getBark();
private:
  char *myBark;
};
```

Here the value of this rule may not seem obvious. But the class designer commits only to supporting the public interface. Today `getBark()` may return `myBark`. Tomorrow it may return a value negotiated with its base class, or perhaps be overridden by some further derived class. Classifying all class data as private minimizes the chances of client code becoming entangled in the implementation details of the class.

Rule 4. Define all public methods as virtual.

This ensures that any method can be overridden by classes derived from this class. The only exception to this rule is the **new** operator, which cannot be virtual. The **delete** operator can and should be virtual.

This rule is important to follow, because a class designer can never predict when a class may become a base for further derivation, and cannot reliably predict which methods the derived classes are likely to want to override. Derived classes cannot override nonvirtual methods. There is no reason a class should prefer nonvirtual methods, except for some questionable performance optimization. Classes whose proper functioning depends on some or all methods being nonvirtual are classes likely to cause future problems.

Once we have defined public methods as virtual, they should be used wherever appropriate in the class implementation. For example, given this definition

```
class dog : public animal {
public:
  virtual void setBark(char *newBark);
  virtual char *getBark();
  virtual void talk()
private:
  char *myBark;
};
```

it would be an error to implement **talk()** as

```
void dog::talk()
{
  printf("I say %s\n", myBark);
}
```

because should the virtual method **getBark()** ever be overridden in a derived class, the semantics will not be respected by **talk()**. The better implementation of **talk()** is

```
void dog::talk()
{
  printf("I say%s\n", getBark());
}
```

This rule needs to be taken with a grain of salt. It will not always be reasonable to make every public method virtual. It is true, however, that every nonvirtual method lessens the chances that the class can form an effective base for future derivations. Any nonvirtual public methods should, therefore, be carefully scrutinized. Remember to always keep the implementation semantics consistent with the virtual definitions.

Rule 5. Make all private methods nonvirtual.

Private methods by definition cannot be accessed outside the class, and derived classes will have no need to override them. If you think a derived class may want to override a private method, then make the method public (and virtual, by rule 4).

For completeness, C++ does support a **protected** access class. A **protected** method can be overriden in a derived class, but not accessed outside the class. The philosophy of this book is that the **protected** attribute falls in that category of C++ features regarded as syntactic fluff, that is, features peripheral to the central issues of object-oriented programming and therefore not discussed here.

Rule 6. Use only C++ constructs described in this text.

If you think you need a construct not described here, your design is too complicated. Put your effort into simplifying your design, not complicating your code.

Once again, take this with a grain of salt. As you continue your studies of C++ you will find useful facilities not described in this book. But always strive to keep your classes as simple as possible. Your classes should be as easy to understand as the examples in this book. If you find, for example, that none of your co-workers are smart enough to understand your highly sophisticated use of C++, the chances are that you are making life more difficult than it needs to be. Strive to simplify.

12.3   Overview of Example

The program we are going to look at is a text processing program, which we call **TP**. A text processor is a program which reads a file of text and creates a nicely formatted output file. The input file contains text that is to be reformatted and text that represents commands to the text processor.

Input text is considered within the context of an environment. The text processor recognizes several environments. Environments are identified by special character sequences in the input file. The initial environment for text is the **setup** environment, which reads initial settings for the output file. Let's look at a simple text example.

This input file, with lines numbered for future reference,

```
1. width 60
2. height 20
3. columns 1
4. [[header]]
5. Romeo and Juliet                    Page: [[page_number]]
6. [[end_environment]]
7. [[footer]]
8. Juliet's Lament
```

```
 9. [[end_environment]]
10. [[indent_paragraphs]]
11. Tis but thy name that is my enemy.
12. Thou art thyself, though not a Montague.
13. What's Montague?  It is
14. [[bulleted_list]]
15. nor hand,
16.
17. nor foot,
18.
19. nor arm,
20.
21. nor face,
22.
23. nor any other part belonging to a man.
24. [[end_environment]]
25. O, be some other name!
26. What's in a name?  That which we call a rose
27. by any other name would smell as sweet.
28.
29. So Romeo would, were he not Romeo call'd,
30. retain that dear perfection which he owes
31. without that title.
32.
33. Romeo, doff thy name;
34. And for that name, which is no part of thee,
35. take all myself.
36. [[end_environment]]
```

gives this output, with page breaks shown as dashed lines:

```
----------------------------------------
Romeo and Juliet                Page: 1

    Tis but thy name that is my enemy. Thou art thyself,
though not a Montague. What's Montague?  It is
    - nor hand,
    - nor foot,
    - nor arm,
    - nor face,
    - nor any other part belonging to a man.
    O, be some other name! What's in a name?  That which we
call a rose by any other name would smell as sweet.
```

> So Romeo would, were he not Romeo call'd, retain that
> dear perfection which he owes without that title.
> Romeo, doff thy name; And for that name, which is no part
> of thee, take all myself.

Juliet's Lament

TP automatically starts up in the **setup** environment. In this environment, **width** identifies a number which defines the width of the output page in characters. Similarly, **height** defines the number of lines a page contains. **columns** defines the number of columns of text you want to appear.

New environments are identified by keywords bracketed by [[...]]. Line 4, for example, identifies a **header** environment. The end of environments are identified by [[end_environment]]. Line 6, for example, terminates the **header** environment started by line 4.

Most environments recognize blank lines as separating paragraphs, although different environments process paragraph breaks differently. Line 16, for example, identifies a paragraph break within a **bulleted_list** environment, which indents and bullets new paragraphs.

Here is our complete list of environments TP recognizes:

[[header]] — Text in this environment will be printed at the head of each page.

[[footer]] — Text in this environment will be printed at the bottom of each page.
[[standard_text]] — Text in this environment is considered to be standard input text. Blank lines are interpreted as paragraph breaks. Output paragraphs are not indented. Input line breaks are ignored. Output text is justified to the left margin.
[[right_justified_text]] — Similar to [[standard_text]], but output text is justified to the right margin.

[[indent_paragraphs]] — Similar to [[standard_text]], but new paragraphs are indented.

[[bulleted_list]] — Like [[indent_paragraphs]], but new paragraphs are started with a bullet, and new lines are indented.

Nonenvironment keywords include

width, **height**, **columns**, within the **setup** environment, as described earlier.

[[end_environment]] — terminates the current environment.

[[page_number]] — valid within [[header]] or [[footer]] environments. This identifies a location where the current page number should be printed.

As we can guess from these descriptions, we can dramatically change the format of **TP** output with small changes in the input file. For example, changing the number 1 in line 3 to a 2 tells **TP** to use double column output instead of single column, with this very different output result:

```
-----------------------------------------
Romeo and Juliet                 Page: 1

    Tis but thy name that is   sweet.
my enemy. Thou art thyself,        So Romeo would, were he
though not a Montague.         not Romeo call'd, retain
What's Montague?  It is        that dear perfection which
    - nor hand,                he owes without that title.
    - nor foot,                    Romeo, doff thy name; And
    - nor arm,                 for that name, which is no
    - nor face,                part of thee, take all
    - nor any other part       myself.
  belonging to a man.
    O, be some other name!
What's in a name?  That
which we call a rose by any
other name would smell as

Juliet's Lament
```

Then changing the **height** from 20 to 15 in line 2 says only 15 lines of text fit on a page, and **TP** then creates two pages of output instead of one

```
-----------------------------------------
Romeo and Juliet                 Page: 1

    Tis but thy name that is     belonging to a man.
my enemy. Thou art thyself,        O, be some other name!
though not a Montague.         What's in a name?  That
What's Montague?  It is        which we call a rose by any
    - nor hand,                other name would smell as
    - nor foot,                sweet.
    - nor arm,                     So Romeo would, were he
    - nor face,                not Romeo call'd, retain
    - nor any other part       that dear perfection which

Juliet's Lament
```

```
------------------------------------------
Romeo and Juliet              Page: 2

he owes without that title.
   Romeo, doff thy name; And
for that name, which is no
part of thee, take all
myself.
```

Juliet's Lament

TP is fairly simple, as far as text processors go. A "real" text processor would contain at least a dozen more environments, and a host of font manipulation commands. As a further simplification, TP always reads from a file named **test.dat** and always writes to **stdout**. These simplifications help keep the code to a reasonable size while still illustrating some complex programming logic.

Next we will give some broad (and somewhat artificial) characterizations of our various TP classes, including some preliminary object-oriented design notes on each. Words meant to convey object-oriented design concepts are first shown in italics, and are generally used as defined by Wirfs-Brock [Wirfs-Brock et al.].

First are the Low-Level Helper Classes, which perform low level functionality. These include

link A generic link in the linked list. The *responsibilities* of this class are limited to providing constructors and destructors.

linkedList A generic linked list. This *container* class has general responsibility for maintaining a collection of generic objects. Wirfs-Brock would say that a **link** is related to a **linkedList** by an *is-part-of* relationship. However, it seems more appropriate to look at the relationship from the **linkedList** point of view, so we will say a **linkedList** *is-composed-of* a **link**.

baseType The base of any class which can be manipulated by the **linkedList** class. This class represents a *contract* between classes which can be contained by a **linkedList** and classes which make use of a **linkedList**. Containable classes must be derived from **baseType**, and they agree to support several methods. Classes which make use of the **linkedList** class agree to use the **linkedList** to contain only objects derived from **baseType**.

fileMgr Provides an object-oriented interface to the file system. This class acts, in the most traditional sense, as a *server* class.

word A generic class which describes a "word" of text. This class agrees to two *contracts*. The first is to fulfill its responsibilities as a derived class from **baseType**. The second is to offer various interfaces to managing a character string.

TPWord A slightly more specialized version of **word**, designed to meet the needs of TP. This class represents a new contract, in addition to those of **word**, in which **TPWord** agrees to support a notion of compartmentalization between different types of words. A **TPWord** *is-kind-of* a **word**.

Next are the Page Layout Classes, which maintain information about different aspects of the current page. These include

columnBlock A linked list of blocks of text. Each block contains one column of text on the page. A **columnBlock** has responsibility for coordinating the activity of the different columns.

textLine An object which contains a line of text. A **textLine** is a specialized *kind-of* **linkedList**.

page An object which contains the different objects making up a page. A **page** *is-composed-of* a **columnBlock**, and **textLines** representing the header and footer of the page. This class has the contract containing the information about a full page of text, and *collaborates* with **columnBlock** and **textLine** to fulfill its responsibilities.

Next are the Option Processing Classes, each controlling some aspect of setting up output options. These include

optionEnvProcessor A base class for other option processing classes, implementing generic option processing functionality. The next three classes are all *kind-of* **optionEnvProcessor**, and each *is-analogous-to* each of the others.

footerProcessor Implements the [[footer]] environment.

headerProcessor Implements the [[header]] environment.

setupEnvProcessor Implements the initial set up environment.

Finally the most visible of the classes, the Text Processing Environment Classes. Each of these has responsibility for controlling one of the text processing environments.

envProcessor A base class for all environment classes which implements all generic environment functionality. The next four classes are all *kind-of* **envProcessors**, and each *is-analogous-to* each of the others.

bulletedList Implements the [[bulleted_list]] environment.

indentedParagraphs Implements the [[indent_paragraphs]] environment.

rightJustifiedText Implements the [[right_justified_text]] environment.

txtEnvProcessor A base class for all text processing environments, which implements those behaviors common to all text processing environments but not used by option processing classes.

A class derivation graph for **TP** shows how these various classes are derived from each other

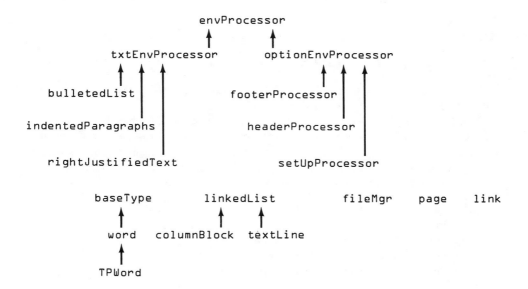

This construction graph shows how the classes use each other as building blocks.

(Read **TPWord** ⟵ **page** as "one of the elements of **page** is a **TPWord**.")

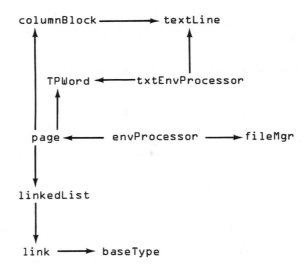

12.4   Helper Classes

Let's go through each of these classes in detail, starting with the helper classes, the simplest and most self-contained group of classes.

The **baseType** is the root class of any class which can be placed on the linked list. It serves as a common handle, exactly as did the **baseType** class of Chapter 8. We are using a slightly different implementation in this chapter. In Chapter 8, **baseType** was implemented as a pure virtual class, meaning that methods were defined, but not implemented. The definition of **baseType** then looked like

```
class baseType {
public:
  virtual int match(void *target) = 0;
  virtual void print(FILE *output) = 0;
  virtual void replace(baseType *dest) = 0;
  virtual baseType *newCopy() = 0;
};
```

Our new definition of `baseType` defines a slightly different set of methods, and provides default implementations of each. The definition file for `baseType` is

```
#ifndef BASETYPE_CLASS
#define BASETYPE_CLASS 1
#include <stdio.h>

class baseType {
public:
  virtual ~baseType();
  virtual int match(void *target);
  virtual void print(FILE *output);
  virtual char *getClassName();
};


#endif
```

The implementation file provides minimal implementations. The first method, the destructor, provides no implementation, and is included to ensure its virtual characteristics.

```
#include "bt.hpp"
#include <stdio.h>
#include <stdlib.h>

static void terminate(char *);

baseType::~baseType()
{
}
```

The next two methods are defined to terminate with an error message.

```
int baseType::match(void *target)
{
  terminate("match");
}

void baseType::print(FILE *output)
{
  terminate("print");
}
```

```
void terminate(char *methodName)
{
  printf("Method %s\n", methodName);
  printf("invoked, but not implemented for this Type\n");
  exit(0);
}
```

Notice the difference in strategies between this **baseType** and the earlier version in handling method overriding. Neither version expects its implementations to be the ones invoked. The earlier version used pure virtual method definitions, with no implementations, forcing derived classes to provide appropriate method implementations. This says, in effect, "If you use me as a base class, you must implement these methods." This new version of **baseType** says, in effect, "I am not going to force you to provide implementations in derived classes. However, if you do not, you had better be sure the method in question is never invoked, because if it is I am going to terminate and make you look foolish."

Either or both of these strategies is acceptable. The following implementations, on the other hand, are asking for problems:

```
int baseType::match(void *target)
{
}

void baseType::print(FILE *output)
{
}
```

The last method in **baseType** is useful for debugging purposes

```
char *baseType::getClassName()
{
  static char *myName = "baseType";
  return myName;
}
```

The assumption here is that every derived class will override this method, using a similar implementation, but replacing the string **baseType** by the name of its own class. Then, at debug time, when say, we have lost track of what kind of object is on our linked list, we can write

```
baseType *thisItem;
linkedList *myList;
/* ... */
```

```
thisItem = myList->head();
printf("thisItem is a %s\n", thisItem->getClassName());
/* ... */
```

Next, let's look at the **linkedList** class, and its close cousin, the **link** class. Both of these are similar to versions already discussed, although the functionality shown here is limited to that needed by TP code.

The **link** class definition is

```
#ifndef LINK_CLASS
#define LINK_CLASS 1
#include "bt.hpp"

class link {
public:
  link(baseType *newContents);
public:
  link *next;
  link *previous;
  baseType *contents;
};


#endif
```

The data portion violates rule 3 by declaring data public instead of private. The **linkedList** class, as implemented, needs access to the **link** data members. We could have implemented **get/set** methods for each of the three data items, thus preserving code integrity according to rule 3. Alternatively, we could have declared the data private, and then used a C++ construct not described in this book to give the **linkedList** class privileged access to **link** data. The following reasons seem sufficient to justify the approach used here.

1. The **link** class is intimately associated with the **linkedList** class. It has no real life of its own. Giving the **linkedList** access to **link** data is reasonable.

2. We want to absolutely minimize our use of fancy C++ features, and stick with some basic, nonlanguage specific, object-oriented programming techniques.

3. The **link** class is effectively insulated from other classes, since it is used only internally within **linkedList** code, and the **linkedList** code never reveals **link** data to non **linkedList** code.

The **link** implementation file is

```
#include "link.hpp"
link::link(baseType *newContents)
{
    contents = newContents;
    next = previous = 0;
}
```

Not much to it.

The linkedList class definition should look familiar. The major change is that most methods have retrieve() functionality built in. The definition is

```
#ifndef LINKED_LIST_CLASS
#define LINKED_LIST_CLASS 1

#include "link.hpp"
#include "bt.hpp"
#include <stdio.h>

#define MAX_INT 30000        // Default maximum list size.

class linkedList : public baseType{
public:
  linkedList();                          // Constructor.
  virtual ~linkedList();                 // Destructor.
  virtual void freeContents();           // Works like constructor,
                                         // but also deletes elements
                                         // stored in list.
  virtual baseType *head();              // head becomes current.
  virtual baseType *tail();              // tail becomes current.

  virtual int length();                  // Returns length of list.
  virtual void setMax(int newMax);       // Sets max length of list.
  virtual int left();                    // max - length.

  virtual baseType *next();              // next becomes current.
  virtual baseType *previous();          // previous becomes current.

  virtual baseType *retrieve();          // retrieve current contents.
  virtual baseType *replace(baseType *newElement);
                                         // replace current contents.
  virtual baseType *promoteTail();       // Move tail to head.
  virtual baseType *addHead(baseType *newElement);
                                         // Add new head.
```

```
    virtual baseType *addTail(baseType *newElement);
                                    // Add new tail.
    virtual baseType *removeHead();  // Delete head
    virtual int isTail();            // Is current the tail?
    virtual void print(FILE *);      // Print list.


private:

    int max;
    int nlinks;
    link *currentLink;
    link *headLink;
    link *tailLink;

};
#endif
```

The code implementation file should be understandable based on previous versions and the documentation in the definition file.

```
    #include <stdlib.h>
    #include "ll.hpp"

    linkedList::linkedList()
    {
        currentLink = headLink = tailLink = 0;
        nlinks = 0;
        max = MAX_INT;
    }

    linkedList::~linkedList()
    {
        while(removeHead());
    }

    void linkedList::freeContents()
    {
      baseType *thisItem;
      while(thisItem = removeHead()) delete thisItem;
    }
```

```
baseType *linkedList::head()
{
   if (!nlinks) return 0;
   currentLink = headLink;
   return currentLink->contents;
}

baseType *linkedList::tail()
{
   if (!nlinks) return 0;
   currentLink = tailLink;
   return currentLink->contents;
}

int linkedList::length()
{
   return nlinks;
}

void linkedList::setMax(int newMax)
{
  max = newMax;
}

int linkedList::left()
{
   return max - length();
}

baseType *linkedList::next()
{
  if (!nlinks) return 0;
  if (currentLink->next) {
     currentLink = currentLink->next;
     return currentLink->contents;
  }
  else {
     return 0;
  }
}
```

```
baseType *linkedList::previous()
{
  if (!nlinks) return 0;
  if (currentLink->previous) {
     currentLink = currentLink->previous;
     return currentLink->contents;
  }
  else {
     return 0;
  }
}

baseType *linkedList::retrieve()
{
  if (!nlinks) return 0;
  return currentLink->contents;
}

baseType *linkedList::replace(baseType *newElement)
{
  if (!nlinks) return 0;
  currentLink->contents = newElement;
  return currentLink->contents;
}

baseType *linkedList::promoteTail()
{
   link *oldTail;
   printf("promoteTail\n");
   if (!nlinks) return 0;
   if (nlinks == 1) return headLink->contents;
   oldTail = tailLink;
   tailLink = tailLink->previous;
   oldTail->previous->next = 0;
   oldTail->previous = 0;
   oldTail->next = headLink;
   headLink->previous = oldTail;
   headLink = oldTail;
   currentLink = headLink;
}
```

```
baseType *linkedList::addHead(baseType *newElement)
{
  link *newLink = new link(newElement);
  if (!left()) {
    head();
    return(replace(newElement));
  }
  if (head()) {
    currentLink->previous = newLink;
  }
  else tailLink = newLink;
  newLink->next = currentLink;
  headLink = currentLink = newLink;
  nlinks++;
  return currentLink->contents;
}

baseType *linkedList::addTail(baseType *newElement)
{
  link *newLink = new link(newElement);
  if (!left()) {
    tail();
    return(replace(newElement));
  }
  if (tail()) {
    currentLink->next = newLink;
  }
  else headLink = newLink;
  newLink->previous = currentLink;
  tailLink = currentLink = newLink;
  nlinks++;
  return currentLink->contents;
}

baseType *linkedList::removeHead()
{
  baseType *thisItem;
  if (!nlinks) return 0;
  thisItem = head();
  if (nlinks == 1) {
    delete headLink;
    headLink = tailLink = currentLink = 0;
  }
```

```
      if (nlinks > 1) {
         next();
         delete headLink;
         headLink = currentLink;
         headLink->previous = 0;
      }
      nlinks--;
      return thisItem;
   }

   int linkedList::isTail()
   {
      return (currentLink == tailLink);
   }

   void linkedList::print(FILE *output)
   {
      baseType *thisItem;
      thisItem = head();
      if (thisItem) {
         while (thisItem) {
            thisItem->print(output);
            thisItem = next();
         }
      }
   }
```

The `fileMgr` class provides an object-oriented interface to the file system, with a few additional functions which will come in handy. Only read functionality is included, since that is all that is needed for the simple TP problem. We leave write functionality as a reader exercise.

The `fileMgr` constructor takes as a parameter a character string identifying the input file. For TP, this will always be invoked with the character string "`test.dat`." The file is opened as part of construction, and closed as part of the destruction.

The `fileMgr` class provides only two other public methods: `getChar()` and `peekChar()`. The first of these returns the next character in the file, and could have been implemented as a front for the standard library function `fgetc()`, were it not for the requirements of `peekChar()`. The method `peekChar()` looks ahead at characters in the file, without affecting what `getChar()` will next return. `peekChar()` takes an integer parameter, which is the offset from the current character at which you wish to peek.

Another way to look at this is to consider a file as a queue of unread characters. When the file is first opened, the entire file is in the unread queue. `getChar()`

removes characters one by one from the unread queue. `peekChar()` allows you to peek ahead in the queue without removing characters. Therefore, if our input file consists of the string

        MINT CHOCOLATE CHIP

then we get this calling sequence:

method	returns
getChar()	'M'
getChar()	'I'
getChar()	'N'
getChar()	'T'
getChar()	' '
peekChar(0)	'C'
peekChar(1)	'H'
getChar()	'C'
getChar()	'H'

    `peekChar()` and `getChar()` could have been implemented as a linked list of characters. `peekChar(n)` would then return the nth character stored on the list. `getChar()` would then return and delete the head of the list. We leave this implementation as an exercise.

    For efficiency, our `fileMgr` is implemented as a ring buffer. A ring buffer has a fixed size, 20 in this case. A ring buffer acts like an array, but the `last+1` element is the same as the first element. We will see how this is actually implemented shortly.

    Remember this important point: the fact that the `fileMgr` uses a ring buffer internally is no concern of the `fileMgr` clients, who care only that the four public methods work as advertised.

    The definition of `fileMgr` is

```
#ifndef CLASS_FILEMGR
#define CLASS_FILEMGR 1
#include <stdio.h>

#define BUFF_SIZE 20

class fileMgr {
public:
  fileMgr(char *newFile);      // Instantiate and open file
  virtual ~fileMgr();          // Deallocate and close file

  virtual int getChar();       // Get next available character
  virtual int peekChar(int n); // Peek n characters ahead
```

```
  private:
    int size();              // Chars in ring buffer
    int incr(int oldNum);    // Increment ring index
    int add(int oldNum, int n);  // Add n to a ring index

    FILE *funit;
    int buffer[BUFF_SIZE];
    int putSide;             // Index to insert next character in
    int getSide;             // Index to read next character from
};
```

```
#endif
```

The three private methods are all involved with different aspects of managing the ring buffer. The method `size()`, for example, returns the number of characters currently on the ring buffer, functionality which is much more complicated than one might think. The method `incr()` serves the purpose of a ++ operator for ring buffer indices. Incrementing a ring buffer index is special only when the index has reached its maximum. Since our ring buffer stores 20 characters, and the first character is stored at buffer location 0, it follows that the twentieth location is the same as the first location, and therefore `incr(19)` is 0. With this in mind, you should be able to follow the implementation of `fileMgr`. First, the constructor, destructor, and private methods.

```
#include "fm.hpp"
#include <stdio.h>
#include <stdlib.h>
#include <string.h>

fileMgr::fileMgr(char *newFile)
{
  funit = fopen(newFile, "r");
  putSide = 0;
  getSide = 0;
}

fileMgr::~fileMgr()
{
  fclose(funit);
}
```

```
int fileMgr::add(int oldNum, int addNum)
{
    return ((oldNum + addNum) % BUFF_SIZE);
}

int fileMgr::incr(int oldNum)
{
    if (oldNum == (BUFF_SIZE -1)) return 0;
    else return (oldNum + 1);
}

int fileMgr::size()
{
    int result;
    if (getSide == putSide) result = 0;
    else if (getSide < putSide) result = putSide - getSide;
    else result = (BUFF_SIZE - getSide - 1) + (putSide + 1);
    return result;
}

int fileMgr::getChar()
{
    int newChar;
    if (size()) {
        newChar = buffer[getSide];
        getSide = incr(getSide);
    }
    else {
        newChar = fgetc(funit);
    }
    return newChar;
}
```

Most of the code for peekChar() is concerned with ensuring there are enough characters in the ring buffer to satisfy the peek request. By the way, peekChar() returns an int instead of a char for the same reason that fgetc() returns an int instead of a char, namely, so that it can return EOF when appropriate.

```
int fileMgr::peekChar(int offset)
{
    int newChar;
    char cChar;
    int n;
```

```
      for (;;) {
        n = size();
        if (n > offset) break;
        newChar = fgetc(funit);
        cChar = newChar;
        buffer[putSide] = newChar;
        putSide = incr(putSide);
      }
      offset = add(getSide, offset);
      newChar = buffer[offset];
      return newChar;
    }
```

The last two of the helper classes are word and TPWord. Both are straight forward. The word definition is

```
#ifndef CLASS_WORD
#define CLASS_WORD 1

#include "bt.hpp"
#include <stdio.h>

class word : public baseType {
public:
  word(char *string);
  word(char newChar, int nChars);
  virtual ~word();

  virtual int match(void *target);  // Does word match target?
  virtual void print(FILE *output); // Print a word
  virtual void replace(char *newChars);
                              // Replace word contents
  virtual int getLength();          // Number of chars in word
  virtual int wordToInt();          // Translate word to int
  virtual char *getClassName();

private:

  char *storage;
  int length;
};

#endif
```

Notice **word** is derived from **baseType**, making it eligible for placement on **linkedLists**.

Four of the **word** methods override virtual declarations in **baseType**. There are two **word** constructors, one which constructs given a character string, and one which construct from a character and a count. The method **wordToInt()** translates a **word** object into an integer. The implementation of **word** is

```
#include "word.hpp"
#include <string.h>
#include <stdlib.h>
#include <stdio.h>

word::word(char *string)
{
  storage = new char[strlen(string)+1];
  strcpy(storage, string);
  length = strlen(string);
}

word::word(char newChar, int nChars)
{
  int n;
  storage = new char[nChars+1];
  for (n=0; n<nChars; n++) {
      storage[n] = newChar;
  }
  storage[n] = '\0';
  length = strlen(storage);
}

word::~word()
{
  int n;
  delete storage;
}

int word::match(void *target)
{
  int nchrs;
  int targetLength = strlen(target);
  return (!strncmp(storage, target, targetLength));
}
```

```
int word::wordToInt()
{
  return atoi(storage);
}

void word::replace(char *newChars)
{
  delete storage;
  storage = new char[strlen(newChars)+1];
  strcpy(storage, newChars);
  length = strlen(newChars);
}

void word::print(FILE *output)
{
  int n;
  for (n=0; n<length; n++) fprintf(output, "%c", storage[n]);
}

int word::getLength()
{
  return length;
}

char *word::getClassName()
{
  static char *myClass = "word";
  return myClass;
}
```

The TPWord class further specializes the word class, adding functionality needed by TP. TPWord objects, unlike word objects, have a type. Types are defined in the TPWord header file, and are determined by the TPWord method type(). TPWord also has a new associated function, readToken(). It is not a method of the class, but is still closely associated with the class. It therefore seems appropriate to include its prototype with the class definition and its code along with the method implementations. The definition of TPWord is

```
#ifndef CLASS_TPWORD
#define CLASS_TPWORD 1

#include "word.hpp"
#include "fm.hpp"
```

```
#define TP_WORD 0
#define TP_LINE_BREAK 1
#define TP_PARAGRAPH_BREAK 2
#define TP_TOKEN 3
#define TP_BLANK_SPACE 4
#define TP_EOF 5

class fileMgr;

class TPWord : public word {
public:
  TPWord(char *newWord);
  TPWord(char newChar, int nChars);
  virtual int type();
  virtual char *getClassName();
};

TPWord *readToken(fileMgr *myFile);

#endif
```

When looking at the implementation file, notice the simple minded definition of type(), which decides the type of a TPWord based on its first few characters. The type() implementation is insulated from the internal representation of a TPWord, which, as private, inherited data, is unknown in any case. type() depends only on the match() function working as advertised in the word definition. This code illustrates how we can keep derived classes free of dependencies on base implementations. The implementation of TPWord starts like

```
#include "tpword.hpp"
#include <string.h>

int TPWord::type()
{
    if (match("[[EOF]]")) return TP_EOF;
    else if(match("[[")) return TP_TOKEN;
    else if (match("\n\n")) return TP_PARAGRAPH_BREAK;
    else if (match("\n")) return TP_LINE_BREAK;
    else if (match(" ")) return TP_BLANK_SPACE;
    else return TP_WORD;
}
```

The function `readToken()` accepts a pointer to a `fileMgr`, and returns a pointer to a newly constructed `TPWord`. The `fileMgr` pointer is assumed to point to an existing `fileMgr` object. From our understanding of `fileMgr`s, we can be sure an existing `fileMgr` is already primed with an existing file. The fact that `readToken()` returns a new `TPWord` object implies that this functionality could have been implemented as a third `TPWord` constructor. We will leave this as an exercise. The code for `readToken()` is

```
TPWord *readToken(fileMgr *myFile)
{
    char buffer[100];
    int nxtChr;
    int n = 0;
    int brackets;
    nxtChr = myFile->peekChar(0);

/* Check for string of blanks.
   -------------------------- */
    if (nxtChr == ' ') {
        while (myFile->peekChar(0) == ' ') {
            buffer[n++] = myFile->getChar();
        }
    }

/* Check for string of newlines.
   ---------------------------- */
    else if (nxtChr == '\n') {
        while (myFile->peekChar(0) == '\n') {
            buffer[n++] = myFile->getChar();
        }
    }

/* Check for EOF.
   ------------- */
    else if (nxtChr == EOF) {
        strcpy(buffer, "[[EOF]]");
        n = strlen(buffer);
    }
```

```
/* Check for special token.
   ----------------------- */
   else if ((nxtChr == '[') && (myFile->peekChar(1) == '[')) {
      brackets = 0;
      while (brackets < 2) {
         nxtChr = myFile->getChar();
         buffer[n++] = nxtChr;
         if (nxtChr == ']') brackets++;
         else brackets = 0;
      }
   }

/* Otherwise, handle as word.
   ------------------------ */
   else {
      for (;;) {
         nxtChr = myFile->peekChar(0);
         if (nxtChr == ' ') break;
         if (nxtChr == '\n') break;
         if (nxtChr == EOF) break;
         if (nxtChr == '[') break;
         buffer[n++] = myFile->getChar();
      }
   }

/* Return converted buffer.
   ----------------------- */
   buffer[n] = '\0';
   return new TPWord(buffer);
}
```

The rest of the file has no surprises. It is

```
TPWord::TPWord(char *newWord) : word(newWord)
{}
TPWord::TPWord(char newChar, int nChars) :
word(newChar, nChars)
{}

char *TPWord::getClassName()
{
   static char *myClass = "TPWord";
   return myClass;
}
```

12.5 Page Layout Classes

The page layout classes are involved with storing text in memory until it is ready to be printed. If you consider the flow of text from an input file to output columns, you will realize that lines cannot be printed until the final page composition is complete.

The most basic building block of the page layout classes is the `textLine`, which contains one contiguous line of related text. The `textLine` will be used to construct a page header, a page footer, or a line of text in one of the text columns.

A `textLine` can contain a maximum number of characters, determined at construction time, and supports queries about the number of characters still left on the line. A `textLine` is derived from a `linkedList`. Its definition is

```
#ifndef CLASS_TEXTLINE
#define CLASS_TEXTLINE 1

#include "ll.hpp"
#include "tpword.hpp"

class textLine : private linkedList {
public:

  textLine(int newSize);

  virtual baseType *addTail(baseType *newElement);
  virtual baseType *addHead(baseType *newElement);

  virtual int charsInLine();
  virtual int charsLeft();

  linkedList::head;
  linkedList::tail;
  linkedList::next;
  linkedList::previous;
  linkedList::retrieve;
  linkedList::promoteTail;
  linkedList::print;
  linkedList::freeContents;
```

```
private:

   int maxSize;
   int totalChars;
};
#endif
```

Although `textLine` is a `linkedList`, it is a `linkedList` which only contains `TPWords`. `linkedLists` already have functionality to track information about the number of objects they contain (e.g., `linkedList::length()`), but `textLines` are more interested in the number of characters in these objects, not the number of objects *per se*. So, the `textLine` class adds some private data members. The first is `maxSize`, which tracks the maximum number of characters permitted in this `textLine`. The second is `totalChars`, which tracks the number of characters currently in the `textLine`.

The `textLine` class overrides two of the `linkedList` methods, `addHead()` and `addTail()`, with versions which first update the new private data of `textLine` and then pass control over to their `linkedList` versions.

`textLine` is derived from `linkedList`, but privately derived, preventing `textLine` clients from calling arbitrary `linkedList` methods. Several of the linkedList methods would not work, and are not needed, for `textLine` objects. We could override them with versions which do work, but this seems wasteful, since we don't need their functionality. We could forget about them and hope they are never called by `textLine` clients, but this seems dangerous. Or we can ensure that invalid methods are never called by specifically declaring those methods which can be safely inherited. That is what we have done by declaring the inheritance private, and explicitly declaring the safe methods as public.

The implementation of `textLine` is

```
// Note: in all these methods,
// we know baseType is really a word

#include "textline.hpp"
#include <stdio.h>
#include <stdlib.h>

textLine::textLine(int newSize)
{
   totalChars = 0;
   maxSize = newSize;
}
```

```
baseType *textLine::addTail(baseType *newElement)
{
   TPWord *myWord = (TPWord *) newElement;
   int newTotal;
   newTotal = totalChars + myWord->getLength();
   if (newTotal <= maxSize) {
      totalChars = newTotal;
      return(linkedList::addTail(newElement));
   }
   else return newElement;
}


baseType *textLine::addHead(baseType *newElement)
{
   TPWord *myWord = (TPWord *) newElement;
   int newTotal;
   newTotal = totalChars + myWord->getLength();
   if (newTotal <= maxSize) {
      totalChars = newTotal;
      return(linkedList::addHead(newElement));
   }
   else return newElement;
}


int textLine::charsInLine()
{
   return totalChars;
}


int textLine::charsLeft()
{
   return maxSize - totalChars;
}
```

The next of the page layout classes is columnBlock. A columnBlock is a linked list of columns, where each column is a linked list of text lines. Pictorially, this can

be represented as

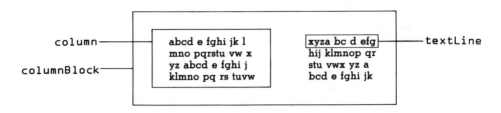

The "column" concept could have been encapsulated in a column class, publicly derived from linkedList. But column would have had no reason to extend (or shrink) linkedList, so the design decision was made to use linkedList directly.

columnBlock, on the other hand, does modify the basic linkedList concept somewhat. The definition is

```
#ifndef CLASS_COLUMNBLOCK
#define CLASS_COLUMNBLOCK
#include "ll.hpp"
#include <stdio.h>

#define SPACE_BETWEEN 3
#define HEADER_SPACE 3
#define FOOTER_SPACE 3

class columnBlock : public linkedList {
public:
  columnBlock(int newColumns, int newHeight, int newWidth);
  virtual int getColumnWidth();
  virtual int linesLeft();
  virtual baseType *addTail(baseType *newLine);
  virtual void print(FILE *output);
private:
  void printBlanks(FILE *output, int nblanks);
  int columnWidth;
};

#endif
```

Several specialized functions are incorporated into `columnBlock`. First, let's consider the constructor. The constructor takes three parameters. The first parameter describes the number of desired columns of text, information which originates from the `columns` description such as that shown at line 3 of the input text file. The second parameter describes the number of lines of text that fit vertically on a page, originating from the `height` line (line 2). The third parameter describes the number of characters that fit horizontally on the page, originating from the `width` line (line 1).

From this information, the constructor decides how wide a single text line can be within a column, and sets itself up as a linked list with one link for each column of text. The constructor is

```
#include "colblk.hpp"
#include "textline.hpp"

columnBlock::columnBlock(int newColumns,int newHeight,int
newWidth)
{
  int n;
  linkedList *newBlock;

  columnWidth = newWidth - ((newColumns - 1) * SPACE_BETWEEN);
  columnWidth = columnWidth / newColumns;

  setMax(newColumns);
  for (n=0; n<newColumns; n++) {
      newBlock = new linkedList();
      newBlock->setMax(newHeight - HEADER_SPACE -
  FOOTER_SPACE);
      linkedList::addTail((baseType *) newBlock);
  }
  head();
}
```

The method `getColumnWidth()` returns the calculated acceptable width of a `textLine` within a column. It is

```
int columnBlock::getColumnWidth()
{
  return columnWidth;
}
```

`addTail()` overrides the `linkedList` version. It adds a `textLine` to the current column, tracking and adjusting, when necessary, which column is considered current.

```
baseType *columnBlock::addTail(baseType *newLine)
{
  linkedList *thisBlock;
  int num;
  void *ptr;
  thisBlock = (linkedList *) retrieve();
  if (!thisBlock) return 0;
  if (!thisBlock->left()) {
    if (!(thisBlock = (linkedList *) next())) {
      return 0;
    }
  }
  return thisBlock->addTail(newLine);
}
```

The next method returns TRUE if there is room for another textLine someplace in the columnBlock, FALSE otherwise.

```
int columnBlock::linesLeft()
{
  linkedList *thisBlock;
  thisBlock = (linkedList *) retrieve();
  if ((thisBlock->left()) || !isTail()) return 1;
  else return 0;
}
```

Finally, the most complicated of the columnBlock logic, the printing logic, which prints the first line of each column, then the second line of each column, and so on.

```
void columnBlock::print(FILE *output)
{
/* Set up.
   ------- */
  int n, blockLength, blankLines;
  linkedList *thisBlock;
  textLine *thisLine;

/* Determine number of lines in typical block.
   ------------------------------------------- */
  thisBlock = (linkedList *) head();
  blockLength = thisBlock->length();
  blankLines = thisBlock->left();
```

```
   /* For each horizontal line...
      -------------------------- */
      for (n=0; n<blockLength; n++) {

/*        For each text block...
          --------------------- */
          thisBlock = (linkedList *) head();
          while (thisBlock) {

/*            Print the column line.
              --------------------- */
              thisLine = (textLine *) thisBlock->head();
              if (thisLine) {
                 thisLine->print(output);
                 thisLine->freeContents();
                 printBlanks(output, thisLine->charsLeft());
              }
              else {
                 printBlanks(output, getColumnWidth());
              }
              thisBlock->removeHead();

/*            Print space between columns.
              --------------------------- */
              printBlanks(output, SPACE_BETWEEN);

/*            Move to next block.
              ------------------ */
              thisBlock = (linkedList *) next();
          }
          fprintf(output, "\n");
      }
   /* Print blank lines.
      ----------------- */
      for (n=0; n<blankLines; n++) {
        fprintf(output, "\n");
      }
   }
```

```
void columnBlock::printBlanks(FILE *output, int nblanks)
{
  int n;
  for (n=0; n<nblanks; n++) {
      fprintf(output, " ");
  }
}
```

The last of the page layout classes is the **page** itself. You might expect page to be very complex, but actually, most of the dirty details have already been taken care of in **columnBlock**. The **page** definition is

```
#ifndef CLASS_PAGE
#define CLASS_PAGE_1
#include <stdio.h>

#include "colblk.hpp"
#include "tpword.hpp"
#include "textline.hpp"

#define DEFAULT_WIDTH 20
#define DEFAULT_HEIGHT 15
#define DEFAULT_COLUMNS 1

class page {
public:

  virtual void print(FILE *output);

  page();                           // New page with defaults
  virtual ~page();
  virtual void setPageHeight        // Reset vertical lines
     (int newHeight);               // per page.
  virtual void setPageWidth         // Reset horizontal
     (int newWidth);                // characters per page.
  virtual void setNumberOfColumns // Reset columns per page
     (int ncolumns);                // from default.
  virtual void setPageNumber        // Set special word to be
     (TPWord *newPageWord);         // page number.

  virtual columnBlock *getColumnBlock();
  virtual textLine *getHeaderBlock();
  virtual textLine *getFooterBlock();
```

```
private:

  int maxColumnWidth();       // Set width of columns.
  void printBlankLines        // Print blank text lines.
    (FILE *output, int nLines);

  int height;
  int width;
  int ncolumns;
  int pageNumber;

  textLine *header;
  textLine *footer;

  columnBlock *columns;
  TPWord *pageWord;
};
#endif
```

There are many methods, but none are too complex. The implementation is

```
#include "page.hpp"
#include <stdio.h>
#define MAX_WORDS_IN_HEADER 100
#define MAX_WORDS_IN_FOOTER 100

page::~page()
{
  textLine *thisLine;
  if (header) {
    header->freeContents();
    delete header;
  }
  if (columns) delete columns;
  if (footer) {
    footer->freeContents();
    delete footer;
  }
}
```

```
page::page()
{
  width = DEFAULT_WIDTH;
  height = DEFAULT_HEIGHT;
  ncolumns = DEFAULT_COLUMNS;
  pageNumber = 0;

  header = 0;
  columns = 0;
  footer = 0;
  pageWord = 0;
}

void page::setPageHeight(int newHeight)
{
  height = newHeight;
}

void page::setPageWidth(int newWidth)
{
  width = newWidth;
}

void page::setNumberOfColumns(int newColumns)
{
  ncolumns = newColumns;
}

columnBlock *page::getColumnBlock()
{
    if (!columns) columns = new columnBlock
       (ncolumns, height, width);
    return columns;
}

textLine *page::getHeaderBlock()
{
    if (!header) header = new textLine(MAX_WORDS_IN_HEADER);
    return header;
}
```

```
textLine *page::getFooterBlock()
{
    if (!footer) footer = new textLine(MAX_WORDS_IN_FOOTER);
    return footer;
}
```

The one slightly interesting method is print(). Notice how page numbers are
handled. This class provides a method which sets a "special" TPWord, which is
assumed to be in the desired location for printing page numbers. Internally, the
location of this special word is stored in pageWord. pageWord, if it exists, should
point to one of the words in either the header or footer of the page. Notice how
the print method uses this location.

```
void page::setPageNumber(TPWord *newPageWord)
{
    pageWord = newPageWord;
}

void page::print(FILE *output)
{
    int done;
    linkedList *thisBlock;
    char buffer[10];

/* Print header.
   ------------- */
    pageNumber++;
    if (pageWord) {
        sprintf(buffer, "%d", pageNumber);
        pageWord->replace(buffer);
    }
    fprintf(output,
        "\n-----------------------------------------\n");
    if (header) header->print(output);
    fprintf(output,"\n\n");

/* Print text.
   ----------- */
    if (columns) columns->print(output);
    fprintf(output,"\n\n");
```

```
/* Print footer.
   ------------ */
   if (footer) footer->print(output);

/* Clear out text from this column block.
   ------------------------------------- */
   delete columns;
   columns = 0;
}
```

12.6   Root Environment Processor

The **page** class represents, in a sense, the culmination of the output classes. A
fully populated **page** object has all the information necessary to print a full page
of output text. The remaining classes can be thought of as the input classes, the
classes which know how to interpret input text and place it into a **page** object.

The root of the input classes is **envProcessor**. It includes methods common to
all text processing environments. Its definition is

```
#ifndef CLASS_ENVPROCESSOR
#define CLASS_ENVPROCESSOR 1

class page;
class fileMgr;
class TPWord;

class envProcessor {
public:
  envProcessor();
  envProcessor(envProcessor *lastEnv);
  virtual ~envProcessor();

  virtual void processEnvironment() = 0;
  virtual void startUpNewEnvironment(TPWord *envName);
  virtual void initializeEnvironment();
  virtual void shutdownEnvironment();
  virtual void prepareForNewEnvironment();
  virtual int  getParagraphIndentation();
  virtual int  getLineIndentation();

  virtual page    *getPage();
  virtual fileMgr *getFileMgr();
```

```
virtual void      setPage(page *newPage);
virtual void      setFileMgr(fileMgr *newFileMgr);

virtual envProcessor *getPreviousEnv();
virtual char *getClassName();

private:

    page          *thisPage;
    fileMgr       *thisFile;
    envProcessor *previousEnv;
};
#endif
```

envProcessor is an abstract base class, meaning that it is not expected to be instantiated directly. Because of the definition of **processEnvironment()**, we know the class cannot be instantiated, only classes derived from it can be instantiated.

The implementation file starts by including the necessary headers.

```
#include "ep.hpp"
#include "tpword.hpp"
#include "txtep.hpp"
#include "header.hpp"
#include "footer.hpp"
#include "rttxt.hpp"
#include "ipep.hpp"
#include "blep.hpp"
#include "page.hpp"

#include <stdio.h>
#include <stdlib.h>
```

Our **TP** system allows text environments to be embedded within each other. Our input text, for example, has an **indent_paragraphs** environment starting on line 10, then a **bulleted_list** environment starting on line 14, then an **end_environment** on line 24, which terminates the **bulleted_list**, and the final **end_environment** terminating the **indent_paragraphs** on line 36. The **bulleted_list**, therefore, starts before the **indent_paragraphs** ends, and we say the **bulleted_list** is embedded inside an **indent_paragraphs**.

The **envProcessor** class includes two constructors, the first to be used when the environment is not embedded such as the **setUp** environment, the second to be used for embedded environments such as the **bulleted_list**. Be sure you do not confuse embedding (a **TP** concept) with derivation (an object-oriented programming concept).

The constructor implementations are

```
envProcessor::envProcessor()
{
  previousEnv = 0;
  thisFile = 0;
  thisPage = 0;
}

envProcessor::envProcessor(envProcessor *lastEnv)
{
  previousEnv = lastEnv;
  thisFile = previousEnv->getFileMgr();
  thisPage = previousEnv->getPage();
}
```

The difference between these two constructors is that the nonembedded constructor is used only once, for **setUp**, whereas the embedded constructor is used for the remaining environments, and makes the assumption that a previous environment has already instantiated a **page** and **fileMgr**. Every environment keeps track of its immediate predecessor environment, and can supply this information through the **getPreviousEnv()** method.

The destructor deletes memory allocated by the constructor, if this is the original environment which allocated the memory. If the environment is an embedded environment, the destructor assumes this memory will be deallocated by some previous environment's destructor.

```
envProcessor::~envProcessor()
{
  if(!previousEnv) {
    delete thisFile;
    delete thisPage;
  }
}
```

The next method is **getClassName()**, and we provide it here for similar reasons as for **baseType** earlier. As before, we assume that future derivations will override this method.

```
char *envProcessor::getClassName()
{
  static char *myClass = "envProcessor";
  return myClass;
}
```

The next set of methods are place holders, defined here to do nothing, but are called where appropriate in case derived classes want to override them.

```
void envProcessor::initializeEnvironment()
{}
void envProcessor::shutdownEnvironment()
{}
void envProcessor::prepareForNewEnvironment()
{}
```

The next method is invoked when we detect a new environment command while processing an existing environment.

```
void envProcessor::startUpNewEnvironment(TPWord *envName)
{
  envProcessor *nextEnv;
  if (envName->match("[[standard_text]]"))
    nextEnv = new txtEnvProcessor(this);
  else if (envName->match("[[header]]"))
    nextEnv = new headerProcessor(this);
  else if (envName->match("[[footer]]"))
    nextEnv = new footerProcessor(this);
  else if (envName->match("[[standard_text]]"))
    nextEnv = new txtEnvProcessor(this);
  else if (envName->match("[[right_justified_text]]"))
    nextEnv = new rightJustifiedText(this);
  else if (envName->match("[[indent_paragraphs]]"))
    nextEnv = new indentedParagraphs(this);
  else if (envName->match("[[bulleted_list]]"))
    nextEnv = new bulletedList(this);
  else {
    printf("Unknown environment: ");
    envName->print(stdout);
    exit(1);
  }
  prepareForNewEnvironment();
  nextEnv->processEnvironment();
  delete nextEnv;
}
```

Notice that **startUpNewEnvironment()** always uses the embedded constructor. This is logical, since we are starting up a new environment from an existing environment. Most of the method is a giant switch statement, attempting to figure out which new environment needs to be instantiated. To be sure we understand the logic, consider which lines will be executed if the new environment is `bulleted_list`. First we will get the appropriate environment instantiated, with the current environment passed into the constructor

```
nextEnv = new bulletedList(this);
```

Next, we invoke the current environment's `prepareForNewEnvironment()`, which, unless we have overridden the version inherited from `envProcessor`, will do nothing

```
prepareForNewEnvironment();
```

Next, we turn over control to the new environment

```
nextEnv->processEnvironment();
```

The `nextEnv` will return control to us when it encounters an `end_environment` command, at which time it is finished, and we can delete it and continue where we left off

```
delete nextEnv;
```

Finally, we have a series of boring **set**/**get** method which require no explanation.

```
page *envProcessor::getPage()
{
  return thisPage;
}

fileMgr *envProcessor::getFileMgr()
{
  return thisFile;
}

void envProcessor::setPage(page *newPage)
{
  thisPage = newPage;
}

void envProcessor::setFileMgr(fileMgr *newFileMgr)
{
  thisFile = newFileMgr;
}

envProcessor *envProcessor::getPreviousEnv()
{
  return previousEnv;
}
```

```
int envProcessor::getParagraphIndentation()
{
  return 0;
}

int envProcessor::getLineIndentation()
{
  return 0;
}
```

Three different virtual method defining methodologies have been used in this class. `processEnvironment()` is defined such that derived classes must implement this method. It is so inconceivable that a derived class would not need its own version of this method that we will force a compile error if such an event occurs. Other methods (e.g., `getPage()`) are not expected to be overridden, and are fully implemented. If any methods were not going to be virtual, these would be good candidates. By following our rule of making all methods virtual, however, we reserve the right to override these should the need arise. Finally, we have methods which are defined with dummy implementations (e.g. `shutdownEnvironment()`). These are methods for which "do nothing" is a valid option for many environments, and we expect derived classes to provide overrides only if they have other needs.

12.7   Option Processing Classes

The option processing classes are concerned with setting up layout information. They are all derived from `optionEnvProcessor`, which doesn't provide a lot of functionality, and is included mostly for esthetics: Since the text processing classes have their common base, it seems only fair that the option processing classes should be treated similarly. Their base definition is

```
#ifndef CLASS_OPTIONENVPROCESSOR
#define CLASS_OPTIONENVPROCESSOR 1
#include "ep.hpp"

class optionEnvProcessor : public envProcessor {
public:
  optionEnvProcessor(envProcessor *lastEnv);
  optionEnvProcessor();
  virtual int readIntWord();
  virtual char *getClassName();
};

#endif
```

Its implementation is

```
#include "opep.hpp"
#include "tpword.hpp"

optionEnvProcessor::optionEnvProcessor(
  envProcessor *lastEnv)
  : envProcessor(lastEnv)
{
}

char *optionEnvProcessor::getClassName()
{
  static char *myClass = "optionEnvProcessor";
  return myClass;
}

optionEnvProcessor::optionEnvProcessor()
{
}

int optionEnvProcessor::readIntWord()
{
  TPWord *thisWord;
  int returnValue;
  thisWord = readToken(getFileMgr());   // Blank
  delete thisWord;
  thisWord = readToken(getFileMgr());   // Number
  returnValue =  thisWord->wordToInt();
  delete thisWord;
  return returnValue;
}
```

The only slightly interesting method is the last one, which is invoked when some `optionEnvProcessor` has just read a word which it expects to be followed by a word containing an integer.

Keep in mind that although this class seems to have minimal functionality, it inherits all the capability of `envProcessor`, including the `startUpNewEnvironment()` method.

The next class is the first of the environments to be instantiated. TP always starts up by instantiating a `setUpEnvProcessor`. This environment processes the set up commands, and turns over control to new environments as it finds them. Its definition is

```
#ifndef CLASS_SETUPENVPROCESSOR
#define CLASS_SETUPENVPROCESSOR 1
#include "opep.hpp"

class setUpEnvProcessor : public optionEnvProcessor {
public:
  setUpEnvProcessor();
  virtual char *getClassName();
private:
  void processOptions();
  char thisFileName[100];
};
#endif
```

Notice that this class defines the private member `thisFileName`, a character string designed to contain the name of the input file. Because this is the first environment that will be instantiated, it takes responsibility for instantiating the `fileMgr`, and needs the name of the input file to do so.

The implementation is

```
#include "suep.hpp"
#include <string.h>
#include <stdio.h>
#include <stdlib.h>
#include "page.hpp"
#include "fm.hpp"
#include "tpword.hpp"

setUpEnvProcessor::setUpEnvProcessor()
{
  strcpy(thisFileName, "test.dat");
  setPage(new page);
  setFileMgr(new fileMgr(thisFileName));
  processOptions();
}

char *setUpEnvProcessor::getClassName()
{
  static char *myClass = "setUpEnvProcessor";
  return myClass;
}
```

The last method does most of the work, reading through input text words and setting appropriate page layout options.

```
void setUpEnvProcessor::processOptions()
{
  int n = 0;
  fileMgr *myfm;
  page *thisPage;
  TPWord *thisWord;

  thisPage = getPage();
  myfm = getFileMgr();

  for (;;) {
    thisWord = readToken(getFileMgr());
    if (thisWord->type() == TP_EOF) {
      delete thisWord;
      break;
    }
    else if (thisWord->type() == TP_TOKEN)
      startUpNewEnvironment(thisWord);
    else if (thisWord->match("width"))
      thisPage->setPageWidth(readIntWord());
    else if (thisWord->match("height"))
      thisPage->setPageHeight(readIntWord());
    else if (thisWord->match("columns"))
      thisPage->setNumberOfColumns(readIntWord());
    delete thisWord;
  }
  thisPage = getPage();
  thisPage->print(stdout);
}
```

While it seems we have a class with minimal functionality, this is far from true. Remember the derivation graph we are working with

setUpEnvProcessor $\longrightarrow$ optionEnvProcessor $\longrightarrow$ envProcessor

setUpEnvProcessor has plenty of functionality, it's just that most of this functionality is reused code inherited from base classes.

The next two classes we will look at are footerProcessor and headerProcessor. Like setUpEnvProcessor, both of these classes are derived from optionEnvProcessor. These two new classes are similar. Both define a constructor which does nothing but pass control back to the base class constructor. Both override the processEnvironment() method, which is almost the same for both classes. In both, processing the environment means returning on end_environment, ignoring line breaks, and offering special treatment to the string [[page_number]].

In fact, the only difference between these two processEnvironment()s is that footerProcessor's places text on the **page**'s footer linked list, and headerProcessor places text on the **page**'s header linked list. Notice which object receives the addTail() method in the two versions of processEnvironment().

The footerProcessor definition is

```
#ifndef CLASS_FOOTERPROCESSOR
#define CLASS_FOOTERPROCESSOR 1
#include "opep.hpp"

class footerProcessor : public optionEnvProcessor {
public:
  footerProcessor(envProcessor *lastEnv);
  virtual void processEnvironment();
};
#endif
```

The footerProcessor implementation is

```
#include "footer.hpp"
#include "page.hpp"
#include "tpword.hpp"

footerProcessor::footerProcessor(envProcessor *lastEnv)
: optionEnvProcessor(lastEnv)
{
}

void footerProcessor::processEnvironment()
{
    page *thisPage;
    textLine *thisFt;

    thisPage = getPage();
    thisFt = thisPage->getFooterBlock();

    for (;;) {
      thisWord = readToken(getFileMgr());
      if (thisWord->match("[[end_environment]]")) {
        delete thisWord;
        return;
      }
```

```
        if (thisWord->type() == TP_LINE_BREAK) {
           delete thisWord;
           continue;
        }
        thisFt->addTail(thisWord);
        if (thisWord->match("[[page_number]]"))
           thisPage->setPageNumber(thisWord);
     }
  }
```

The `headerProcessor` definition is

```
#ifndef CLASS_HEADERPROCESSOR
#define CLASS_HEADERPROCESSOR 1
#include "opep.hpp"

class headerProcessor : public optionEnvProcessor {
public:
  headerProcessor(envProcessor *lastEnv);
  virtual void processEnvironment();
};
#endif
```

The `headerProcessor` implementation is

```
#include "header.hpp"
#include "page.hpp"
#include "tpword.hpp"

headerProcessor::headerProcessor(envProcessor *lastEnv)
: optionEnvProcessor(lastEnv)
{
}

void headerProcessor::processEnvironment()
{
    page *thisPage;
    textLine *thisHd;
    TPWord *thisWord;
    thisPage = getPage();
    thisHd = thisPage->getHeaderBlock();
```

```
    for (;;) {
      thisWord = readToken(getFileMgr());
      if (thisWord->match("[[end_environment]]"))  {
        delete thisWord;
        return;
      }
      if (thisWord->type() == TP_LINE_BREAK) {
        delete thisWord;
        continue;
      }
      thisHd->addTail(thisWord);
      if (thisWord->match("[[page_number]]"))
        thisPage->setPageNumber(thisWord);
    }
}
```

12.8 Text Processing Environment Classes

The last set of classes are those that process regular input text. All of these classes are based on `txtEnvProcessor`. The strategy employed is that `txtEnvProcessor` defines a default text processor in a generic manner. Each derived text processor overrides only those methods which are different in their respective environments.

For example, a bulleted list environment is similar in many ways to a standard text environment. Both process words, blanks, and line breaks the same. The bulleted list environment is different only in how it processes new paragraphs. We, therefore, expect the bulleted list environment to override only those methods which are involved with processing new paragraphs.

The definition of `txtEnvProcessor` is

```
#ifndef CLASS_TXTENVPROCESSOR
#define CLASS_TXTENVPROCESSOR 1
#include "ep.hpp"

class textLine;
class TPWord;
class columnBlock;

class txtEnvProcessor : public envProcessor {
public:
  txtEnvProcessor(envProcessor *lastEnv);
  virtual ~txtEnvProcessor();
```

```
virtual void shutdownEnvironment();
virtual void initializeEnvironment();
virtual void prepareForNewEnvironment();
virtual void processEnvironment();
virtual void processWord();
virtual void processBlanks();
virtual void processLineBreak();
virtual void processFullLine();
virtual void processFullPage();
virtual void processNewLine();
virtual void processNewParagraph();

virtual char *getClassName();

virtual int       getParagraphIndentation();
virtual int       getLineIndentation();
virtual textLine *getLine();
virtual void      setLine(textLine *newLine);

private:

  TPWord        *thisWord;
  textLine      *thisLine;
  columnBlock   *thisCB;
};
#endif
```

The **txtEnvProcessor** implementation starts with

```
#include "txtep.hpp"
#include "tpword.hpp"
#include "textline.hpp"
#include "page.hpp"
#include <string.h>
#include <stdlib.h>
#include <stdio.h>

#define PARAGRAPH_INDENTATION 0
#define LINE_INDENTATION 0
```

The constructor is responsible for making sure that the private **thisCB** is set. The destructor makes sure any memory allocated during the run of this class is deallocated.

```
txtEnvProcessor::txtEnvProcessor(envProcessor *lastEnv)
                  : envProcessor(lastEnv)
{
  page *thisPage;
  thisWord = 0;
  thisLine = 0;

  thisPage = getPage();
  thisCB = thisPage->getColumnBlock();
}

txtEnvProcessor::~txtEnvProcessor()
{
  if(thisWord) delete thisWord;
  if(thisLine) delete thisLine;
}
```

The next method prepares to turn control back to the previous environment, if there is one.

```
void txtEnvProcessor::shutdownEnvironment()
{
  envProcessor *lastEnv;
  lastEnv = getPreviousEnv();
  if (lastEnv) lastEnv->initializeEnvironment();
}
```

The `initializeEnvironment()` method is invoked when another environment is ready to return control to `txtEnvProcessor`. The method assumes that the line just read consists of `[[end_environment]]`, and starts out by discarding the following linefeed character.

```
void txtEnvProcessor::initializeEnvironment()
{
  int charsToIndent;
  TPWord *blanks;
  TPWord *lineFeed;
  textLine *thisLine;
  fileMgr *thisFile;

  thisFile = getFileMgr();
  lineFeed = readToken(thisFile);
  delete lineFeed;
  charsToIndent = getParagraphIndentation();
  processNewLine();
```

```
        thisLine = getLine();
        if (charsToIndent) {
            blanks = new TPWord(' ', charsToIndent);
            thisLine->addTail((baseType *) blanks);
        }
    }
```

The next method is called before turning over control to a new environment.

```
    void txtEnvProcessor::prepareForNewEnvironment()
    {
      processFullLine();
    }
```

Next is the primary method for the class, the method that defines the overall process of processing a generic text environment. Notice how it maintains a policy neutral description of text processing. For example, upon reading a newline character, it does not invoke any special newline processing algorithm, instead it invokes the virtual method processLineBreak(), giving later derived classes the opportunity to decide for themselves what processing a new line means. This generic algorithm gives considerable flexibility in reuse through class derivation.

```
    void txtEnvProcessor::processEnvironment()
    {
    /* Declare local variables.
       ----------------------- */
        textLine *currentLine;
        textLine *thisLine;
        page *thisPage;
        fileMgr *thisFile;
        int n = 0;
        char *myClass = getClassName();
        thisPage = getPage();
        thisFile = getFileMgr();

    /* Prepare for looping.
       -------------------- */
        initializeEnvironment();
```

```
/* Loop until end of file.
   ---------------------- */
while (thisWord = readToken(thisFile)) {
   if (thisWord->type() == TP_EOF) {
      delete thisWord;
      break;
   }
   if (thisWord->match("[[end_environment]]")) {
      shutdownEnvironment();
      break;
   }

   switch (thisWord->type()) {
     case TP_LINE_BREAK:
        processLineBreak();
        continue;
     case TP_WORD:
        processWord();
        continue;
     case TP_PARAGRAPH_BREAK:
        processNewParagraph();
        continue;
     case TP_BLANK_SPACE:
        processBlanks();
        continue;
     case TP_TOKEN:
        startUpNewEnvironment(thisWord);
        delete thisWord;
        continue;
   }
}
processFullLine();
}
```

Next comes a series of methods which define default behaviors. Some of the defaults such as `processWord()` will be appropriate for many class derivations. Others such as `processLineBreak()` will often be overridden. However, this class does not make judgement calls. By defining specific behaviors, and packaging those behaviors as virtual methods, the opportunity exists for any of these behaviors to be redefined as necessary in later derivations.

```cpp
void txtEnvProcessor::processWord()
{
    textLine *thisLine = getLine();
    page *thisPage;
    thisPage = getPage();
    thisCB = thisPage->getColumnBlock();
    if (!thisCB->linesLeft()) processFullPage();
    if (thisWord->getLength() > thisLine->charsLeft()) {
        processFullLine();
        processNewLine();
        thisLine = getLine();
    }
    thisLine->addTail((baseType *) thisWord);
}

void txtEnvProcessor::processBlanks()
{
    textLine *thisLine = getLine();
    if (!thisLine->charsLeft()) {
        delete thisWord;
        return;
    }
    processWord();
}

void txtEnvProcessor::processLineBreak()
{
    textLine *thisLine = getLine();
    delete thisWord;
    if (!thisLine->charsInLine()) return;
    if (!thisLine->charsLeft()) return;
    thisWord = new TPWord(" ");
    processWord();
}
```

```
void txtEnvProcessor::processFullLine()
{
  textLine *thisLine = getLine();
  page *thisPage;
  thisPage = getPage();
  thisCB = thisPage->getColumnBlock();
  thisCB->addTail((baseType *) thisLine);
  setLine(new textLine(thisCB->getColumnWidth()));
}

void txtEnvProcessor::processFullPage()
{
  page *thisPage;
  thisPage = getPage();
  thisPage->print(stdout);
  thisCB = thisPage->getColumnBlock();
}

void txtEnvProcessor::processNewLine()
{
  int charsToIndent;
  TPWord *blanks;
  textLine *thisLine;
  charsToIndent = getLineIndentation();
  if (charsToIndent) {
     thisLine = getLine();
     blanks = new TPWord (' ', charsToIndent);
     thisLine->addTail((baseType *) blanks);
  }
}

void txtEnvProcessor::processNewParagraph()
{
  int charsToIndent;
  TPWord *blanks;
  textLine *thisLine;

  charsToIndent = getParagraphIndentation();
  processFullLine();
  processNewLine();
  thisLine = getLine();
```

```
        if (charsToIndent) {
            blanks = new TPWord(' ', charsToIndent);
            thisLine->addTail((baseType *) blanks);
        }
        delete thisWord;
    }
```

Next is our old friend getClassName().

```
    char *txtEnvProcessor::getClassName()
    {
        static char *myClass = "txtEnvProcessor";
        return myClass;
    }
```

The next two methods return the number of characters that lines and paragraphs should be indented. The default version, provided here, provides whatever indentation the previous environment defined, if there was a previous environment, and no indentation otherwise.

```
    int txtEnvProcessor::getParagraphIndentation()
    {
        envProcessor *previousEnv;
        previousEnv = getPreviousEnv();
        if (previousEnv)
            return previousEnv->getParagraphIndentation() +
            PARAGRAPH_INDENTATION;
        else return 0;
    }

    int txtEnvProcessor::getLineIndentation()
    {
        envProcessor *previousEnv;
        previousEnv = getPreviousEnv();
        if (previousEnv) return previousEnv->getLineIndentation() +
            LINE_INDENTATION;
        else return 0;
    }
```

Next, a standard pair of **get**/**set** methods.

```
textLine *txtEnvProcessor::getLine()
{
  if (!thisLine) thisLine = new
      textLine(thisCB->getColumnWidth());
  return thisLine;
}

void txtEnvProcessor::setLine(textLine *newLine)
{
  thisLine = newLine;
}
```

Now we start with a series of classes, all derived from **txtEnvProcessor**, which subtly redefine selected aspects of the generic text environment behavior. Perhaps the simplest is **indentedParagraphs**, which overrides only the methods responsible for determining indentation. The class definition is

```
#ifndef CLASS_INDENTEDPARAGRAPHS
#define CLASS_INDENTEDPARAGRAPHS 1

#include "txtep.hpp"

class indentedParagraphs : public txtEnvProcessor {
public:
  indentedParagraphs(envProcessor *lastEnv);
  virtual int getParagraphIndentation();
  virtual int getLineIndentation();
};
#endif
```

and its implementation is

```
#include "ipep.hpp"

#define PARAGRAPH_INDENTATION 3
#define LINE_INDENTATION 0

indentedParagraphs::indentedParagraphs(
  envProcessor *lastEnv)
  : txtEnvProcessor(lastEnv)
{}

int indentedParagraphs::getParagraphIndentation()
{
  return PARAGRAPH_INDENTATION;
}
```

```
int indentedParagraphs::getLineIndentation()
{
  envProcessor *lastEnv = getPreviousEnv();
  if (lastEnv) return lastEnv->getLineIndentation() +
      LINE_INDENTATION;
  else return LINE_INDENTATION;
}
```

The next class is `bulletedList`, which is only slightly more complicated. It not only overrides the indentation methods, but those which process a new paragraph, since, by definition, paragraphs in a `bulleted_list` environment are each bulleted. The definition is

```
#ifndef CLASS_BULLETEDLIST
#define CLASS_BULLETEDLIST 1

#include "txtep.hpp"

class bulletedList : public txtEnvProcessor {
public:
  bulletedList(envProcessor *lastEnv);
  virtual int getParagraphIndentation();
  virtual int getLineIndentation();
  virtual void initializeEnvironment();
  virtual void processNewParagraph();
};
#endif
```

and the implementation is

```
#include "blep.hpp"
#include "tpword.hpp"
#include "textline.hpp"

#define PARAGRAPH_INDENTATION 0
#define LINE_INDENTATION 2
#define BULLET " - "

bulletedList::bulletedList(envProcessor *lastEnv)
: txtEnvProcessor(lastEnv)
{}

int bulletedList::getParagraphIndentation()
{
  return PARAGRAPH_INDENTATION;
}
```

```
int bulletedList::getLineIndentation()
{
  int result;
  envProcessor *lastEnv = getPreviousEnv();
  if (lastEnv) return lastEnv->getLineIndentation() +
    LINE_INDENTATION;
  else return LINE_INDENTATION;
}

void bulletedList::processNewParagraph()
{
  textLine *thisLine;
  txtEnvProcessor::processNewParagraph();

  TPWord *bullet = new TPWord(BULLET);
  thisLine = getLine();
  thisLine->addTail((baseType *) bullet);
}

void bulletedList::initializeEnvironment()
{
  textLine *thisLine;
  txtEnvProcessor::initializeEnvironment();

  TPWord *bullet = new TPWord(BULLET);
  thisLine = getLine();
  thisLine->addTail((baseType *) bullet);
}
```

The `rightJustifiedText` environment moves spaces from the end of the line to the beginning of the line. This is not a particularly useful environment. A more useful version would take the leftover spaces and distribute them evenly throughout the line, but this is more complex than we want for an example. We leave this as an exercise. The definition is

```
#ifndef CLASS_RIGHTJUSTIFIEDTEXT
#define CLASS_RIGHTJUSTIFIEDTEXT 1

#include "txtep.hpp"
```

```
class rightJustifiedText : public txtEnvProcessor {
public:
  rightJustifiedText(envProcessor *lastEnv);
  virtual void processFullLine();
  virtual char *getClassName();
};
#endif
```

and the implementation is

```
#include "rttxt.hpp"
#include "textline.hpp"
#include "tpword.hpp"
#include <stdio.h>

rightJustifiedText::rightJustifiedText(envProcessor *lastEnv)
: txtEnvProcessor(lastEnv)
{
}

char *rightJustifiedText::getClassName()
{
  static char *myClass = "rightJustifiedText";
  return myClass;
}

void rightJustifiedText::processFullLine()
{
  textLine *currentLine;
  textLine *thisLine;
  TPWord *thisWord;
  int size;

  thisLine = getLine();
  if (thisLine) {
    size = thisLine->charsLeft();
    thisWord = new TPWord(' ', size);
    thisLine->addHead(thisWord);
    thisWord = (TPWord *) thisLine->tail();
    if (thisWord->type() == TP_BLANK_SPACE)
        thisLine->promoteTail();
  }
  txtEnvProcessor::processFullLine();
}
```

12.9   Text Processing Program

Given all of these classes, what does it take to write a program to open the file test.dat and format it to the screen according to the rules of the **TP** system? The following program does exactly that

```
#include "suep.hpp"
int main()
{
  setUpEnvProcessor *nextEnv;
  nextEnv = new setUpEnvProcessor;
  delete nextEnv;
  return 0;
}
```

This may strike you as a little unbelievable. Nevertheless, as you trace through the code path, starting with the **setUpEnvProcessor** constructor, you can watch the program unfold. We leave this as an exercise.

12.10   Code Reuse

Let's consider the code reuse story. In Chapter 7 we discussed a method of calculating code savings by use of class derivations. Here we will analyze the **TP** system according to this methodology. Rewriting the class derivation graph, with counts for lines of code used to program each class, we get

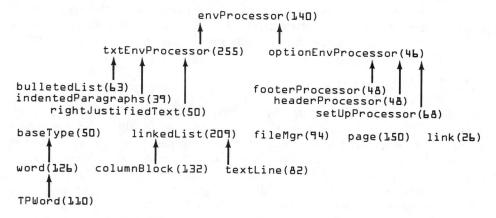

We can use this class derivation graph to calculate the cost of writing **TP** *with* and *without* using the class hierarchies of an object-oriented programming language.

Class	WITH cost	WITHOUT cost
envProcessor	140	140
txtEnvProcessor	255	255+140
optionEnvProcessor	46	46+140
bulletedList	63	63+255+140
footerProcessor	48	48+46+140
indentedParagraphs	39	39+255+140
headerProcessor	48	48+46+140
rightJustifiedText	50	50+255+140
setUpProcessor	68	68+46+140
baseType	50	50
linkedList	209	209+50
fileMgr	94	94
page	150	150
link	26	26
word	126	126+50
columnBlock	132	132+209+50
textLine	82	82+209+50
TPWord	110	110+126+50
	----	----------
Totals	1736	4553

Based on this analysis, we can say that our 1736 lines of object-oriented code have as much functionality as 4553 lines of non object-oriented code, an excellent ratio of 2.62 effective lines of code per 1 actual line of code. Of course this analysis is crude. On the one hand we give ourselves extra credit by assuming that every line in a base class is really contributing to the derived classes. But on the other hand, we have not given ourselves credit for *composed-of* relationships. It seems likely these pluses and minuses balance out, and that our analysis is not far off.

12.11 Summary

This chapter shows two important advantages of object-oriented programing. First, it lends itself nicely to writing reusable code. Second, it allows large, complex systems to be considered as a series of small, manageable programming problems, each with clear goals which can be specified, coded, and tested with considerable independence of work being done elsewhere on the system.

One should not be misled by this. It is not necessary to use an object-oriented programming language to achieve either of these goals. It is also not a guarantee that by using an object- oriented language you will be able to achieve these goals. Nevertheless, object-oriented programming is the best paradigm yet devised for expressing programming problems in a way that encourages reuse and encapsulation. For the programmer that understands the importance of reuse and encapsulation, object-orient programming will feel very natural.

12.12 Postscript

One of the factors hampering communication within the various related object-oriented fields is the lack of a common sample application. If you attend a conference on object-oriented programming, you might find yourself attending sessions on different programming languages and on object-oriented design and analysis methodologies. Most likely, each of these sessions will be using a different application to illustrate the important points.

This causes two problems. First, it is very difficult for the participant to compare equivalent features across presentations. Second, it forces the presenter to use trivial examples, since, within the short time available for a presentation, it is not possible to describe a sophisticated application.

The object-oriented community would be well served by having one common sample application which can be used in a variety of situations. The example should be complex enough to illustrate many different aspects of programming. It should be widely distributed so that familiarity can eventually be assumed.

As this example becomes well known, it will be reasonable to expect language advocates to describe how their favorite new language solves some of the difficult aspects of the common sample application. It will be reasonable to expect proponents of different design and analysis tools to show how their tools model the common sample application better than other tools.

If we can achieve this state, the object-oriented community as a whole will be well served. Languages will become easier to compare, since we can see how they all solve the same complex application. Tool demonstrations will be able to use a much more sophisticated example, since the demonstrators will be able to assume participants are already familiar with the application.

The application discussed in this chapter seems to be a good candidate for such a common sample application. It is complex enough to illustrate many difficult programming issues, such as keeping track of memory allocation and ensuring all allocated memory has been properly freed. It uses many classes with a wide variety of interrelationships. It is a good application for discussing both programming and design issues.

In the hope of encouraging the widespread adoption of this application as a common sample application, permission is hereby granted to freely copy any or all of the code in this chapter providing only that the following acknowledgement be given

*Class Construction in C and C++, Object-Oriented
Programming Fundamentals* by Roger Sessions, Copyright ©
1992 Prentice Hall. Reprinted with permission.

It should be noted that this permission to copy extends to the code only, and
to this chapter only. It does not extend to the discussion in this chapter, nor to the
code or the discussions of any other chapters.

12.13 Exercises

Exercise 12.1 The `fileMgr` class provides only read functionality. Redesign the
class so that it also provides appropriate write functionality. Decide which methods
need changing, and which new methods need to be added. Test your methods.

Exercise 12.2 Redesign the `fileMgr` class so that it is based on a linked list
instead of a ring buffer. The linked list implementation has the advantage of being
unlimited in size. The ring buffer implementation has the advantage of faster
performance. Test the performance of the two classes, and see if the performance
difference is significant.

Exercise 12.3 Write a generic ring buffer class similar to the generic linked list
class. Rewrite the `fileMgr` to make use of your generic ring buffer.

Exercise 12.4 A large number of `TPWords` are allocated and deallocated through
the course of this program. Figure out a way to count the number of invocations
of the constructor and destructor, and show that the two numbers are the same.
Do the same for the `link` constructor and destructor.

Exercise 12.5 The `word` class defines seven virtual methods, and the claim was
made in the text that only four of these override `baseType` methods. Which are
the four, and which `baseType` methods do they override?

Exercise 12.6 Write a third `TPWord` constructor which takes a pointer to a
`fileMgr` and returns a new `TPWord`.

Exercise 12.7 We read in this chapter that `pageWord`, a data member of `page`, should point only to a `TPWord` which lives in either the header or footer. Why would it cause problems if this pointed to some other `TPWord`?

Exercise 12.8 Rewrite the `setUpEnvProcessor` constructor to take the name of the input data file, instead of assuming the name is `test.dat`.

Exercise 12.9 The classes `headerProcessor` and `footerProcessor` both inadvertently forgot to override `getClassName()`. Add the appropriate overrides.

Exercise 12.10 The class `rightJustifiedText` does a crude job of right justification. It simply takes any leftover spaces and moves them to the beginning of the line. Write a better version which spreads the spaces out evenly throughout the text line.

Exercise 12.11 Start tracing the code path starting with the `setUpEnvProcessor` constructor, and show how the text processor works.

*If we wish to achieve an effect, we must first
investigate the nature of the forces in question and
ascertain their proper place. If we can bring these
forces to bear in the right place, they will have the
desired effect, and completion will be achieved. But
in order to handle external forces properly, we must
above all arrive at the correct standpoint ourselves,
for only from this vantage can we work correctly.*

*- I Ching
Wei Chi Hexagram — Before Completion
Translated by Richard Wilhelm and Cary F. Baynes*

Epilogue

This seems to be a logical stopping point. You should now be comfortable with what object-oriented programming is all about, and why the technology is an important one to the field of software development. You should be feeling comfortable with constructing classes and using objects in the most widespread and important of the object-oriented programming languages, C++.

This is the end of one phase of your journey, and, I hope, the beginning your next phase. Object-oriented programming is an interesting technology, one with many avenues to explore.

You might decide to continue your studies of C++. There are several features of the language which are quite important, though orthogonal to the issues of object-oriented programming, and therefore not covered here. These include stream IO, general operator overloading, templates, and exception handling. *The C++ Primer, Second Edition* [Lippman] and *The C++ Programming Language, Second Edition* [Stroustrup] are both good choices to continue your studies in C++. *The Annotated C++ Reference Manual* [Ellis and Stroustrup] is an essential reference document needed for debating the fine points of the language.

You might move into the closely related field of object-oriented design and analysis. This area focuses its attention on how systems are organized: how classes are identified, how methods are partitioned across classes, and how complex inter-class relationships are modelled. Excellent books in this area include *Designing*

Object-Oriented Software [Wirfs-Brock et al.], *Object-Oriented Modeling and Design* [Rumbaugh et al.], *Object-Oriented Design* [Booch], and *Object-Oriented Analysis* [Coad and Yourdon].

You might decide to study some other object-oriented languages, to see the similarities and differences in philosophies. One good candidate is Smalltalk, an interpreted language complete with a programming environment. *Inside Smalltalk* [LaLonde and Pugh] describes this language. Another good candidate language is Eiffel, which pays close attention to the notion of object correctness. The best known introduction to Eiffel is *Object-Oriented Software Construction* [Meyer]. A book which is specifically about Objective C, but makes many good points about object-oriented programming in general is *Object-Oriented Programming, Second Edition* [Cox and Novobilski].

Any of these directions will take you into interesting realms, with much to explore. There are two traps you should immediately learn to avoid.

First, don't assume you are now an expert. Learning to use object-oriented programming effectively is hard work and the payoff is not immediate. Reading any of the books mentioned in this chapter will give you valuable new insights. Talk to friends who are using the technology. Read the journals. Attend the conferences.

Second, don't believe everything you hear. Claims about object-oriented technology often border on the absurd. Very few, if any, of us fully understand this new technology. Most of us are still trying new approaches and constantly re-adjusting our thinking about how best to write object-oriented programs.

I hope your experiences with object-oriented technology in general, and object-oriented programming in particular, are rich and varied, and leave you well prepared to meet whatever new technologies tomorrow brings.

Appendix B

References

[Booch] *Object-Oriented Design with Applications*, by Grady Booch.
The Benjamin/Cummings Publishing Company, Inc., Redwood City, Calif. (1991)

[Coad and Yourdon] *Object-Oriented Analysis*, by Peter Coad and Edward Yourdon.
Prentice Hall, Englewood Cliffs, N.J. (1990)

[Cox] *Object-Oriented Programming*, Second Edition, by Brad J. Cox and Andrew
J. Novobilski.
Addison-Wesley Publishing Company, Reading, Mass. (1991)

[Ellis and Stroustrup] *The Annotated C++ Reference Manual*, by Margaret A. Ellis
and Bjarne Stroustrup.
Addison-Wesley Publishing Company, Reading, Mass. (1990)

[LaLonde and Pugh] Inside Smalltalk (Volume I and II), by Wilf R. LaLonde and
John R. Pugh.
Prentice Hall, Englewood Cliffs, N.J. (1991)

[Lippman] *The C++ Primer*, Second Edition, by Stanley B. Lippman.
Addison-Wesley Publishing Company, Reading, Mass. (1991)

[Meyer] *Object-Oriented Software Construction*, by Bertrand Meyer.
Prentice Hall, Englewood Cliffs, N.J. (1988)

[Nelson] An Object-Oriented Tower of Babel, by M.L. Nelson.
OOPS Messenger (USA) Vol. 2, No. 3 July 1991 P3–11.

[Rumbaugh et al.] Object-Oriented Modeling and Design, by James Rumbaugh,
Michael Blaha, William Premerlani, Frederick Eddy, and William Lorensen.
Prentice-Hall, Englewood Cliffs, N.J. (1991)

[Sessions] Reusable Data Structures for C, by Roger Sessions.
Prentice Hall, Englewood Cliffs, N.J. (1989).

[Stroustrup] The C++ Programming Language, Second Edition, by Bjarne
Stroustrup.
Addison-Wesley Publishing Company, Reading, Mass. (1991)

[Wirth, 74] On the Composition of Well-Structured Programs by Niklaus Wirth.
ACM Computing Surveys, December 1974.

[Wirfs-Brock et al.] *Designing Object-Oriented Software*, by Rebecca Wirfs-Brock,
Brian Wilkerson, and Lauren Wiener.
Prentice Hall, Englewood Cliffs, N.J. (1990)

[Wirth, 90] Modula-2 and Object-Oriented Programming, by Niklaus Wirth.
Microprocessors and Microsystems, Vol. 14 No. 3, 3 April 1990.

Index